Prescriptive Analytics

Prescriptive Analytics

The Final Frontier for Evidence-Based Management and Optimal Decision Making

Dursun Delen, PhD

Pearson

Editor-in-Chief: Mark L. Taub

Executive Editor: Kim Spenceley

Development Editor: Chris Zahn

Managing Editor: Sandra Schroeder

Senior Project Editor: Lori Lyons

Production Manager:
Aswini Kumar/codeMantra

Copy Editor: Gill Editorial Services

Indexer: Cheryl Lenser

Proofreader: Betty Pessagno

Cover Designer: Chuti Prasertsith

Compositor: codeMantra

I want to dedicate this book to my parents, both of whom I have recently lost; to my wife, Handan; and to our children, Altug and Serra.

Contents

Preface

Largely driven by the need to make better and faster decisions, business analytics has been gaining popularity faster than any management trends we have seen in recent history. Some of the most reputed consultancy companies are projecting business analytics to grow three times the rate of other business segments in upcoming years, and named analytics as one of the top business trends of this decade. Since Thomas H. Davenport and Jeanne G. Harris's 2007 book, *Competing on Analytics: The New Science of Winning*, many books and research studies have asserted that embracing business analytics strategically leads to making better and faster decisions toward improving customer satisfaction, competitive posture, and shareholder value. Because of these testaments, in recent years we have seen tremendous growth in adoption of analytics-enhanced managerial practices from all types of businesses and organizations.

Within the analytics ecosystem, almost all providers have their own definition of business analytics—each purposefully focusing on some combination of hardware and/or software capabilities—collectively resulting in more confusion than clarification. As an attempt to unify the understanding of "what business analytics is," the business community along with the educational community have developed a simple taxonomy where they defined analytics using three progressive phases/echelons: descriptive/diagnostic analytics → predictive analytics → prescriptive analytics. This book is about prescriptive analytics, the highest echelon in the analytics continuum, which is the one closest to "making accurate and timely decisions." While the first two echelons (descriptive/diagnostic analytics and predictive analytics) focus on discovering and creating insight from data, prescriptive analytics focuses on making the best decisions. Based on the insight generated by descriptive/diagnostics and predictive analytics, prescriptive analytics identifies, estimates, and compares all the possible outcomes/alternatives and chooses the best action toward achieving business objectives.

Prescriptive analytics and optimization are often used synonymously. Generally speaking, to optimize means "to improve" or "to make some outcome better." In business analytics, however, to optimize means a proven mathematical modeling process to find the best possible solution—optimal use of the limited resources toward achieving the business objectives while complying with a number of constraints. Although, at least conceptually, optimization suitably describes the purpose behind prescriptive analytics, the practicality and generalizability of the same extends beyond optimization to include simulation, multi-criteria decision modeling, heuristics and inferential knowledge representation, as well as the new and highly promising enablers such as Big Data, deep learning, and cognitive computing. These latest trends allow for richer and better insight creation toward immediate and accurate courses of action.

Who This Book Is For

This book is written for professionals who are interested in developing a holistic understanding about business analytics—especially about prescriptive analytics—and for college students at graduate and undergraduate levels who need a book nicely balanced between theory and practice in explaining prescriptive analytics as the top layer in the business analytics continuum. This book aims to provide an end-to-end, all-inclusive, holistic approach to prescriptive analytics—not only covering optimization and simulation, but also including multi-criteria decision-making methods along with inference- and heuristic-based decisioning techniques. The book is enhanced with numerous conceptual illustrations, example problems and solutions, and motivational case and success stories.

What This Book Covers

This book is organized into six chapters. The goal of Chapter 1, "Introduction to Business Analytics and Decision-Making," is to provide an overview of business analytics, its longitudinal perspective and a simple taxonomy, and where prescriptive analytics fits into this big picture. This chapter also provides a thorough description of the human decision-making process. Chapter 2, "Optimization and Optimal Decision-Making," introduces the topic of optimization and describes different types of optimization methods using simple yet practical examples and application cases. Chapter 3, "Simulation Modeling for Decision-Making," explains simulation, including Monte Carlo simulation and discrete and continuous simulation, as a powerful tool to analyze complex systems to make better decisions. Chapter 4, "Multi-Criteria Decision-Making," introduces multi-criteria decision making along with a simple taxonomy, and provides descriptions and examples of a variety of popular techniques used for multi-criteria problems commonly found in practice. Chapter 5, "Decisioning Systems," is about expert systems and case-based reasoning. These mature decisioning techniques are making a renewed impact on the decision systems where both data and expertise are used synergistically to support the decision-making process. Chapter 6, "The Future of Business Analytics," introduces the latest techniques in analytics, namely, Big Data, deep learning, and cognitive computing, as the leading edge for the next generation of automated decisioning and prescriptive analytics.

Register Your Book

Register your copy of **Prescriptive Analytics** at informit.com for convenient access to downloads, updates, and corrections as they become available. To start the registration process, go to informit.com/register and log in or create an account. Enter the product ISBN **9780134387055** and click Submit. Once the process is complete, you will find any available bonus content under "Registered Products."

Acknowledgments

A book usually is the reflection of its author's own perspective on a given topic. This book is no exception; it is the manifestation of the author's more than three decades of analytics experiences, created through numerous research projects, consultancy engagements, in-school and professional teaching, mentoring, and graduate advising. Hence, I want to acknowledge my colleagues, clients, and students for their contribution in creating my analytics knowledge base.

I also would like to acknowledge the people from whom I have received emotional and psychological support and encouragement throughout the process. In particular, I want to acknowledge the following individuals: Hamide and Musa Delen, Ceyhan and Erol Elibol, Leman and Yilmaz Tomak, Candan Bulmus, Inanc and Dincer Elibol, Erhan Sayin, Ali Mutlu, Ahmet Murat Fis, Selim Zaim, Enes Eryarsoy, and Nihat Kasap.

I also would like to thank the staff at Pearson Education for their professionalism and dedication to make this book a reality—especially Debra Williams and her team for their help and attention to details.

About the Author

Dursun Delen, PhD, is the holder of the William S. Spears Endowed Chair in Business Administration, Patterson Family Endowed Chair in Business Analytics, Director of Research for the Center for Health Systems Innovation, and Regents Professor of Management Science and Information Systems in the Spears School of Business at Oklahoma State University (OSU). He received his PhD in Industrial Engineering and Management from OSU in 1997. Prior to his appointment as an Assistant Professor at OSU in 2001, he worked for a privately owned research and consultancy company, Knowledge Based Systems Inc., in College Station, Texas, as a research scientist for five years, during which he led a number of decision support, information systems, and advanced analytics-related research projects funded by federal agencies including DoD, NASA, NIST, and DOE.

Dr. Delen provides professional education and consultancy services to companies and government agencies on analytics and information systems-related topics.

He is often invited to national and international conferences for invited talks and keynote addresses on topics related to data/text mining, business intelligence, decision support systems, business analytics, and knowledge management. He served as the general co-chair for the 4th International Conference on Network Computing and Advanced Information Management in Seoul, South Korea, and regularly chairs tracks and mini-tracks at various business analytics and information systems conferences.

He has published more than 150 peer-reviewed articles. His research has appeared in major journals, including *Decision Sciences, Decision Support Systems, Communications of the ACM, Computers and Operations Research, Computers in Industry, Journal of Production Operations Management, Artificial Intelligence in Medicine,* and

Expert Systems with Applications. He recently authored/co-authored ten books/textbooks within the broad areas of business analytics, decision support systems, data/text mining, and business intelligence.

He is the editor-in-chief for the *Journal of Business Analytics, AI in Business,* and *International Journal of Experimental Algorithms,* senior editor for *Decision Support Systems and Decision Sciences,* associate editor for *Journal of Business Research, Decision Analytics,* and *International Journal of RF Technologies,* and is on the editorial boards of several other academic journals.

1 ⎯⎯⎯⎯⎯⎯⎯⎯⎯⎯⎯⎯⎯⎯⎯⎯⎯⎯⎯

Introduction to Business Analytics and Decision-Making

Business analytics is a relatively new term that has been gaining popularity in the business world like nothing else in recent history. Before diving into the specifics about business analytics and one of its echelons—prescriptive analytics, which is closest to the decision-making stage and the main focus of this book—it would be helpful to first define business analytics and how its echelons relate to managerial decision-making. In most general terms, **business analytics** is the art and science of identifying or discovering novel insight from large volumes and varieties of data by means of using sophisticated machine learning, mathematical, and statistical models to support more accurate and timely managerial decision-making. So, in a sense, business analytics is all about decision-making and problem-solving. Nowadays, business analytics can simply be stated as "the process of discovering meaningful and actionable insight in data."

Data and Business Analytics

Because we are living in an era of data, the business analytics definitions are mostly focused on that—the digitization of data that is constantly flowing in, both from within and from outside the organization, in large quantities and many varieties. Figure 1.1 shows the process of creating information and knowledge through a systematic and scientific transformation of data. Various data, both structured and unstructured, is converted into knowledge and wisdom through a scientific process known as **data analytics**.

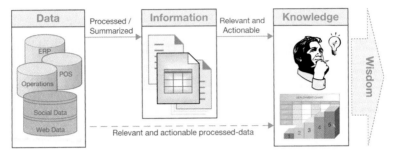

Figure 1.1 The process of converting data into information, knowledge, and wisdom.

Although the most current definitions of analytics are primarily data focused, there are and there have been many applications of analytics involving little or no data; instead, those analytics projects used mathematical models that relied on process description and expert knowledge (for example, optimization and simulation models, expert systems, and multi-criteria decision-modeling methods; all of which and more are explained in due details in the following chapters of this book).

Business analytics is the application of analytics models and methodologies, tools, and techniques to solve ever-so-complex business problems. Organizations commonly apply analytics to large collections of data to describe (better understand the internal factors), predict (foresee the future trends), and prescribe (find the best possible course of action) for improving business performance. Analytics have been shown to help firms do the following:

- Improve their relationships with their customers (encompassing all phases of customer relationship management—acquisition, retention, enrichment), employees, and other stakeholders.
- Identify fraudulent transactions and odd behaviors, saving firms money.

- Enhance product and service features and their pricing, which leads to better customer satisfaction and profitability.

- Optimize marketing and advertising campaigns, reaching more customers with the right kind of message and promotions with the least amount of expenses.

- Minimize operational cost by optimally managing inventories and allocating resources to wherever and whenever they are needed by means of optimization and simulation modeling.

- Empower employees with the information and insight they need to make faster and better decisions while they are facing customers or customer-related issues.

Analytics, perhaps because of its rapidly increasing popularity as a buzzword, is being used to replace several previously popularized terms such as **intelligence**, **mining**, and **discovery**. For example, the term **business intelligence** is now **business analytics**; **customer intelligence** is now **customer analytics**; **Web mining** is now **Web analytics**; and **knowledge discovery** is now **data analytics**. Because modern-day analytics can require extensive computation (due to the volume, variety, and velocity of data—the Big Data), the tolls, techniques, and algorithms used for analytics projects leverage the most current, state-of-the-art methods developed in fields that include management science, computer science, statistics, data science, computational linguistics, and mathematics.

As mentioned, analytics is all about problem-solving and decision-making. To better understand the motivation for business analytics and to further accentuate its role in managerial decision-making, in the following section we provide a brief discussion of the human decision-making process using one of the most widely cited decision theories.

An Overview of the Human Decision-Making Process

At the most basic level, decision-making is the process of choosing among two or more alternative courses of action for the purpose of attaining one or more goals. As it relates to business analytics, the alternatives are usually generated through descriptive and predictive levels of analytics by a process of data collection and information creation, and the optimal decision is made through the prescriptive level of the analytics continuum. Managerial decision-making is synonymous with the entire management process. Consider, for instance, the critical managerial function of planning, which involves a series of decisions such as what should be done, when, where, why, how, and by whom. Every phase in the planning process involves managerial decision-making, and the collective accuracy, or the optimality, of the decision made determines the value of the outcome obtained.

Are problem-solving and decision-making synonymous? A problem occurs when a system does not meet its established goals, does not yield the expected or predicted results, or does not work as planned. An opportunity may also be considered a problem; if it is not leveraged in a timely fashion, somebody else could take advantage of it, resulting in an even bigger problem down the road. Generally speaking, decision-making can be considered a step in the problem-solving process. That is, one way to distinguish between the two is to examine the phases of the decision process: 1. intelligence, 2. design, 3. choice, and 4. implementation. Some consider the entire process (phases 1–4) as problem-solving, with the choice phase as the real decision-making. Others view phases 1–3 as formal decision-making, ending with a recommendation, with problem-solving additionally including the actual implementation of the recommendation (phase 4). Note that a problem may include situations in which a person must decide which opportunity to exploit. In this book, we use the terms, problem solving and decision making, interchangeably.

There have been numerous attempts to describe the human decision-making process. Although every person, based on life experiences, develops and employs a different set of logically ordered steps to identify and solve problems and make decisions, common sense suggests that there ought to be a generalized approach to human decision-making, maybe not at the detailed level, but at a high level of conceptualization. Among the related theories suggested, the one by Newell and Simon (1972) and Simon (1982) stands ahead of the rest and has stood against the time for the past 50 years. Herbert Alexander Simon (1916–2001) was an American economist and political scientist whose primary interest was the human decision-making process within organizations. He received the Nobel Prize in Economics in 1978 and the Turing Award in 1975. He was at Carnegie Mellon University for most of his career, from 1949 to 2001.

Simon's Theory of Decision-Making

Although, historically, decision-making has been viewed as a creative, experience-driven, ad-hoc practice, today it is widely perceived as a systematic, evidence-driven, scientific process. Therefore, to enhance the likelihood of obtaining the best possible outcomes, the decision-makers are advised to follow a standardized, systematic, and logical decision-making process. Simon (1977) said that such a systematic process involves three major phases: intelligence, design, and choice. He later added a fourth phase: implementation. Monitoring can be considered a fifth phase—a form of feedback. However, we view monitoring as the *intelligence phase* applied to the outputs of the *implementation phase*. Simon's model is widely accepted as the most concise and yet most complete characterization of rational decision-making. A conceptual picture of the decision-making process, proposed by Simon, is shown in Figure 1.2.

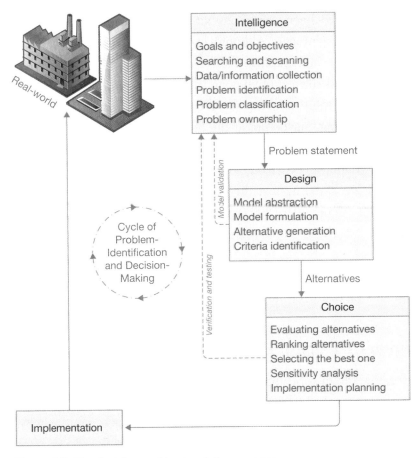

Figure 1.2 The decision-making/modeling process.

There is a continuous flow of activity from intelligence to design, from design to choice; but at any phase, there may be a return to a previous phase—feedback—for validation, verification, and refinement. The seemingly complex nature of the haphazard path from problem discovery to solution development and implementation via decision-making can be explained by the continuous improvement achieved through these feedback loops. Following is a brief description of the phases in this decision-making process.

Phase 1. Intelligence

The intelligence phase in the decision-making process involves scanning the environment, either intermittently or continuously. It includes several activities aimed at identifying problem situations or opportunities. It may also include monitoring the results of the implementation phase of a previously completed decision-making process.

Problem (or Opportunity) Identification   The intelligence phase begins with the identification of organizational goals and objectives related to issues of concern—such as inventory management, job selection, and lack of or incorrect Web presence—and the determination of whether those goals and objectives are being met. Problems occur because of the dissatisfaction with the status quo. Dissatisfaction is the result of a difference between what people desire or expect and what is occurring. In this first phase, a decision-maker attempts to determine whether a problem exists, identify its symptoms, determine its magnitude, and explicitly define it. Often, what is described as a problem, such as excessive costs, may be only a symptom or measure of a problem, such as improper inventory levels. Because real-world problems are usually complicated by many interrelated factors, it is sometimes difficult to distinguish between the symptoms and the real problem. New opportunities and problems certainly may be uncovered while investigating the causes of symptoms.

The existence of a problem can be determined by monitoring and analyzing the organization's productivity level. The measurement of productivity and the construction of a model ought to be based on real data. The collection of data and the estimation of future data are among the most difficult steps in the analysis. The following are some issues that may arise during data collection and estimation and thus plague decision-makers:

- Data are not available. As a result, the model is made with, and relies on, potentially inaccurate estimates.

- Obtaining data may be expensive.

- Data may not be accurate or precise enough.

- Data estimation is often subjective.

- Data may be insecure.

- Important data that influence the results may be qualitative (soft).

- There may be too much data, resulting in information overload.

- Outcomes (or results) may occur over an extended period. As a result, revenues, expenses, and profits will be recorded at different points in time. To overcome this difficulty, a present-value approach can be used if the results are quantifiable.

- It is assumed that future data will be similar to historical data. If this is not the case, the nature of the change has to be predicted and included in the analysis.

When the preliminary investigation is completed, it is possible to determine whether a problem really exists, where it is located, and how significant it is. A key issue is whether an information system is reporting a problem or only the symptoms of a problem. For example, in the case of "sales are down," there is a problem, but the sales being down is a symptom, indicating existence of a real problem. It is imperative to identify the real problem, and not the symptom, to solve and thereby create a real business value.

Problem Classification   Problem classification is the conceptualization of a problem in an attempt to place it in a definable category, possibly leading to a standard solution approach. An important approach classifies problems according to the degree of structure evident in them. This ranges from completely structured, or programmed, to completely unstructured, or unprogrammed.

Problem Decomposition   Many complex problems can be divided into subproblems. Solving the simpler subproblems may help in solving a complex problem. Also, seemingly poorly structured problems sometimes have highly structured subproblems. Just as a semistructured problem results when some phases of decision-making are structured whereas other phases are unstructured, when some subproblems of a decision-making problem are structured while others are unstructured, the problem itself is semistructured. Decomposition also facilitates communication among decision-makers. Decomposition is one of the most important aspects of the analytic hierarchy process (AHP is discussed in Chapter 4, "Multi-Criteria Decision Making"), which helps decision-makers incorporate both qualitative and quantitative factors into their decision-making process.

Problem Ownership   In the intelligence phase, it is important to establish problem ownership. A problem exists in an organization only if someone or some group takes on the responsibility of attacking it and if the organization has the ability to solve it. The assignment of authority to solve the problem is called **problem ownership**. For example, a manager may feel that there's a problem because interest rates are too high. Because interest rate levels are determined at the national and international levels and most managers can do nothing about them, high interest rates are the problem of the government, not a problem for a specific company to solve. The problem companies actually face is how to operate in a high–interest-rate environment. For an individual company, the interest rate level should be handled as an uncontrollable (environmental) factor to be predicted. When problem ownership is not established, either someone is not doing his job, or the problem at hand has yet to be identified as belonging to anyone. It is then important for someone to either volunteer to own it or assign it to someone. The intelligence phase ends with a formal problem statement.

Phase 2.   Design

The design phase involves finding or developing and analyzing possible courses of action. These include understanding the problem and testing solutions for feasibility. A model of the decision-making problem is constructed, tested, and validated. Modeling involves conceptualizing a problem and abstracting it to quantitative or qualitative form. For a mathematical model, the variables are identified, and their mutual relationships are established. Simplifications are made, whenever necessary, through assumptions. For example, a relationship between two variables may be assumed to be linear even though in reality there may be some nonlinear effects. A proper balance between the level of model simplification and the representation of reality must be obtained because of the cost-benefit trade-off. A simpler model leads to lower development costs, easier manipulation, and a faster solution but is less representative of the real problem and can produce inaccurate results. However, a simpler model generally requires less data, or the data is aggregated and easier to obtain.

The process of modeling involves a combination of art and science. As a science, there are many standard model classes available, and, with practice, an analyst can determine which one is applicable to a given situation. As an art, creativity and finesse are required when determining what simplifying assumptions can work, how to combine appropriate features of the model classes, and how to integrate models to obtain valid solutions.

Principle of Choice   A **principle of choice** is a criterion that describes the acceptability of a solution approach. In a model, it is a result variable. Selecting a principle of choice is not part of the choice phase but involves how a person establishes decision-making objectives and incorporates the objectives into the models. Are we willing to assume high risk, or do we prefer a low-risk approach? Are we attempting to optimize or satisfice? It is also important to recognize the difference between a criterion and a constraint.

The Difference Between a Criterion and a Constraint

Many people new to the formal study of decision-making inadvertently confuse the concepts of criterion and constraint. Often, this is because a criterion may imply a constraint, either implicit or explicit, thereby adding to the confusion. For example, there may be a distance criterion that the decision-maker does not want to travel too far from home. However, there is an implicit constraint that the alternatives from which he selects must be within a certain distance from his home. This constraint effectively says that if the distance from home is greater than a certain amount, the alternative is not feasible—or, rather, the distance to an alternative must be less than or equal to a certain number. (This would be a formal relationship in some models; in the model in this case, it reduces the search, considering fewer alternatives.) This is similar to what happens sometimes when selecting a university, where schools beyond a single day's driving distance would not be considered by most people, and, in fact, the utility function (criterion value) of distance can start out low close to home, peak at about 70 miles (about 100 km)—say, the distance between Atlanta (home) and Athens, Georgia—and sharply drop off thereafter. In short, constraints helps in defining the feasible solution space while a criterion helps in ranking and selecting the best feasible solution.

Normative Models   **Normative models** are models in which the chosen alternative is demonstrably the best of all possible alternatives. To find it, the decision-maker should examine all the alternatives and prove that the one selected is indeed the best, which is what the person would normally want. This process is basically **optimization**. In operational terms, optimization can be achieved in one of three ways:

1. Get the highest level of goal attainment from a given set of resources. For example, which alternative will yield the maximum profit from an investment of $10 million?

2. Find the alternative with the highest ratio of goal attainment to cost (profit per dollar invested) or maximize productivity.

3. Find the alternative with the lowest cost (or smallest amount of other resources) that will meet an acceptable level of goals. For example, if your task is to select hardware for an intranet with a minimum bandwidth, which alternative will accomplish this goal at the least cost?

Normative decision theory is based on the following assumptions of rational decision-makers·

- Humans are economic beings whose objective is to maximize the attainment of goals. The decision-maker is rational. In other words, more of a good thing (revenue, fun) is better than less; less of a bad thing (cost, pain) is better than more.

- For a decision-making situation, all viable alternative courses of action and their consequences, or at least the probability and the values of the consequences, are known.

- Decision-makers have an order or preference that enables them to rank the desirability of all consequences of the analysis from best to worst.

Are decision-makers really rational? See Schwartz (2005) for anomalies in rational decision-making. Although there may be major anomalies in the presumed rationality of financial and economic behavior, we take the view that they could be caused by incompetence, lack of knowledge, multiple goals being framed inadequately, misunderstanding of a decision-maker's true expected utility, and time-pressure impacts.

Are Decision-Makers Really Rational?

Some researchers question the concept of rationality in decision-making. There are countless cases of individuals and groups behaving irrationally in real-world and experimental decision-making situations. For example, suppose you need to take a bus to work every morning, and the bus leaves at 7:00 a.m. If it takes you one hour to wake up, prepare for work, and get to the bus stop, you should always awaken at or before 6:00 a.m. However, sometimes you may sleep until 6:30, knowing that you will miss breakfast and not perform well at work. Or you may be late and arrive at the bus stop at 7:05, hoping that the bus will be late, too. So, why are you late? Multiple objectives and hoped-for goal levels may lead to this situation. Or your true expected utility for being on time might simply indicate that you should go back to bed most mornings!

Suboptimization   By definition, optimization requires a decision-maker to consider the impact of each alternative course of action on the entire organization because a decision made in one area may have significant effects on other areas. Consider, for example, a marketing department that implements an electronic commerce (e-commerce) site. Within hours, orders far exceed production capacity. The production department, which plans its own schedule, cannot meet demand. It may gear up for as high demand as is possible to meet. Ideally and independently, the department should produce only a few products in extremely large quantities to minimize manufacturing costs. However, such a plan might result in large, costly inventories and marketing difficulties caused by the lack of a variety of products, especially if customers start to cancel orders that are not met in a timely way. This situation illustrates the sequential nature of decision-making.

A systems point of view assesses the impact of every decision on the entire system. Thus, the marketing department should make its plans in conjunction with other departments. However, such an approach may require a complicated, expensive, time-consuming analysis. In practice, the information builder may close the system within narrow boundaries, considering only the part of the organization under study (the marketing or production department, in this case). By simplifying, the model then does not incorporate certain complicated relationships that describe interactions with and among the other departments. The other departments can be aggregated into simple model components. Such an approach is called **suboptimization**.

If a suboptimal decision is made in one part of the organization without considering the details of the rest of the organization, then an optimal solution from the point of view of that part may be inferior for the whole. However, suboptimization may still be a practical approach to decision-making, and many problems are first approached from this perspective. It is possible to reach tentative conclusions—and generally usable results—by analyzing only a portion of a system, without getting bogged down in too many details. After a solution is proposed, its potential effects on the remaining departments of the organization can be tested. If no significant negative effects are found, the solution can be implemented.

Suboptimization may also apply when simplifying assumptions are used in modeling a specific problem. There may be too many details or too much data to incorporate into a specific decision-making situation, so not all of it is used in the model. If the solution to the model seems reasonable, it may be valid for the problem and thus be adopted. Suboptimization may also involve simply bounding the search for an optimum (by a heuristic) by considering fewer criteria or alternatives or by eliminating large portions of the problem from evaluation. If it takes too long to solve a problem, a good-enough solution found already may be used and the optimization effort terminated.

Good Enough or Satisficing?

According to Simon (1977), most human decision-making, whether organizational or individual, involves a willingness to settle for a satisfactory solution, "something less than the best." When **satisficing**, the decision-maker sets up an aspiration, a goal, or a desired level of performance and then searches the alternatives until one is found that achieves this level. The usual reasons for satisficing are time pressures (e.g., decisions may lose value over time), the inability to achieve optimization (e.g., solving some models could take longer than until when the sun is supposed to become a supernova), and recognition that the marginal benefit of a better solution is not worth the marginal cost to obtain it. In such a situation, the decision-maker is behaving rationally, though he or she is actually satisficing. Essentially, satisficing is a form of suboptimization. There may be a best solution, an optimum, but it would be difficult to attain it. With a normative model, too much computation may be involved; with a descriptive model, it may not be possible to evaluate all the sets of alternatives.

Bounded Rationality Related to satisficing is Simon's idea of **bounded rationality**. Humans have a limited capacity for rational thinking; they generally construct and analyze a simplified model of a real situation by considering fewer alternatives, criteria, or constraints than actually exist. Their behavior with respect to the simplified model may be rational. However, the rational solution for the simplified model may not be rational for the real-world problem. Rationality is bounded not only by limitations on human processing capacities, but also by individual differences, such as age, education, knowledge, and attitudes. Bounded rationality is also why many models are descriptive rather than normative. This may also explain why so many good managers rely on intuition, an important aspect of good decision-making (see Stewart, 2002; and Pauly, 2004).

Because rationality and the use of normative models lead to good decisions, it is natural to ask why so many bad decisions are made in practice. Intuition is a critical factor that decision-makers use in solving unstructured and semistructured problems. The best decision-makers recognize the trade-off between the marginal cost of obtaining further information and analysis versus the benefit of making a better decision. But sometimes decisions must be made quickly, and, ideally, the intuition of a seasoned, excellent decision-maker is called for. When adequate planning, funding, or information is not available, or when a decision-maker is inexperienced or ill trained, disaster can strike.

Developing (Generating) Alternatives   A significant part of the model-building process is generating alternatives. In optimization models (such as linear programming), the alternatives may be generated automatically by the model. In most decision situations, however, it is necessary to generate alternatives manually. This can be a lengthy process that involves searching and creativity, perhaps utilizing electronic brainstorming in a group support system (GSS). It takes time and costs money. Issues such as when to stop generating alternatives can be important. Too many alternatives can be detrimental to the process of decision-making. A decision-maker may suffer from information overload. Generating alternatives is heavily dependent on the availability and cost of information and requires expertise in the problem area. This is the least formal aspect of problem-solving. Alternatives can be generated and evaluated using heuristics. The generation of alternatives from either individuals or groups can be supported by electronic brainstorming software in a Web-based GSS. Note that the search for alternatives usually occurs after the selection of the criteria for evaluating the alternatives are determined. This sequence can ease the search for alternatives and reduce the effort involved in evaluating them, but identifying potential alternatives can sometimes aid in identifying criteria. The outcome of every proposed alternative must be established. Depending on whether the decision-making problem is classified as one of certainty, risk, or uncertainty, different modeling approaches may be used.

Measuring Outcomes   The value of an alternative is evaluated in terms of goal attainment. Sometimes an outcome is expressed directly in terms of a goal. For example, profit is an outcome, profit maximization is a goal, and both are expressed in dollar terms. An outcome such as customer satisfaction may be measured by the number of complaints, by the level of loyalty to a product, or by ratings found through surveys. Ideally, a decision-maker would want to deal with a single goal, but in practice, it is not unusual to have multiple goals. When groups make decisions, each group participant may have a different agenda. For example, executives might want to maximize profit, marketing might want to maximize market penetration, operations might want to minimize costs, and stockholders might want to maximize the bottom line. Typically, these goals conflict, so special multiple-criteria methodologies have been developed to handle this. One such method is the AHP, which is covered in detail in Chapter 4.

Risk   All decisions are made in an inherently unstable environment. This is due to far too many unpredictable events occurring in both the economic and the physical environments. Some risk (measured as probability) may be due to internal organizational events, such as a valued employee quitting or becoming ill, whereas others may be due to natural disasters, such as a hurricane. Aside from the human toll, one economic aspect of Hurricane Katrina was that the price of a gallon of gasoline doubled overnight due to uncertainty in the port capabilities, refining, and pipelines of the southern United States. What can a decision-maker do in the face of such instability?

In general, people have a tendency to measure uncertainty and risk poorly. People tend to be overconfident and have an illusion of control in decision-making. This may perhaps explain why people often feel that one more pull of a slot machine will definitely pay off.

However, methodologies for handling extreme uncertainty do exist. Aside from estimating the potential utility or value of a particular decision's outcome, the best decision-makers are capable of accurately estimating the risk associated with the outcomes that result from making each decision. Thus, one important task of a decision-maker is to attribute a level of risk to the outcome associated with each potential alternative being considered. Some decisions may lead to unacceptable risks in terms of success and can therefore be discarded or discounted immediately.

In some cases, some decisions are assumed to be made under conditions of certainty simply because the environment is assumed to be stable. Other decisions are made under conditions of uncertainty, where risk is unknown. Still, a good decision-maker can make working estimates of risk. Also, the process of developing a business intelligence/decision support system (BI/DSS) involves learning more about the situation, which leads to a more accurate assessment of the risks.

Scenarios   A **scenario** is a statement of assumptions about the operating environment of a particular system at a given time; that is, it is a narrative description of the decision-situation setting. A scenario describes the decision and uncontrollable variables and parameters for a specific modeling situation. It may also provide the procedures and constraints for the modeling.

Scenarios originated in the theater, and the term was borrowed for war gaming and large-scale simulations. Scenario planning and analysis is a DSS tool that can capture a whole range of possibilities. A manager can construct a series of scenarios or what-if cases, perform computerized analyses, and learn more about the system and decision-making problem while analyzing it. Ideally, the manager can identify an excellent, possibly optimal, solution to the model of the problem.

Scenarios are especially helpful in simulations and what-if analyses. In both cases, we change scenarios and examine the results. For example, we can change the anticipated demand for hospitalization (an input variable for planning), thus creating a new scenario. Then we can measure the anticipated cash flow of the hospital for each scenario.

Scenarios play an important role in management support system (MSS) because they do the following:

- Help identify opportunities and problem areas
- Provide flexibility in planning
- Identify the leading edges of changes that management should monitor
- Help validate major modeling assumptions
- Allow the decision-maker to explore the behavior of a system through a model
- Help to check the sensitivity of proposed solutions to changes in the environment, as described by the scenario

There may be thousands of possible scenarios for every decision situation. However, the following are especially useful in practice:

- The worst possible scenario
- The best possible scenario
- The most likely scenario
- The average scenario

Errors in Decision-Making   The model is a critical component in the decision-making process, but a decision-maker may make a number of errors in its development and use. Validating the model before it is used is critical. Gathering the right amount of information, with the right level of precision and accuracy, to incorporate into the decision-making process is also critical. Sawyer (1999) described "the seven deadly sins of decision-making," most of which are behavior or information related.

Phase 3.   Choice

Choice is the critical act of decision-making. The choice phase is the one in which the actual decision and the commitment to follow a certain course of action are made. The boundary between the design and choice phases is often unclear because certain activities can be performed during both phases and because the decision-maker can return frequently from choice activities to design activities, such as by generating new alternatives while performing an evaluation of existing ones. The choice phase includes the search for, evaluation of, and recommendation of an appropriate solution to a model. A solution to a model is a specific set of values for the decision variables in a selected alternative.

Note that solving a model is not the same as solving the problem the model represents. The solution to the model yields a recommended solution to the problem. The problem is considered solved only if the recommended solution is successfully implemented.

Solving a decision-making model involves searching for an appropriate course of action. Search approaches include analytical techniques (solving a formula), algorithms (step-by-step procedures), heuristics (rules of thumb), and blind searches (shooting in the dark, ideally in a logical way).

Each alternative must be evaluated. If an alternative has multiple goals, each must be examined and balanced against the other. **Sensitivity analysis** is used to determine the robustness of any given alternative; slight changes in the parameters should ideally lead to slight or no changes in the alternative chosen. **What-if analysis** is used to explore major changes in the parameters. Goal-seeking helps a manager determine values of the decision variables to meet a specific objective.

Phase 4. Implementation

In *The Prince*, Machiavelli astutely noted some 500 years ago that there was "nothing more difficult to carry out, nor more doubtful of success, nor more dangerous to handle, than to initiate a new order of things." The implementation of a proposed solution to a problem is, in effect, the initiation of a new order of things or the introduction of change. And change must be managed. User expectations must be managed as part of change management.

The definition of *implementation* is somewhat complicated because implementation is a long, involved process with vague boundaries. Simplistically, the **implementation phase** involves putting a recommended solution to work, not necessarily implementing a computer system. Many generic implementation issues, such as resistance to change, degree of support of top management, and user training, are important in dealing with managerial decisions.

An Overview of Business Analytics

Is there a difference between analytics and analysis? Even though these two terms are being used interchangeably, analytics is not exactly the same as analysis. In its basic definition, **analysis** refers to the process of separating a whole problem into its parts so that the parts can be critically examined at the granular level. It is often used for complex systems where the investigation of the complete system is not feasible or practical; therefore, the analysis definition needs to be simplified by decomposing it into its more descriptive/understandable components. Once the improvements at the granular level are realized and the examination of the parts is completed, the whole system (either a conceptual or a physical system) is then put together using a process called synthesis. **Analytics**, on the other hand, is the variety of methods, technologies, and associated tools used for creation of new knowledge/insight to solve complex problems and to make better and faster decisions. In essence, analytics is a multi-faceted and multi-disciplined approach to addressing complex situations. Analytics takes advantage of data and mathematical models to make sense of the ever-so-complicated world that we are living in. Even though analytics includes the act of analysis at different stages of the discovery process, it is not just analysis but analysis, synthesis, and everything else. More than anything else, analytics is a methodology that encompasses a multitude of methods and practices.

Why the Sudden Popularity of Analytics?

Analytics is the buzzword of business circles nowadays. No matter what business journal or magazine you look at, it is likely you will see articles about analytics and how it is changing the way managerial decisions are being made. It has become a new label for evidence-based management (evidence/data-driven decision-making). The question is why analytics has become so popular, and why now? The reasons (or forces) behind this popularity can be grouped into three categories: need, availability and affordability, and culture change.

- **Need.** As we all know, business is anything but "as usual" today. Previously characterized progressively as local, then regional, then national, the competition is now global. Large to medium to small, every business is under the pressure of global competition. The barrier that sheltered companies in their respective geographic locations with tariffs and transportation costs are no longer as protective. In addition to—and perhaps because of—the global competition, customers have become more demanding. They want the highest quality of products and services with the lowest prices in the shortest possible time. Success or mere survival depends on businesses being agile and their managers making the best possible decisions in a timely manner to respond to market-driven forces (rapidly identifying and addressing problems and taking advantage of the opportunities). Therefore, the need for fact-based, better, and faster decisions is more critical now than ever before. In the midst of these unforgiving market conditions, analytics is promising to provide managers with the insight they need to make better and faster decisions, which would improve their competitive posture in the marketplace. Analytics nowadays is widely perceived as the savior of business managers from the complexities of global business practices.

- **Availability and affordability.** Thanks to recent technological advances and the affordability of software and hardware, organizations are collecting tremendous amounts of data. Automated data collections systems—based on a variety of sensors/RFID—significantly increased the quantity and quality of organizational data. Coupled with the content-rich data collected from the Internet-based technologies including social network/media, businesses now can have more than they can handle. As the saying goes, "they are drowning in data but starving for knowledge." In addition to the data-collection technologies, the data-processing technologies have improved significantly. The machines with numerous processors and large memory capacity make it possible to process considerable and complex data in a reasonable time frame, often in real time. These advances in hardware and software technology are also reflected in pricing, continuously reducing the cost of ownership for such systems. In addition to the ownership model came the software (or hardware) as a service (SaaS or HaaS) business model that allowed businesses—especially small to medium businesses with limited financial power—to rent analytics capabilities and pay only what they use of them.

- **Cultural change.** At the organizational level, there is a shift from old-fashioned intuition-driven decision-making to new-age fact/evidence-based decision-making. Most successful organizations are making a conscious effort toward shifting into a data/evidence-driven business practice. Because of the availability of data and supporting IT infrastructure, such a paradigm shift is taking place faster than many have thought. As the new generation of quantitatively savvy managers replaces the baby boomers, this evidence-based managerial paradigm shift will only intensify.

What Are the Application Areas of Analytics?

Even though the business analytics wave is somewhat new, there are numerous applications of analytics covering almost every aspect of business practices. For instance, there are numerous success stories in customer relationship management (CRM) where sophisticated models are developed to identify new customers and up-sell/cross-sell opportunities and customers who have a high propensity to attrite. Using social media analytics and sentiment analysis, businesses are trying to stay on top of what people are saying about their product/ services and brands. Fraud detection, risk mitigation, product pricing, marketing campaign optimization, financial planning, employee retention, talent recruiting, and actuarial estimation are among the many business applications of analytics. It would be hard to find a business issue where a number of analytics applications cannot be identified. From business reporting to data warehousing, from data mining to optimization, analytics techniques are used widely in almost every facet of business.

What Are the Main Challenges of Analytics?

Even though the advantages as well as the enabling reasons for analytics are evident, there still are many businesses hesitant to jump on the analytics bandwagon. Even though they may all have their specific reasons, at the highest level, the main roadblocks/hurdles to analytics adaptation can be listed as follows:

- **Analytics talent.** Data scientists, as many people today call the quantitative geniuses who can convert data into actionable insight, are scarce in the market, and the really good ones are difficult to find. Because analytics is relatively new, the talent for analytics is still in the process of development. Many colleges have started master's and undergraduate programs to address the analytics talent gap. As the popularity of analytics increases, so will the need for people who have the knowledge and skills to convert "Big Data" into information and knowledge that managers and other decision-makers need to tackle complexities of the real world.

- **Culture.** As the saying goes, "old habits die hard." Changing from a traditional management style (which is often characterized with intuition and gut feelings as the basis of making decisions) to a contemporary management style (which is based on data and scientific models, to base managerial decisions, to data/evidence and collective organizational knowledge) is not an easy process to undertake for any organization. People do not like to change. Change means losing what you have learned or mastered in the past and having to learn how to do what you do all over again. It suggests that the knowledge, or power, you've accumulated over the years will disappear or partially will be lost. Cultural shift may be the most difficult part of adopting analytics as the new management paradigm.

- **Return on investment.** Another factor behind analytics adoptions is the difficulty in clearly justifying its return on investment (ROI). Because analytics projects are complex and costly endeavors and their return is not clearly and immediately related, many executives are having a hard time investing in analytics, especially in large scales. One has to answer the question "Will, and if so when, will the value gained from analytics outweigh the investment?" It is hard to convert the value of analytics into justifiable numbers. Most of the value gained from analytics is somewhat intangible and holistic. If done properly, analytics could transform an organization to new and improved levels. A combination of tangible and intangible factors needs to be brought to bear to numerically rationalize investment and movement toward analytics and analytically savvy management practice.

- **Data.** The media is taking about "Big Data" in a positive way, characterizing it as an invaluable asset for better business practices. That is mostly true, especially if the business understands and knows what to do with it. For the others, who have no clue, Big Data is a big challenge. As we will reiterate on the topic later in the book, Big Data is not just big; it is unstructured and is arriving at a speed that prohibits traditional means from collecting and processing it. Not to mention that it usually is messy and dirty. For organizations to succeed in analytics, they need to have a well-thought-out strategy for handling Big Data so that it can be converted to actionable insight.

- **Technology.** Even though it is capable, available, and to some extent, affordable, technology adoption poses another challenge for traditionally less technical businesses. Despite being affordable, it still takes significant money to establish an analytics infrastructure. Without financial means and a clear ROI, management of those businesses may not be willing to invest in needed technology. For those, perhaps an analytics as a service (AaaS) model (which would include both software as well as infrastructure/hardware needed to implement analytics) would be less costly and easier to implement.

- **Security and privacy.** One of the most commonly pronounced criticisms of data and analytics is security. As we often hear in the news about data bridges for sensitive information, there is no completely secured data infrastructure unless it is isolated and disconnected from all other networks (which would be something that goes against the very reason of having data and analytics). The importance of data security has made information assurance one of the most popular concentration areas in information systems departments all over the world. Although the techniques are increasing in sophistication to protect the information infrastructure, so are the methods and techniques used by the adversaries. In addition to security, there are concerns about personal privacy. Use of personal data about the customers (existing or prospect), even if it is within the legal boundaries, should be avoided or highly scrutinized to prevent the organization from bad publicity and public outcry.

Despite the hurdles in the way, analytics adoption is growing, and it is inevitable for today's enterprises, regardless of the size and industry segment. As the complexity in conducting business increases, businesses are trying to find order in the midst of the chaotic behaviors. The ones that succeed in doing so will be the ones fully leveraging the capabilities of analytics.

A Longitudinal View of Analytics

Because of its recent buzz and popularity, many people are asking if analytics is something new. The short answer is "it is not," at least not for the true meaning of what analytics stands for. One can find references to corporate analytics as far back as 1940s during the World War II era when more effective methods were needed to maximize output using only limited resources. Most of the optimization and simulation techniques were developed then. Analytics (or, as it was called, analytical techniques) have been used in business since the early days of time-and-motion studies that were initiated by Frederick Winslow Taylor in the late 19th century. Henry Ford measured pacing of the assembly line, which led to mass production initiatives. But analytics began to command more attention in the late 1960s when computers were used in decision support systems. Since then, analytics have evolved with the development of enterprise resource planning (ERP) systems, data warehouses, and a variety of other hardware and software tools and applications.

The timeline depicted in Figure 1.3 shows the terminology used to describe analytics in the past sixty years. During the early days of analytics, prior to the 1970s, there was very little data, often obtained from the domain experts using manual processes (interviews and surveys) to build mathematical or knowledge-based models to solve constraint optimization problems. The idea was to do the best with limited resources. These decision support models were generally named as operations research (OR). The problems that were too complex to solve optimally (using linear or nonlinear mathematical programming techniques) were tacked with heuristic methods like simulation models.

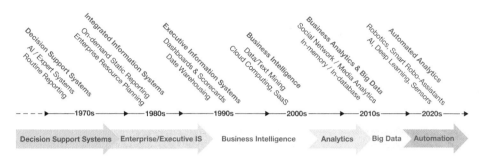

Figure 1.3 A longitudinal view of the evolution of analytics.

In the 1970s, in addition to matured OR models that were now being used in many industries and government systems, a new and exciting line of models emerged: rule-based expert systems (ES). These systems were promising to capture the experts' knowledge in a machine-processable form (for example, a collection of if-then rules) so that they could be used for consultation in much the same way one would use domain experts to identify a structured problem and to prescribe the most probable solution. That way, the scarce expertise can be made available to whomever wherever they would need it using an "intelligent" decision support system. During the 1970s, businesses created routine reports to help/inform decision-makers (managers) about what had happened in the previous day, week, month, or quarter. Although it was useful to know what had happened in the past, managers needed more than what was available: a variety of reports at different levels of granularity to better understand and address changing needs and challenges of the business.

The 1980s saw a significant change in the way organizations captured their business-related data. The old practice of having multiple disjointed information systems that were tailored to capture transactional data of the organizational unit/function (accounting, marketing and sales, finance, manufacturing) left its place to integrated enterprise-level information systems that we commonly call ERP systems today. The old, mostly sequential, and nonstandardized data representation schemas left their places to relational database management (RDBM) systems. These systems made it possible to improve capturing, storing, and relating organizational data fields to one another while significantly reducing the replication of information. The need to have RDBM and ERP systems emerged when data integrity and consistency became an issue, significantly hindering the effectiveness of business practices. With ERP, all the data from every corner of the enterprise is collected and integrated into a consistent schema so that every part of the organization would have access to the single version of the truth when and where they needed it. In addition to the emergence of ERP systems, or perhaps because of these systems, business reporting became an on-demand as-needed business practice. That way, the decision-makers can, when they need to or want to, create a specialized report to investigate organizational problems and opportunities.

In the 1990s, the need for having more versatile reporting led to executive information systems (a decision support system that was designed and developed specifically for executives and their decision-making needs). These systems were designed as graphical dashboards and scorecards so that they could serve as visually appealing displays while focusing on the most important factors for decision-makers to keep track of—key performance indicators. To make this highly versatile reporting possible while maintaining the transactional integrity of the business information systems intact, they had to create a middle data tier as a repository to specifically support business reporting and decision-making. This new tier is called data warehouse (DW). In a short time, most large to medium-sized businesses adopted data warehousing as their platform for enterprise-wide decision-making. The dashboards and scorecards were getting their data from DW, and by doing so, were not hindering the efficiency of the business transaction systems—mostly referred to as ERP systems.

In the 2000s, these DW-driven decision support systems were named as business intelligence systems. As the longitudinal data accumulated in the DWs, so did the capabilities of hardware and software to keep up with the rapidly changing and evolving needs of the decision-makers. As a necessity of the globalized competitive marketplace, decision-makers needed the most current information in a digestible form to address business problems and to take advantage of market opportunities in a timely manner. Because the data in a DW is updated periodically, it does not reflect the latest information. To elevate this information latency problem, DW vendors developed a system to update the data more frequently, which led to coining the term "real-time data warehousing" or, more realistically, "right-time data warehousing," which differs from the former by adopting a data refreshing policy based on the needed freshness of the data items. (Not all data items need to be refreshed in real time.) Because the data collected in a DW was large and feature rich, the emerging computational trends like data mining and text mining have become popular for "mining" the corporate data to "discover" new and useful knowledge nuggets to improve business processes and practices. With the increasing volumes and verities of data, the need for more storage and more processing power emerged. While large corporations had the means to tackle the problem, small to medium-sized companies looked for financially more manageable business models. This need led to service-oriented architecture and software and infrastructure as a service (IaaS)-type analytics business models. That way, smaller companies had access to analytics capabilities on an as-needed basis and paid only for what they used, as opposed to investing in financially prohibitive hardware and software resources.

In the 2010s, we have seen and still are seeing yet another paradigm shift in the way the data is captured and used. Largely attributed to the widespread use of the Internet, new data generation mediums have emerged. Of all the new data sources, including RFID tags, digital energy meters, clickstream Web logs, smart home devices, and wearable health monitoring equipment, perhaps the most interesting and challenging one is the social network/media data. Even though it is rich in information content, analysis of such unstructured data sources poses significant challenges to computational systems from both a software as well as a hardware perspective. Recently, the term "Big Data" was coined to highlight these challenges the new data streams have brought upon us. Many advancements in both hardware—massively parallel processing with huge computational memory and highly parallel multi-processor computing systems—as well as software/algorithms—Hadoop with MapReduce and NoSQL—have been developed to address the challenges of Big Data.

What the next decade will bring, what new terms will be used to name analytics, are hard to predict. The time between new paradigm shifts in information systems and particularly in analytics has been shrinking, and the trend of such will continue for the foreseeable future. Today, the reality is that even though analytics is not new, the explosion in its popularity is. With the recent explosion of Big Data, means to collect and store this data, and intuitive software tools, data and data-driven insight have become more accessible to business professionals than ever before. Therefore, in the midst of global competition, there is a huge opportunity to make better managerial decisions using data and analytics to increase revenue while decreasing cost by building better products, improving customer experience, catching fraud before it happens, and improving customer engagement through targeting and customization—all with the power of analytics and data. More and more companies are now preparing/schooling their employees with the know-how of business analytics to drive effectiveness and efficiency in their day-to-day decision-making processes.

A Simple Taxonomy for Analytics

Because of the multitude of factors related to both needing to make better and faster decisions as well as the availability and affordability of hardware and software technologies, analytics is gaining popularity faster than any trends we have seen in recent history. Will this upward exponential trend continue? Many industry experts think that it will, at least for the foreseeable future. Some of the most respected consultancy companies project analytics to grow three times the rate of other business segments in upcoming years, naming analytics as one of the top business trends of this decade (Robinson, Lewis, and Bennett, 2010). As the interest and adoption of analytics have grown rapidly, a need to characterize analytics into a simple taxonomy has emerged. Along with the top consultancy companies (Accenture, Gartner, IDT, among others), several technologically oriented academic institutions embarked on a mission to create a simple taxonomy for analytics. Such taxonomy, if developed properly and adopted universally, could create a contextual description of analytics, thereby facilitating a common understanding of what analytics is, what is included/excluded in analytics, and how analytics-related terms such as business intelligence, predictive modeling, and data mining would relate to each other. One of the academic institutions that took this challenge was the Institute for Operations Research and Management Science (INFORMS). To reach a wide audience, INFORMS hired Capgemini, a strategic management consulting firm, to carry out the study of characterizing analytics.

The study produced a concise definition of analytics: "Analytics facilitates realization of business objectives through reporting of data to analyze trends, creating predictive models for forecasting and optimizing business processes for enhanced performance." As this definition implies, one of the key findings from the study was that analytics is seen (by the executives inquired from a wide range of industries) as a core function of businesses that use it and spans many departments and functions within organizations and, in mature organizations, the entire business. As far as identifying the main categories of analytics is concerned, the study identified three hierarchical but sometimes overlapping groupings: descriptive, predictive, and prescriptive analytics. These three groups are hierarchical in terms of the level of analytics maturity of the organization. Most organizations start with descriptive analytics, then move into predictive analytics, and finally reach the top level in analytics hierarchy: prescriptive analytics. Even though these three groupings of analytics are hierarchical in complexity and sophistication, moving from a lower level to a higher level is not clearly separable. That is, a business can be in the descriptive analytics level while at the same time using predictive and even prescriptive analytics capabilities, in a somewhat piecemeal fashion. Therefore, moving from one level to the next essentially means that the maturity at one level is completed and the next level is being widely exploited. Figure 1.4 shows a graphical depiction of the simple taxonomy developed by INFORMS and widely adopted by most industry leaders as well as academic institutions.

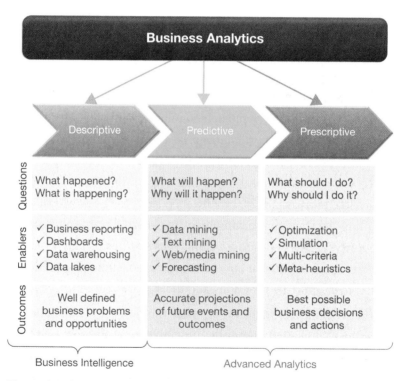

Figure 1.4 A simple taxonomy for analytics.

Descriptive analytics is the entry level in analytics taxonomy. It is often called business reporting because most of the analytics activities at this level deal with creating a report to summarize business activities to answer the question "What happened?" or "What is happening?" The spectrum of these reports includes static snapshots of business transactions delivered to knowledge workers (decision-makers) on a fixed schedule; dynamic views of business performance indicators delivered to managers and executives in an easily digestible form—often in a dashboard-looking graphical interface—on a continuous manner; and ad-hoc reporting where the decision-maker is given the capability of creating her own specific report (using an intuitive, drag-and-drop graphical user interface) to address a specific or unique decision situation.

Descriptive analytics is also called BI, and predictive and prescriptive analytics are collectively called advanced analytics. The logic behind calling part of the taxonomy advanced analytics is that moving from descriptive to predictive or prescriptive is a significant shift in the level of sophistication, which warrants the label of "advanced." BI has been one of the most popular technology trends for information systems designed to support managerial decision-making since the start of the century. It was popular until the arrival of the analytics wave. (To some extent, it still is popular in certain business circles.) Analytics characterizes BI as the entrance level to the world of analytics, setting the stage and paving the way toward more sophisticated decision analysis. These descriptive analytics systems usually work off a data warehouse, which is a large database specifically designed and developed to support BI functions and tools.

Predictive analytics comes right after the descriptive analytics in the three-level analytics hierarchy. Organizations that are matured in descriptive analytics move into this level, where they look beyond what happened and try to answer the question "What *will* happen?" As we will cover the predictive capabilities of these analytics techniques in depth in the following chapters as part of data mining, herein we provide only a short description of main prediction classes. Prediction essentially is the process of making intelligent/scientific estimates about the future values of some variables like customer demand, interest rates, and stock market movements. If what is being predicted is a categorical variable, the act of prediction is called **classification**; otherwise, it is called **regression**. If the predicted variable is time-dependent, the prediction process is often called **time-series forecasting**.

Prescriptive analytics is the highest echelon in analytics hierarchy. It is where the best alternative among many—that are usually created/ identified by predictive or descriptive analytics—courses of action is determined using sophisticated mathematical models. Therefore, in a sense, this type of analytics tries to answer the question "What should I do?" Prescriptive analytics uses optimization, simulation, and heuristics-based decision-modeling techniques. Even though prescriptive analytics is at the top of the analytics hierarchy, the methods behind it are not new. Most of the optimization and simulation models that constituted prescriptive analytics were developed during and right after World War II in the 1940s, when there was a dire need to do the best and the most with limited resources. Since then, prescriptive analytics has been used by some businesses for specific problem types, including yield/revenue management, transportation modeling, and scheduling. The new taxonomy of analytics made it popular again, opening its use to an array of business problems and situations.

Figure 1.5 shows the progressive nature of the three hierarchical levels of analytics along with the questions answered and techniques used at each level. As can be seen, the main subject of the book, pre-scriptive analytics is the top most layer in the analytics hierarchy, one that is closest to the decision being made.

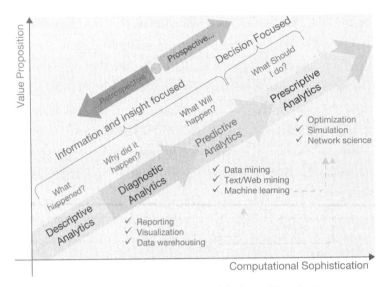

Figure 1.5 Three levels of analytics and their enabling techniques.

Business analytics is gaining popularity because it promises to provide decision-makers with information and knowledge that they need to succeed. The effectiveness of business analytics systems, no matter what level in the analytics hierarchy, depends largely on the quality and quantity of the data (volume and representational richness); the accuracy, integrity, and timeliness of the data management system; and the capabilities and sophistication of the analytical tools and procedures used in the process. Understanding the analytics taxonomy helps organizations be smart about selecting and implementing analytics capabilities to efficiently navigate through the maturity continuum. Following is a case study that shows the magnitude of impact that can be obtained from proper implementation of a large-scale analytics project.

Analytics Success Story: UPS's ORION Project

Arguably, as one of the largest prescriptive analytics and operations research projects in the world to date, UPS's On-Road Integrated Optimization and Navigation (ORION), has become an iconic figure for exemplifying the most successful analytics applications. Using a variety of inputs (most of which originating from its fleet telematics) and advanced analytics algorithms, ORION calculates optimal routing for its drivers. Because of its tremendous success, in 2016, UPS's ORION project won the prestigious Franz Edelman Award for Achievement in Operations Research and the Management Sciences, presented annually by INFORMS, which recognizes excellence in the execution of prescriptive analytics and operations research projects on the organizational level. (Since its inception in 1971, cumulative benefits from Edelman finalist projects well exceeded $250 billion.)

Background

United Parcel Service, or UPS, one of the leading logistics providers in the world, has been competing in a highly competitive and rapidly changing global business environment. Securing and sustaining success with a compelling competitive edge in such an environment requires a persistent and relentless pursuit for perfection by inventing and innovating new and improved business processes and practices.

The success of UPS can partially be attributed to its long-standing culture of "constructive dissatisfaction," which is credited to UPS founder, Jim Casey. It is the belief that companies and people should always be looking for ways to improve themselves. As is the case for most successful companies in the logistics business, UPS is committed to continuous improvement through investments in technologies— investing approximately $1 billion a year in operational efficiency and customer solution projects. In the case of ORION, the company not only had to invest in technologies to develop the desired solution, but get creative in the way it used leading-edge predictive and prescriptive analytics.

Just to create a context of the problem space, consider this: for any given business day, each UPS driver makes an average of about 120 delivery stops (Rosenbush and Stevens, 2015). The number of route combinations a driver can make is nearly infinite, a far greater number than the nanoseconds the earth has existed. Identifying the most efficient route, especially after considering variables such as special delivery times, road regulations, and the existence of private roads that don't appear on a map, is a near-impossible endeavor for a human being. The ORION project was initiated to take on this seemingly impossible-to-solve optimization problem. With the goal to ensure that UPS drivers use the most optimized delivery routes in regard to distance, fuel, and time, UPS developed ORION.

Motivated by a perfectionist view, the ORION project is the result of a long-term operational technology investment and commitment by UPS. ORION was more than a decade in the making from the initial development of the algorithm to full deployment to nearly 55,000 routes in North America. 2013 marked the first major ORION deployment by a team of 500 dedicated resources to roll out ORION to 10,000 UPS routes. As results exceeded expectations, UPS sped up the U.S. deployment and completed it by the fall of 2016.

Development of ORION

Optimal solutions that rely on analytics need data—rich, timely, and accurate data. In 2008, UPS deployed its telematics technologies on delivery trucks to gather all kinds of transactional and locational data to understand where efficiencies can be improved. By installing GPS tracking equipment and vehicle sensors, combined with a driver's handheld wireless mobile devices, UPS started to capture data related to traveled routes, amount of time vehicles idled, and even whether drivers were wearing seatbelts (Peterson, 2018).

Successful implementation of the real-time data-gathering modules set the stage for the development of ORION, which consists of a number of advanced analytics modules—based on optimization and other prescriptive analytics models—that could quickly and optimally solve seemingly unsolvable, tremendously complex routing problems.

The resulting algorithm in ORION includes about 1,000 pages of code and turns the captured real-time data into easy-to-follow instructions for drivers to optimize their routes. The ORION algorithm was initially developed in a lab and tested at various UPS sites from 2003 to 2009. The company prototyped ORION at eight sites between 2010 and 2011 and deployed it to six beta sites in 2012. The final system-wide deployment of the project was in 2016.

Today, ORION can solve an individual route in seconds and is constantly running in the background evaluating routes before drivers even leave the facility. This level of route evaluation conducted through the ORION program requires extensive hardware and architectural provisions. Running on a bank of servers in Mahwah, New Jersey, ORION is constantly evaluating the best way for a route to run based on real-time information. While most of America is sleeping, ORION is solving tens of thousands of route optimizations per minute. In addition to architectural enhancements, the driver's delivery information acquisition device (DIAD) is enhanced to serve as the tool for communicating optimized routes to drivers while on the road (Paterson, 2018).

Results

Costing $250 million to build and deploy, ORION is expected to save UPS $300 to $400 million annually. By building efficient routes and reducing the miles driven and fuel consumption, ORION contributes to UPS's sustainability efforts by reducing 100,000 metric tons of greenhouse gas emissions.

The success UPS has seen as a result of implementing ORION is the ramification of a decade-long effort that has gone into its development. The company has already seen an average daily reduction of six to eight miles per route for drivers who are using ORION routes. Once fully deployed systemwide, ORION will save UPS about 100 million miles per year. That's a reduction of 10 million gallons of fuel consumed. It also reduces carbon dioxide emissions by about 100,000 metric tons. Initial results show miles reduced with each route using ORION; a reduction of just one mile per driver per day over one year can save UPS up to $50 million.

ORION also benefits customers because it enables more personalized services, even on peak business days. This includes the UPS My Choice service, which allows consumers to have online and mobile access to see their incoming UPS home deliveries and enables them to actively choose delivery preferences, reroute shipments, and adjust delivery locations and dates as needed. Currently, millions of customers take advantage of the UPS My Choice service, and ORION technologies will continue to make possible even more personalized services, with international service on the future roadmap (Peterson, 2018).

Summary

Analytics has become the chief enabler for modern-day businesses. With a series of innovative analytics projects in the past several decades, UPS has expanded its intelligent decision-making capabilities by using rich data sources (Big Data that comes from GPS devices, vehicle sensors, and driver handhelds as well as the transactional data that come from business practices) along with advanced modeling techniques—from descriptive to predictive to prescriptive analytics.

Analytics Success Story: Man Versus Machine

It has been a relentless pursuit by humans since the emergence of computing systems to develop machines that are capable of competing against humans on intelligence-requiring tasks. These developments have been tested on a number of games and computing scenarios. Following are the most notable ones in the span of history. Once we look at these examples, we no longer can say that machine learning is just for making predictions. Machine learning can be used to compute and make intelligent decisions. Behind these games and contests, the intention has always been to push forward the ability of computers to handle the kinds of complex calculations needed to help discover new medical drugs; do the broad financial modeling needed to identify trends and carry out risk analysis; handle large database searches; and perform massive calculations needed in advanced fields of science.

Checkers

Perhaps the earliest known example of machine learning within the context of games is Arthur Samuel's work on a program that learned how to play checkers better than he could. Samuel used machine learning to learn how to make the right decisions. He developed the checkers playing game on IBM 700 series computers while he was working at IBM in the 1960s and 1970s. Arthur Lee Samuel was an American pioneer in the field of computer gaming and artificial intelligence. He coined the term **machine learning** in 1959. The Samuel Checkers-Playing Program was among the world's first successful self-learning programs, and as such an early demonstration of the fundamental concept of artificial intelligence (AI).

Chess

Deep Blue was a chess-playing computer developed by IBM. It is known for being the first computer chess-playing system to win both a chess game and a chess match against a reigning world champion under regular time controls. Deep Blue won its first game against a world champion on 10 February 1996, when it defeated Garry Kasparov in game one of a six-game match. However, Kasparov won three and drew two of the following five games, defeating Deep Blue by a score of 4–2. Deep Blue was then heavily upgraded and played

Kasparov again in May 1997. The match lasted several days and received massive media coverage around the world. It was the classic plot line of man versus machine. Deep Blue won game six, thereby winning the six-game rematch 3½–2½ and becoming the first computer system to defeat a reigning world champion in a match under standard chess tournament time controls.

Jeopardy!

After Deep Blue, a little more than a decade later, in another attempt to develop smart machines, IBM developed Watson in 2011 to compete against the best human players on the popular game show, *Jeopardy!*. Watson defeated the best two players (most money winner and most consecutive winner) at *Jeopardy!*. IBM Watson is designed as a learning machine (also called a cognitive machine at IBM) from unstructured data sources, or textual knowledge repositories. It was given numerous digital information sources to digest, and then it was trained with pairs of question answers from *Jeopardy!*. As it trained, its performance at answering *Jeopardy!* questions improved until it was able to best top human players. IBM Watson learned how to answer questions. It learned how to decide which answer was best given a question it had never seen before. A detailed description of IBM Watson's story on *Jeopardy!* and its technical capabilities is given below.

Go

In December 2016, Google AlphaGo won a match against one of the top Go players. AlphaGo is an artificial intelligence machine learning that is based on **deep learning**. It was first trained on a large set of recorded Go games between top players. Then it trained against itself. As it trained, its performance at Go increased until it became better than a top human player. AlphaGo learned how to decide what the best next move was for any Go board configuration.

IBM Watson Explained

IBM Watson is perhaps the smartest computer system built to date. After a little more than a decade from the successful development of Deep Blue, IBM researchers came up with another, perhaps more challenging idea: a machine that can not only play *Jeopardy!* but beat the best of the best of human champions on the game show. Compared to chess, *Jeopardy!* is much more challenging. While chess is well structured, has simple rules, and therefore is a good match for computer processing, *Jeopardy!* is a game designed for human intelligence and creativity. It should be built like a cognitive computing system, much like a natural extension of what humans can do at their best. To be competitive, Watson needed to work and think like a human. Making sense of the imprecision inherent in human language was the key to success. With Watson, cognitive computing forged a new partnership between humans and computers that scales and augments human expertise.

Watson is an extraordinary computer system—a novel combination of advanced hardware and software—designed to answer questions posed in natural human language. It was developed in 2010 by an IBM research team as part of a DeepQA project and was named after IBM's first president, Thomas J. Watson. The motivation behind Watson was to look for a major research challenge (one that could rival the scientific and popular interest of Deep Blue), which would also have clear relevance to IBM's business interests. The goal was to advance computational science by exploring new ways for computer technology to affect science, business, and society at large. Accordingly, IBM Research undertook a challenge to build a computer system that could compete at the human champion level in real time on the American TV quiz show *Jeopardy!* The extent of the challenge included fielding a real-time automatic contestant on the show—capable of listening, understanding, and responding—not merely a laboratory exercise.

In 2011, as a test of its abilities, Watson competed on the quiz show *Jeopardy!*, which was the first ever human-versus-machine matchup for the show. In a two-game, combined-point match (broadcast in three *Jeopardy!* episodes during February 14–16), Watson beat Brad Rutter, the biggest all-time money winner on *Jeopardy!*, and Ken Jennings, the record holder for the longest championship streak (75 days). In these episodes, Watson consistently outperformed its human opponents on the game's signaling device but had trouble responding to a few categories, notably those having short clues containing only a few words. Watson had access to 200 million pages of structured and unstructured content consuming 4 terabytes of disk storage. During the game, Watson was not connected to the Internet.

Meeting the *Jeopardy!* challenge required advancing and incorporating a variety of QA technologies (text mining and natural language processing), including parsing, question classification, question decomposition, automatic source acquisition and evaluation, entity and relation detection, logical form generation, and knowledge representation and reasoning. Winning at *Jeopardy!* required accurately computing confidence in one's answers. The questions and content are ambiguous and noisy, and none of the individual algorithms are perfect. Therefore, each component must produce a confidence in its output, and individual component confidence must be combined to compute the overall confidence of the final answer. The final confidence is used to determine whether the computer system should risk choosing to answer at all. In *Jeopardy!* parlance, this confidence is used to determine whether the computer will "ring in" or "buzz in" for a question. The confidence must be computed during the time the question is read and before the opportunity to buzz in. This is roughly between 1 and 6 seconds with an average around 3 seconds.

How Does Watson Do It?

The system behind Watson, which is called DeepQA, is a massively parallel, text mining–focused, probabilistic evidence-based computational architecture. For the *Jeopardy!* challenge, Watson used more than 100 different techniques for analyzing natural language, identifying sources, finding and generating hypotheses, finding and scoring evidence, and merging and ranking hypotheses. What is far more important than any particular technique that Watson used was how it combined techniques in DeepQA such that overlapping approaches could bring their strengths to bear and contribute to improvements in accuracy, confidence, and speed. DeepQA is an architecture with an accompanying methodology that is not specific to the *Jeopardy!* challenge. The overarching principles in DeepQA are massive parallelism, many experts, pervasive confidence estimation, and integration of the-latest-and-greatest in text analytics.

- **Massive parallelism.** Exploit massive parallelism in the consideration of multiple interpretations and hypotheses.

- **Many experts.** Facilitate the integration, application, and contextual evaluation of a range of loosely coupled probabilistic question and content analytics.

- **Pervasive confidence estimation.** No component commits to an answer; all components produce features and associated confidences, scoring different question and content interpretations. An underlying confidence-processing substrate learns how to stack and combine the scores.

- **Integrate shallow and deep knowledge.** Balance the use of strict semantics and shallow semantics, leveraging many loosely formed ontologies.

Figure 1.6 illustrates the DeepQA architecture at a high level. More technical details about the various architectural components and their specific roles and capabilities can be found in Ferrucci et al. (2010).

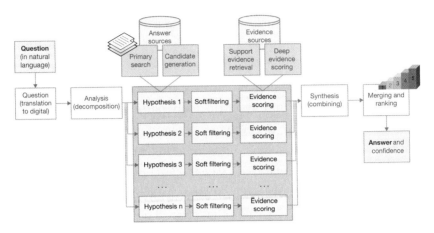

Figure 1.6 A high-level depiction of the DeepQA architecture.

The *Jeopardy!* challenge helped IBM address requirements that led to the design of the DeepQA architecture and the implementation of Watson. After three years of intense research and development by a core team of about 20 researchers and a significant amount of R&D money, Watson managed to perform at human expert levels in terms of precision, confidence, and speed at the *Jeopardy!* quiz show. At that point in time, perhaps the big question was "so what now?" Was it all for a quiz show? Absolutely not! After showing the rest of the world what Watson (and the cognitive system behind Watson) could do, it became an inspiration for the next generation of intelligent information systems. For IBM, it was a demonstration of what is possible (and perhaps what the company is capable of doing) with the cutting-edge analytics and computational sciences. The message was clear: if a smart machine can beat the best of the best in humans at what they are the best at, think about what it can do for your organizational problems. The first industry that utilized Watson was health care, followed by finance, retail, education, public services, and advanced science.

Conclusion

Business analytics is all about decision-making—not the way it was done in the past, which relied heavily on experience, gut feeling, and intuition, but the one that relies on data/evidence and computational/mathematical/statistical sciences. Because of the need to make faster and better decisions in today's highly competitive business world and the availability of large and feature-rich data sources along with the advanced computing resources (both on hardware and software side), managerial decision-making is experiencing a paradigm shift. This chapter provided an overview of the human decision-making process and how business analytics can enhance this process toward more accurate and actionable outcomes.

As discussed in this chapter and illustrated in Figures 1.4 and 1.5, the simple taxonomy of business analytics is composed of three echelons: descriptive/diagnostic, predictive, and prescriptive. Prescriptive analytics is the highest echelon in this hierarchical relationship; it is closest to the decision-making. That is, whereas descriptive, diagnostic, and predictive analytics aim to create information to explain what happened, why it happened, and what will happen, prescriptive analytics focuses on the use of the information generated by these earlier echelons to identify the best course of action—to answer the question of what to do or what the optimal solution is to the problem. The following five chapters cover some of the most popular family of techniques that are collectively called **prescriptive analytics** with plenty of exemplary case studies and simple hands-on exercises.

References

Bi, R. (2014). "When Watson Meets Machine Learning" at www.kdnuggets.com/2014/07/watson-meets-machine-learning.html (accessed June 2014).

DeepQA (2011). DeepQA Project: FAQ. IBM Corporation, http://www.research.ibm.com/deepqa/faq.shtml (accessed April 2014).

Feldman, S., Hanover, J., Burghard, C., and Schubmehl, D. (2012). "Unlocking the Power of Unstructured Data," IBM white paper, found at http://www-01. ibm.com/software/ebusiness/jstart/downloads/unlockingUnstructuredData.pdf (accessed May 2017).

Ferrucci, D. et al. (2010). "Building Watson: An Overview of the DeepQA Project." *AI Magazine*, 31(3), 59–79.

IBM (2014). "Implement Watson" at www.ibm.com/smarterplanet/us/en/ibmwatson/ implement-watson.html (accessed July 2014).

Liberatore, M., and Luo, W. (2011). "INFORMS and the Analytics Movement: The View of the Membership." *Interfaces*, 41(6), 578–589.

Newell, A., Shaw, J. C., & Simon, H. A. (1958). "Elements of a Theory of Human Problem Solving." *Psychological Review*, 65(3): 151–172.

Newell, A., & Simon, H. A. (1972). *Human Problem Solving*, 104(9). Englewood Cliffs, NJ: Prentice-Hall.

Pauly, M. V. (2004). "Split Personality: Inconsistencies in Private and Public Decisions." In S. J. Hoch, H. C. Kunreuther, and R. E. Gunther (eds.). *Wharton on Making Decisions*. New York: Wiley.

Peterson, K. (2018). "ORION Backgrounder," UPS Pressroom, available at https:// pressroom.ups.com/pressroom/ContentDetailsViewer.page?ConceptType= FactSheets&id=1426321616277-282 (accessed January 2019).

Robinson, A., Levis, J. and Bennett, G. (2010, October). "INFORMS to Officially Join Analytics Movement." *ORMS Today*, INFORMS Publication.

Rosenbush, S. and Stevens, L. (2015). "At UPS, the Algorithm Is the Driver." *The Wall Street Journal*. [Online] February 16, 2015. http://www.wsj.com/articles/at-ups-the-algorithm-is-the-driver-1424136536 (accessed January 2019).

Sawyer, D. C. (1999). *Getting It Right: Avoiding the High Cost of Wrong Decisions*. Boca Raton, FL: St. Lucie Press.

Schwartz, K. D. (2005). "Decisions at the Touch of a Button," August 19, 2005, found at dssresources.com/cases/coca-colajapan/index.html

Simon, H. A. (1977), The New Science of Management Decision (3rd revised edition; first edition 1960). Prentice-Hall, Englewood Cliffs, NJ.

Simon, H. A. (1982). *Models of Bounded Rationality: Empirically Grounded Economic Reason*. Cambridge, MA: MIT Press.

Stewart, T. A. (2002, November). "How to Think with Your Gut." *Business 2.0*.

2

Optimization and Optimal Decision-Making

Optimization is usually perceived as a positively connotated word that relates to rational or normative decision-making—a process that is concerned with identifying the best decision to make, under the assumption that an ideal decision-maker is fully informed, able to compute with perfect accuracy, and fully rational. Generally speaking, optimization is being used to refer to the process of achieving "the best" possible outcome from a given situation—that is, identifying the best possible choice-of-action from within a given set of options or alternatives. This set of options may sometimes be deterministic—all related variables and their possible values are known with certainty, yet near infinite in count—and other times it may contain missing variables or variable values that are imprecise or stochastic in nature.

Although in daily discussions optimization can be used somewhat loosely to refer to a good or better-off choice or decision-outcome, its true meaning ought to refer to nothing other than "the best." Webster's dictionary defines optimization as "… an act, process, or methodology of making something (such as a design, system, or decision) as fully perfect, functional, or effective as possible." Specifically, in mathematical procedures, optimization refers to maximizing or minimizing a predetermined goal or outcome, often referred to as an **objective function** in mathematical formulation of optimization problems. Because the maximum or minimum of any given numerical value would go to either positive or negative infinity, respectively, there usually are limiting factors, or constraints, associated with the situations that keep the outcome's values within measurable/calculable limits.

Optimizing, or finding an optimal solution to a given problem, can be a straightforward process if the number of feasible alternatives to consider is limited. In such a situation, one would evaluate each alternative against the goal and select the one that produces the best results, which would be the largest in goal-value for a maximization-type optimization situation and the smallest for a minimization-type situation. It is worth noting here that a feasible solution-alternative is the one that complies with all the limitations/constraints, and optimization is the process or identifying the best out of all those feasible solutions as per the goal or objective function or fitness function. What if there are no feasible alternatives? Well, in that case, there would be no optimal solution, or any solution, to that problem; hence, the problem would be classified as unsolvable. For such an unsolvable problem, the decision-maker would strive to remove or relax one or more of the most pressing limitations or constraints, and by doing so effectively, create a feasible solution space.

The problems that fall into a feasibly solvable category can further be classified as either optimally solvable or heuristically solvable. Some problems can be solved optimally—that is, the best possible solution can be identified mathematically for certainty—and some can be solved only heuristically—the best possible solution cannot be mathematically identified with certainty, so a good or satisfying solution is often the end result. These nonoptimal solutions providing techniques are often called heuristic methods that help find good or better solutions but do not have the capability to identify or confirm the best possible solution. Whereas heuristic methods include simulation and a number of search techniques, optimization techniques include linear, nonlinear, and heuristic mathematical programming techniques. In the next section, we delve into linear programming (LP), arguably the most popular mathematical optimization technique, to explain the mechanics and the process of algebraically formulating and optimally solving a number of different real-world decision problems.

Common Problem Types for LP Solution

The most common optimization models that can be solved with LP formulation include the following:

- **Product mix.** Finding the optimal quantities of products to maximize the total profit. A detailed description of this linear programming model type along with a sample problem is given later in the chapter.

- **Blending.** Finding the optimal proportion of materials to achieve the best-performing composite.

- **Assignment.** Finding the best matching of objects (for example, airplane, crew, and gate) to maximize the system outcome.

- **Investment.** Finding the optimal mix of investment products that yield the maximum rate of return.

- **Replacement.** Finding the optimal set of items to replace to maximize the system output while minimizing the process improvement cost.

- **Inventory.** Finding the optimal inventory levels of items to minimize total inventory cost.

- **Transportation.** Finding the optimal shipment schedule between origins and destinations to minimize the total transportation cost. A detailed description of this linear programming model type along with a sample problem is given later in the chapter.

- **Production planning.** Finding the optimal schedule of orders to process to maximize production output or minimize the production cost.

- **Network models.** Finding the optimal path to minimize the distance. A detailed description of this linear programming model type along with a sample problem is given later in the chapter.
- **Scheduling.** A generic group of problems whose goal is to find the optimal sequence and timing of activities and decisions to optimize the expected outcome, whether job scheduling, crew scheduling, or something else.
- **Telecommunications.** Finding an optimal network of nodes— switches, towers, and relays—that maximizes the quality of service or minimizes the total cost of the system.

Types of Optimization Models

The various types of optimization models include linear programming, integer and mixed-integer programming, nonlinear programming, and stochastic programming.

Linear Programming

Linear programming is the most straightforward to understand and the most commonly used optimization model type. A detailed coverage along with a set of representative examples of this popular optimization technique is given in one of the following main sections.

Integer and Mixed-Integer Programming

In linear programming models, one of the key assumptions is the unrestricted nature of the decision variable values. That is, the decision variables can assume real/fractional values, although, in most cases, the decision variables cannot have quantity fractional values, such as the optimal quantity of each product to produce. Technically speaking, an **integer programming** problem is a mathematical optimization program in which the decision variables are restricted to be integers. **Mixed-integer programming** is similar to integer programming in that some, but not all, of the decision variables are required to assume integer values.

The key difference between linear programming and integer programming is rather trivial; in linear programming, the decision variables are allowed to assume real values, whereas in integer programming they are required to have integer values. The solution mechanism for linear programming and integer programming is quite different, where integer programming solution methods require significantly longer processing time and more computational resources.

Nonlinear Programming

Nonlinear programming is the process of solving an optimization problem where some of the constraints or the objective function are expressed in nonlinear algebraic formulation. An optimization problem is the calculation of the **extrema** (maxima, minima, or stationary points) of an objective function over a set of unknown real variables and conditionals to the satisfaction of a system of equalities and inequalities, collectively termed **constraints**. It is the subfield of mathematical optimization that deals with problems that are not linear.

A typical nonconvex problem is that of optimizing transportation costs by selecting from a set of transportation methods, one or more of which exhibit economies of scale, with various connectivity and capacity constraints. An example would be petroleum product transport given a selection or combination of pipeline, rail tanker, road tanker, river barge, or coastal tankship. Owing to economic batch size, the cost functions may have discontinuities in addition to smooth changes.

In experimental science, some simple data analysis, such as fitting a spectrum with a sum of peaks of known location and shape but unknown magnitude, can be done with linear methods, but in general these problems, also, are nonlinear. Typically, one has a theoretical model of the system under study with variable parameters in it and a model of the experiment or experiments, which may also have unknown parameters. One tries to find a best fit numerically. In this case, one often wants a measure of the precision of the result and the best fit itself.

Stochastic Programming

In the field of mathematical optimization, stochastic programming is a framework for modeling optimization problems that involve uncertainty. Whereas deterministic optimization problems are formulated with known parameters, real-world problems almost invariably include some unknown parameters. When the parameters are known only within certain bounds, one approach to tackling such problems is called **robust optimization**. Here the goal is to find a solution that is feasible for all such data and optimal in some sense. Stochastic programming models are similar in style but take advantage of the fact that probability distributions governing the data are known or can be estimated. The goal here is to find some policy that is feasible for all (or almost all) the possible data instances and maximizes the expectation of some function of the decisions and the random variables. More generally, such models are formulated, solved analytically or numerically, and analyzed to provide useful information to a decision-maker.

As an example, consider two-stage linear programs. Here the decision-maker takes some action in the first stage, after which a random event occurs affecting the outcome of the first-stage decision. A recourse decision can then be made in the second stage that compensates for any bad effects that might have been experienced as a result of the first-stage decision. The optimal policy from such a model is a single first-stage policy and a collection of recourse decisions (a decision rule) defining which second-stage action should be taken in response to each random outcome.

Stochastic programming has applications in a broad range of areas ranging from finance to transportation to energy optimization.

Linear Programming for Optimization

Linear programming (LP) is undoubtedly the best-known technique in the family of optimization tools called mathematical programming, also known as mathematical optimization. LP is a method to achieve the best outcome (such as highest profit or lowest cost) in a mathematical model whose formulation and requirements are represented with linear relationships. Mathematically speaking, LP is a technique for optimizing (either minimizing or maximizing) a goal, or objective function. It is represented as a linear function, subject to a number of constraints, each of which is portrayed in the form of linear equality or linear inequality. In LP formulation, the feasible region, if it exists, forms a convex multi-dimensional shape (a polyhedron) with many corners. The corner that holds the optimal solution is determined by the slope characteristics of the objective function, which is a real-valued linear function defined by the same set of decision variables. In other words, using the objective function characteristics as the guideline, a linear programming algorithm identifies a corner in the polyhedron where the objective function has the optimal value.

George Bernard Dantzig, an American mathematical scientist who made contributions to industrial engineering, operations research, computer science, economics, and statistics, is often credited for developing the general LP formulation and solving it with the simplex method. In the mid-1940s, he applied LP to the formulation and solution of planning problems in the U.S. Air Force. Dantzig's original example was to find the best assignment of 70 people to 70 jobs. The computing power required to evaluate all the permutations to select the best assignment was beyond attainable; the number of possible configurations exceeded the number of particles in the observable universe. However, it took only a moment to find the optimum solution by formulating the problem as a linear program and applying the simplex algorithm. The theory behind linear programming drastically reduces the number of possible solutions that must be checked. Optimally solving seemingly unsolvable problems made linear programming a focal point for many researchers and practitioners, and since then, many variations of the original algorithm have been developed to solve a range of complex decision problems.

LP Assumptions

There are a number of assumptions one needs to be aware of before considering the use of LP for optimization problems. The core assumptions that everyone agrees on are (1) linearity, (2) divisibility, (3) certainty, and (4) non-negativity. Additionally, some also include these four plus (5) fitness and (6) optimality. Let us briefly explain these LP assumptions.

Linearity

In LP, it is assumed that proportionality exists in the formulation of the objective function and constraints. This means that if production of 1 unit of product consumes 6 hours of labor, then making 10 units of the same product consumes 60 hours of the same type of labor hours. The formulation of the objective function and the constraints does not allow for multiplication or square (or higher power) representation of the decision variables.

Divisibility

It is assumed that solutions, or values assigned to the decision variables, need not be in whole numbers, or integers. Instead, they can be divisible and may take any fractional value. The removal of this assumption, where the integer value of decision variables is a requirement, led to a derivative programming algorithm called integer programming.

Certainty

Numerical values—constants and coefficients—used in the formulation of the objective function and constraints are known with certainty and do not change during the time window being modeled and studied. For instance, the unit profit for each product type (used in the objective function as multiplier of decision variables—the production quantities for each product type) is assumed to be known as a constant value.

Non-Negative

In LP, it is assumed that the solution, or the values for the decision variables, must be non-negative because having negative values of physical quantities is illogical and impossible. Unless such a constraint is added to the LP formulation, the solution algorithms could assign negative values to the decision variables to obtain an optimal solution.

Finiteness

There are finite (i.e., limited) quantities of things (e.g., row materials, labor hours, product quantities, and so on) involved in the optimization problem. An optimal solution cannot be computed in a situation where there are an infinite number of alternative activities and resource restrictions.

Optimality

In LP problems, the optimality—maximum profit or minimum cost solutions—always occurs at a corner point (or a corner line, a corner hyperplane) of the multi-dimensional representation of the feasible region.

Components of an LP Model

The structure of an LP model is composed of a set of four components:

1. **Decision variables.** These are the variables whose values determine the solution/answer to the posed optimization problem. For instance, in a product-mix problem, the decision variables are the production quantities of all products that collectively constitute the maximum profit. In this exemplary case, it is necessary to note that each product may require different types and quantities of resources and different unit profit margins.

2. **Objective function.** This function algebraically defines the goal of the optimization problem at hand. Using the decision variables and related parameters or coefficients in a linear mathematical representation, objective function defines what needs to be optimized—either minimized (for something in which smaller is better, such as cost) or maximized (for something in which larger is better, such as profit).

3. **Constraints.** These are the limitations that need to be complied with toward achieving the optimal value for the objective function. Constraints help in defining the feasible solution space. Less restrictive constraints produce a larger feasible solution space, whereas overly restrictive constraints may lead to an infeasible solution space. In the case of an infeasible solution space, one would need to relax, or expand, some of the constraints to create a feasible solution space with alternatives. Constraints can be any combination of material, labor, time, and demand.

4. **Parameters.** These are the constant numerical values used in the formulation of the objective function and constraints. For instance, in the objective function of profit maximization, we use unit profit values of all product types as parameters multiplied

with respective decision variables and summed together to formulate the total profit. Similarly, in constraints, each decision variable is multiplied with unit material used in production of each product type, summed together, made less than or equal to the total available quantity of that material type.

Figure 2.1 shows the graphical depiction of the interactions among these LP modeling components. As can be seen, the decision variables $(X_1, X_2, ..., X_n)$ and the parameters $(c_1, c_2, ..., c_n$ in the objective function and $a_{11}, a_{22}, ..., a_{nn}$ in the constraints) are used to construct the algebraic representation of the LP problem. The overall objective is to identify the values of decision variables that optimize the value of the objective function while complying with each one of the constraints.

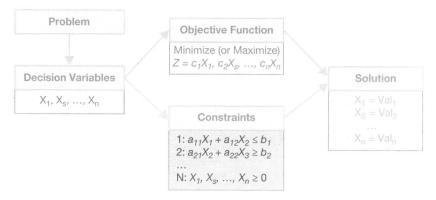

Figure 2.1 A graphical depiction of the component interactions in LP modeling.

Process of Developing an LP Model

Problems are a part of the real world, with all its complexities and uncertainties. The first step in LP modeling is to summarize the real-world situation in a concise verbal description. The second step is to convert the verbal description into the algebraic representation, where the decision variables are identified and used in formulating the objective function and constraints. Once the algebraic representation of the LP model is created, based on the complexity of the model and the availability of software tools, a graphical or a spreadsheet or a specialized software tool is used to find the optimal solution. The optimal solution is defined as the values of the decision variables that produce the best objective function value. A graphical solution can be used if the LP models have only two decision variables. Although moderate size and complex LP models can be solved with the Excel Solver add-in, more complex, large-scale problems may require special optimization software packages such as LINDO, CPLEX, SAS/OR, AMPL, and AIMMS. An illustrative example of this model development and solution process is described in the next section.

The process of developing and solving an LP model is explained in the following section. Using a simple optimization problem type, called the **product mix problem**, the individual steps in the process are explained and exemplified.

Hands-On Example: Product Mix Problem

This example begins with a verbal description of the problem and then presentation of the algebraic representation.

Verbal Description

The ABC Company custom-builds (i.e., installs, configures, verifies) and sells two types of computing equipment/workstations for AI/deep-learning projects—DL1 and DL2—to individual researchers for for-profit businesses and universities over the Internet. DL1 is the slightly less costly, less capable, and less sophisticated of the two workstations. Each workstation requires a certain amount of time for hardware and software installation and configuration, followed by a thorough quality control procedure, before shipping out to the customers. The time it takes to carry out each of these three tasks for each workstation type is given in Table 2.1.

Table 2.1 Summary of Time and Tasks for Workstation Type

Workstation Type	Tasks (Installation, Configuration, and Quality Control)		
	1 - Hardware	*2 - Software*	*3 - Quality Control*
DL1	5	3	2
DL2	8	4	2
Monthly available total man-hours:	1,200	800	400

Each DL1 sells for $1,400, and each DL2 brings in $2,375. The profit margin for DL1 is 25%, whereas the profit margin for DL2 is 20%. The company has a few loyal corporate customers with a total perpetual order of 50 DL1 and 50 DL2 each month. The total man-hours that can be dedicated to the three tasks are given in the last row of Table 2.1. The company wants to determine the product mix—the exact number of DL1 and DL2—to produce each month to maximize its total monthly profit.

Algebraic Representation

The algebraic representation of an LP problem includes decision variables, an objective function, and several constraints.

Decision Variables　First, we need to determine the **decision variables**—identification and characterization of what it is that we are trying to decide. In this problem, it is rather straightforward: we are trying to determine the exact number of DL1 and DL2 to produce. Let us call these two numbers X_1 (number of DL1 to produce each month) and X_2 (the number of DL2 to produce each month).

Objective Function   From the verbal description, we need to formulate an objective function. The **objective function** is the goal we are trying to achieve by identifying the best possible values for the decision variables. In this problem, the objective is to maximize the total monthly profit. Although the unit profit for each workstation is not explicitly given, we can easily calculate it by using the unit cost and the profit margin numbers as follows:

Unit profit for a DL1 = $1,400 * 0.25 = $350

Unit profit for a DL2 = $2,375 * 0.20 = $475

Using the already determined unit profits and the decision variables, the objective function (Z) can be algebraically written as follows:

Maximize (total monthly profit = Z) = $350 * X_1 + 475 * X_2$

Constraints   In the absence of limitations, or **constraints**, this objective function value would go to plus infinity. However, in this problem, as is the case in any real-world situation, we have limited resources—the limited man-hours available for the production processes—and some demand constraints. Specifically, for this problem we have three resource constraints: hardware, software, and quality control. Furthermore, we have two demand constraints: we must produce at least 50 DL1 and 30 DL2 to meet the perpetual monthly orders. Hence, the algebraic representation of the constraints, in terms of the decision variables, can be written as follows:

C1 – Hardware:	$5 * X_1 + 8 * X_2 \leq 1,200$
C2 – Software:	$3 * X_1 + 4 * X_2 \leq 800$
C3 – Quality:	$2 * X_1 + 2 * X_2 \leq 400$
C4 – DL1 (Demand):	$X_1 \geq 50$
C5 – DL2 (Demand):	$X_2 \geq 50$

We also need to have the non-negativity constraints. Although it is obvious to humans, mathematical algorithms need to know that negative values for decision variables are not acceptable. We can show the non-negativity constraints as follows:

C6 – Non-negativity: $X_1, X_2 \geq 0$ or $X_1 \geq 0; X_2 \geq 0$

Graphical Depiction of the LP Model for a Simple Solution

Because we have only two decision variables, X_1 and X_2, we can use a two-dimensional graphical depiction for solving this LP problem. To illustrate the modeling process toward the optimal solution to the problem, we need to properly represent the two decision variables, all the constraints, and the objective function on this graphical depiction. Here are the steps we follow in this graphical solution procedure:

1. Show the decision variables as the two axes: X_1 as the x-axis and X_2 as the y-axis. It does not matter which decision variable is represented on which axis.

2. Starting with the non-negativity constraint, show all constraints, and identify the feasible solution region on the two-dimensional space.

3. Using the algebraic representation of the objective function, identify the optimal solution within the feasible region.

4. Using the optimal values of the decision variables, calculate the objective function value, or the maximum possible total monthly profit.

Step 1 and Step 2: As can be seen in Figure 2.2, by identifying the decision variables as x- and y-axes and shading the non-negativity region on these decision variables, we now have the feasible solution region: an unbounded rectangle. This region will be further reshaped/reduced by the other constraints.

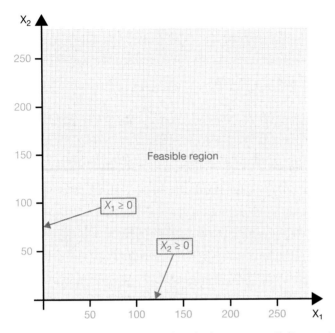

Figure 2.2 Feasible region with only the non-negativity constraints (C6) applied.

Step 3 is where we draw the remaining constraint onto the output of Step 2 to create the feasible region shown in Figure 2.2. While drawing the constraint onto the graphical space, we follow the following simple procedure for each constraint.

1. If the constraint is an inequality type (containing >, ≥, <, or ≤ signs between the left-hand side and the right-hand side of the constraint), we convert the inequality into equality. If the constraint is of the type "equality," we leave it as is.

2. To calculate the intercepts of the constraint line with the two axes, we equalize one of the two decision variables to zero and solve the remaining simple equation. Then we repeat the

process for the other decision variable. At the end, we would have the intercept values for both decision variables by marking and connecting them onto the graphical solution.

3. Based on the inequality, we shade either the below (if the inequality is of "<" or "≤" type) or the above (if the inequality is of ">" or "≥" type) of the newly drawn constraint line to signify the new feasible region, as shown in Figure 2.3.

4. By repeating the process of plotting and shading the graphical region for all the constraints, we would end up with a feasible region, as shown in Figure 2.4.

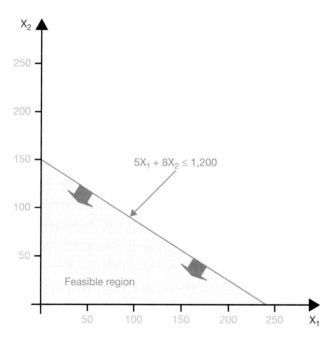

Figure 2.3 Feasible region with the non-negativity and the first resource constraints (C1 and C6) applied.

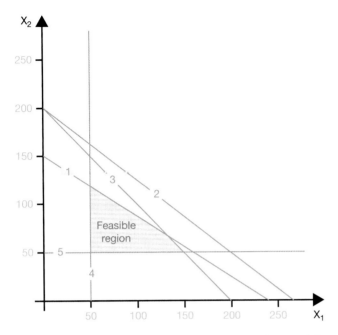

Figure 2.4 Feasible region with all constraints (C1 true C6) applied.

Once we determine the final feasible region, with the help of the objective function, we can identify the optimal solution. For that, we first equalize the objective function to an arbitrarily large number. Preferably, this number is easily divisible by the two objective function coefficients. Then we identify the decision variable values and plot the line into the two-dimensional space, the same way we have done for the constraints C1, C2, and C3. Following that, and in keeping the angle of the objective line function unchanged, we move the line forward and backward to identify the corner that it touches the last before moving out of the feasible region. For a maximization-type optimization problem, this corner will be at the upper-right side of the feasible region, toward the larger values of the decision variables. In contrast, the corner will be at the lower-left sides of the feasible region for minimization-type optimization problems. Specifically, for this problem we equalized the objective function to 33,250 and solved for the decision variable. By doing so, we identified the values of

X_1 and X_2 as 95 and 70, respectively. The corresponding line is shown in Figure 2.5. Also shown in the figure is the corner at which the objective function line touched before moving out of the feasible region, which is corresponding to the optimal values of the decision variables.

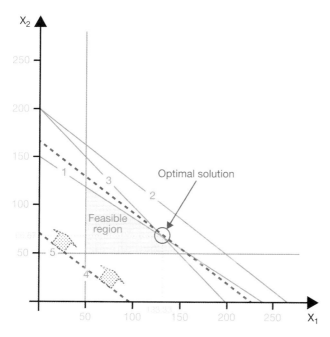

Figure 2.5 Identification of the optimal value via the objective function line.

Although this graphical procedure reveals the optimal solution, it relies on precise drawing of the lines, which may not be possible especially if you are doing it by hand. Instead, a more accurate method is advised, which is often called the enumeration approach—trying each candidate solution (outer corners of the feasible region) for optimality. Specifically, it involves identifying the X_1 and X_2 values for each candidate solution, or corner, replacing those values in the objective function to calculate the sum, and identifying the candidate that produces the best (in this case the maximum) value for the objective function as the optimal solution.

The graphical solution procedure is an excellent way to understand and explain the formulation of an LP problem and the identification of the optimal solution. However, when the number of decision variables is more than two, use of the graphical solution procedure may not be practical or even possible. Instead, for a more complex optimization problem formulation and solution, we use Microsoft Excel with its add-in Solver or specialized LP software products. The following section explains the process of formulating and solving the previously listed LP problem with the Microsoft Excel and Solver add-in.

Formulating and Solving the Same Product-Mix Problem in Microsoft Excel

Excel has an add-in, called Solver, that can solve a variety of optimization problems. By default, the Solver add-in is not activated in a typical Excel installation. To activate the Solver add-in in Excel 2019 or Excel 2016, follow this sequence of actions: File → Options → Add-ins → Manage: Excel Add-ins ☑ Solver Add-in. The graphical depiction of the same procedure is shown in Figure 2.6. For older versions of Excel, one can find similar step-by-step instructions to turn on the Solver add-in by executing a simple search on an Internet browser using the key phrase "How to activate Excel Solver in <Excel version>."

In an Excel sheet, we can use several cells to specify (1) decision variable value holders, (2) parameter values, (3) objective function formulation, and (4) constraints' formulations. In Figure 2.7, we show an intuitive layout to specify these parameter values and formulations.

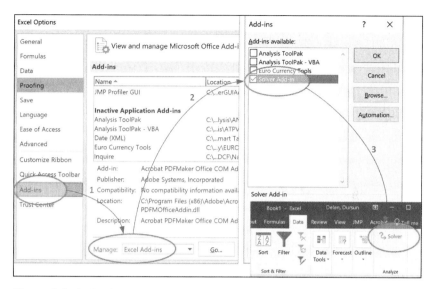

Figure 2.6 Activation procedure for Solver add-in in Excel 2019.

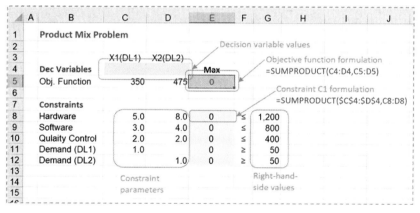

Figure 2.7 Formulation of the LP problem in an Excel sheet.

Once the formulation of the LP problem is completed in an Excel sheet, the Solver add-in can be executed. Assuming that the Solver add-in is already activated in your Excel (if not, you can do so by following the instruction above) you can find the Solver option under the Data tab. Clicking on Solver pops up a dialog window. In this window, you have to specify the cells that contain the objective function formulations, decision variable values, and constraint formulations. Additionally, in the dialog window, you need to select the direction of the optimization (whether maximizing or minimizing) as well as the method to use to solve the optimization problem. The Solver dialog window and the selections/specifications made therein are shown in Figure 2.8.

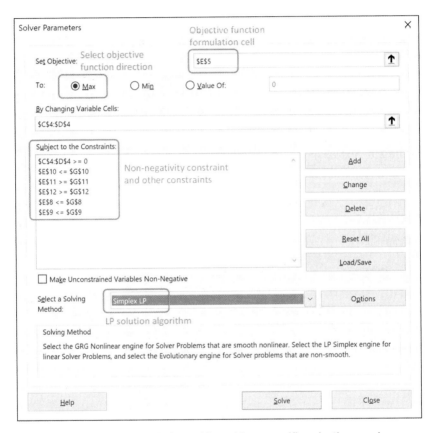

Figure 2.8 Solver dialog window with problem-specific selections and specifications.

In the Solver dialog window, all selections and specifications are straightforward, except specification of the constraints. For each constraint, including the one for a non-negativity constraint, you can click on Add. In the pop-up dialog box, specify the cell that contains the left-hand side value, select the inequality, and specify the cell that contains the right-hand-side value. A screen shot of this process is shown in Figure 2.9.

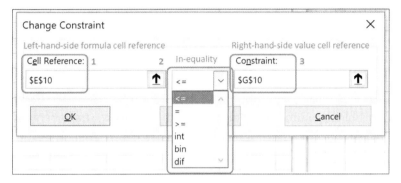

Figure 2.9 Defining the constraints in the Excel Solver add-in.

Once the definition of the LP problem is completed, you can click on the lower-right corner of the Solver dialog window to solve the problem. If all the problem definitions are accurate, Solver generates the optimal solution and fills in the related values in the Excel sheet. Specifically, it inserts the optimal values of the decision variables and calculates and shows the values of the objective function and the left side of the constraint formulations. See Figure 2.10 for the screenshot of the solution to the LP problem.

	A	B	C	D	E	F	G	H
1		SOLUTION: Product Mix Problem						
2						Optimal decision variable values		
3			X1(DL1)	X2(DL2)			Max objective	
4		Dec Variables	133.33	66.67	Max		function value	
5		Obj. Function	350	475	78,333			
6								
7		Constraints						
8		Hardware	5.0	8.0	1,200	≤	1,200	
9		Software	3.0	4.0	667	≤	800	
10		Qulaity Control	2.0	2.0	400	≤	400	
11		Demand (DL1)	1.0		133	≥	50	
12		Demand (DL2)		1.0	67	≥	50	
13								
14					Left-hand-		Right-hand-	
15					side values		side values	

Figure 2.10 Excel Solver generated an optimal solution to the product-mix problem.

Sensitivity Analysis in LP

In addition to the optimal solution, Excel Solver provides an optimal sensitivity analysis report on the provided solution. To generate a sensitivity analysis report, you need to select Sensitivity on the dialog box that pops up at the end of the Solver solution procedure (see Figure 2.11). A sensitivity analysis report helps improve better understanding of the optimal solution and its level of sensitivity to certain problem parameters. This information can potentially be used by a decision-maker to further improve the objective function value by manipulating the values in the problem definition.

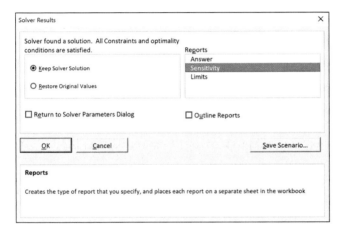

Figure 2.11 Asking to generate a sensitivity analysis report for the optimal solution.

Specifically, the sensitivity analysis report provides two sets of measures: (1) sensitivity of the objective function coefficients, and (2) sensitivity of the constraints' right-hand-side values. An annotated screenshot of the sensitivity analysis report for the product-mix LP solution is shown in Figure 2.12. In the sensitivity analysis report, the section on the objective function coefficients (in the report output, labeled as Variable Cells) provides the following information:

- **Final Value.** The optimal values of the decision variables.

- **Reduced Cost.** If the value of a decision variable is found to be zero, this metric shows the increase (or decrease) that needs to take place on the respective objective function coefficient for that decision variable to assume a non-zero, positive value.

- **Objective Coefficient.** The values of the objective function coefficients.

- **Allowable Increase.** This value shows the allowable increase in the respective objective function coefficient value to maintain the current optimal solution. In other words, if the value is larger than the specified value, the optimal solution—the decision variable values—would change. Therefore, a new LP solution needs to be calculated.

- **Allowable Decrease.** Similarly, this value shows the allowable decrease in the respective objective function coefficient value to maintain the current optimal solution.

In the sensitivity analysis report, the section on the right-hand side values of the constraints, labeled as Constraints in the report output, provides the following information:

- **Final Value.** The left-hand-side values of the constraint. These numbers show the consumption or utilization levels of the constraints. If, for a given constraint, this number is equal to the right-hand-side value, the constraint is said to be fully consumed or utilized (also called a binding constraint).

- **Shadow Price.** The value, which applies only to binding constraints, shows the realizable increase in the objective function value when the right-hand-side value of this constraint is increased by one unit.

- **Constraint R.H. Side.** Shows the constraint's right-hand-side values.

- **Allowable Increase.** This value shows the allowable increase in the respective constraint's right-hand-side value to maintain the current optimal solution. In other words, if the value is larger than the specified value, the optimal solution—the decision variable values—would change. Therefore, a new LP solution needs to be calculated.

- **Allowable Decrease.** Similarly, this value shows the allowable decrease in the respective constraint's right-hand-side value to maintain the current optimal solution.

A	B	C	D	E	F	G	H
1	Microsoft Excel 16.0 Sensitivity Report						
2	Worksheet: [LP Excel Examples for MyBook - ProdMix - Transp - Network 2.xlsx]ProdMix						
3	Report Created: 1/25/2019 8:30:27 PM						
4							
5							
6	Variable Cells	Sensitivity of the objective function coefficients					
7			Final	Reduced	Objective	Allowable	Allowable
8	Cell	Name	Value	Cost	Coefficient	Increase	Decrease
9	C4	Dec Variables X1(DL1)	133.3333333	0	350	125	53.125
10	D4	Dec Variables X2(DL2)	66.66666667	0	475	85	125
11							
12	Constraints	Sensitivity of the constraint right-hand-side values					
13			Final	Shadow	Constraint	Allowable	Allowable
14	Cell	Name	Value	Price	R.H. Side	Increase	Decrease
15	E10	Qulaity Control Max	400	70.83333333	400	20	62.5
16	E11	Demand (DL1) Max	133.3333333	0	50	83.33333333	1E+30
17	E12	Demand (DL2) Max	66.66666667	0	50	16.66666667	1E+30
18	E8	Hardware Max	1200	41.66666667	1200	250	50
19	E9	Software Max	666.6666667	0	800	1E+30	133.3333333
20							

Figure 2.12 Sensitivity analysis report for the product-mix problem.

A potential problem that we have ignored so far in this product-mix problem is the nature of the optimal solution, or the obtained decision variable values. The optimal values of the decision variable are given in real (fractional) values as 133.33 for X_1 and 66.67 for X_2. Because these are quantities of two products—DL1 and DL2—fractional values do not really make sense. The reason for this somewhat unrealistic optimal solution is attributed to one of the assumptions or limitations of LP: the divisibility assumption, as explained above. To remove this assumption and to produce more realistic and actionable results, researchers have developed a derivative of LP and named it integer programming, or IP for short. The key difference between LP and

IP is the nature of the decision variable values: real versus integer. A more detailed explanation of IP and its variant mixed-integer programming is provided earlier in this chapter.

Implementing an IP solution to the previously given product-mix problem in Excel Solver is trivial. All you have to do is add another constraint to the existing list of constraints in the LP definition and resolve the problem. The steps and screenshots of this process are given in Figure 2.13.

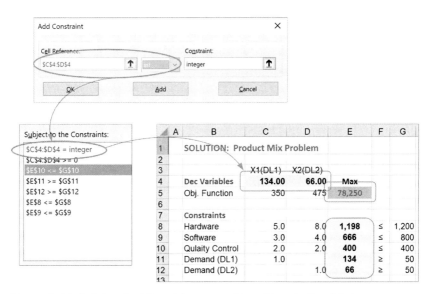

Figure 2.13 Solving the LP problem as an IP problem in Excel Solver.

As can be seen in Figure 2.13, the real numbers of the decision variables in the LP solution (X_1 = 133.33 and X_2 = 66.67) are converted to whole/integer numbers (X_1 = 134 and X_2 = 66) in the IP solution. Instead of using IP, one could also reach the same results by starting with the LP solution and systematically rounding up and down the decision variable values. The caveat in such an experimental process is to obtain a set of integer values for the decision variables that (1) optimizes the objective function value and (2) complies with all the constraints.

Transportation Problem

The transportation problem is a popular operational research topic whose goal is to minimize the total cost of transportation—shipping products from sources (supply centers such as production plants) to sinks (demand centers such as warehouses)—while complying with supply and demand constraints. Whereas supply constraints limit the number of products shipped out of a source, demand constraints enforce the number of products to be sent to each sink.

Hands-On Example: Transportation Cost Minimization Problem

A graphical depiction of an exemplary transportation system is shown in Figure 2.14. In this example, we have three sources, or plants, located in Tulsa (T), Mexico City (M), and Shanghai (S), and we have four sinks, or warehouses, located in Atlanta (A), Baltimore (B), Chicago (C), and Dallas (D). The capacity limitations for the plants—the supply constraints—and the requirements for the warehouses—the demand constraints—are given under each location, as are the unit transportation costs between each source and each sink, as shown in the connection links. The decision variables for the problem are the shipment quantities from each source to each destination. Naturally, most of these shipment quantities would be zero. In the formulation of this LP problem, we can represent the decision variables as X_{ij}, where i denotes the indices for the sources (having the values as the first letter of the source cities—T, M, and S), and j denotes the indices for the sinks (having the values as the first letter of the sink cities—A, B, C, and D). For instance, X_{TB} represents the shipment quantity, one of the decision variables, from T (Tulsa plant) to B (Baltimore warehouse). Because, in this example, we have three sources and four sinks, we have 12 decision variables to find optimal values. The algebraic representation of the LP formulation is given in the following:

Objective function (minimizing the total cost of transportation):

$$Z = Min \left(50X_{TA} + 84X_{TB} + 76X_{TC} + 56X_{TD} + 256X_{MA} + 198X_{MB} \right.$$

$$\left. + 288X_{MC} + 304X_{MD} + 310X_{SA} + 284X_{SB} + 332X_{SC} + 346X_{SD} \right)$$

Subject to
Supply constraints:

$$X_{TA} + X_{TB} + X_{TC} + X_{TD} \leq 150$$

$$X_{MA} + X_{MB} + X_{MC} + X_{MD} \leq 250$$

$$X_{SA} + X_{SB} + X_{SC} + X_{SD} \leq 200$$

Demand constraints:

$$X_{TA} + X_{MA} + X_{SA} \geq 180$$

$$X_{TB} + X_{MB} + X_{SB} \geq 156$$

$$X_{TC} + X_{MC} + X_{SC} \geq 110$$

$$X_{TD} + X_{MD} + X_{SD} \geq 110$$

Non-negativity constraint:

$$X_{TA}, X_{TB}, X_{TC}, X_{TD}, X_{MA}, X_{MB}, X_{MC}, X_{MD}, X_{SA}, X_{SB}, X_{SC}, X_{SD} \geq 0$$

As can be seen in the preceding algebraic representation of the transportation problem example, the supply constraints have less-than or equal-to ($\leq$) between the left- and right-hand sides, whereas the demand constraints have greater-than or equal-to ($\geq$) between the left- and right-hand sides.

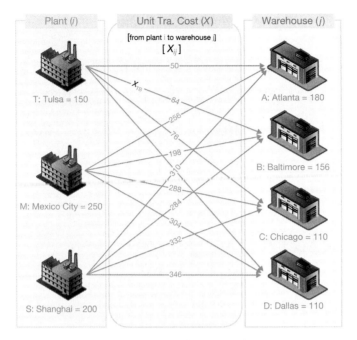

Figure 2.14 Transportation problem example.

Figure 2.15 shows the same transportation problem example in a matrix representation. Each source has a capacity-related supply constraint, shown in the last column, and each sink has a demand constraint, shown in the last row. The numbers at the upper-right corner of each cell represent the unit transportation cost—an aggregate measure of all shipment-related costs—of shipping a single unit between respective source to the sink.

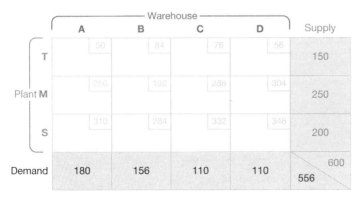

Figure 2.15 Matrix representation of a transportation problem.

A Heuristic Solution

This transportation problem can be solved heuristically. We can use a common-sense logical rule to assign shipment quantities into the 12 decision cells to minimize the total transportation cost while complying with the supply and demand constraints. A commonly used heuristic is called "maximizing shipment quantities for minimum unit cost options." In execution of this heuristic, one would find the minimum unit transportation cost cell and assign the largest possible value (quantity on that cell) while complying with the supply and demand constraints. This procedure is repeated until all 12 cells are filled with zeros and some non-zero integer numbers. The heuristic solution to the earlier defined transportation problem is shown in Figure 2.16. The objective function value of this solution would be as follows:

$$Z = 50X_{TA} + 84X_{TB} + 76X_{TC} + 56X_{TD} + 256X_{MA} + 198X_{MB}$$

$$+ 288X_{MC} + 304X_{MD} + 310X_{SA} + 284X_{SB} + 332X_{SC} + 346X_{SD}$$

$$Z = 50^*150 + 84^*0 + 76^*0 + 56^*0 + 256^*30 + 198^*156 + 288^*64$$

$$+ 304^*0 + 310^*0 + 284^*0 + 332^*46 + 346^*110$$

$$Z = 117.832$$

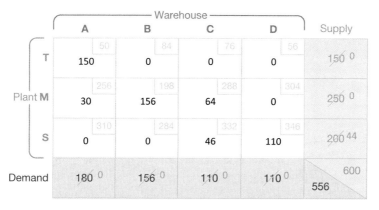

Figure 2.16 The heuristic solution to the transportation problem example.

The Optimal Solution with Excel Solver

The same problem can be solved optimally using Excel Solver. The formulation of the problem in an Excel sheet, a specification of the optimization problem parameters, and the solution of the problem are shown in the annotated screenshots in Figure 2.17. As can be seen, the decision variable values are slightly different from the heuristic solution, and the objective function value is $3,940 (117,832 – 113,892) better/smaller (for the minimization problem) than the one obtained with the heuristic solution.

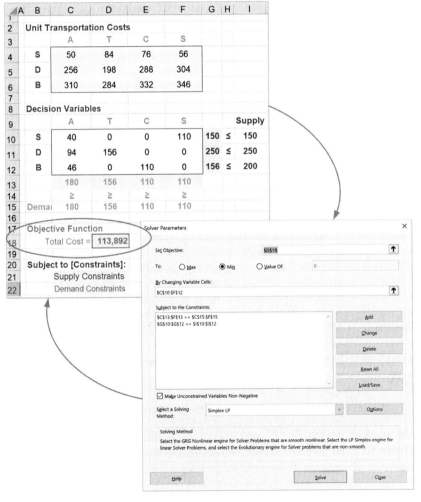

Figure 2.17 Optimal to the transportation model using Excel Solver.

Network Models

Network models are among the most useful classes of optimization problems. The keyword **network** refers to the fact that the model is composed of connected points on a physical or conceptual system of things. An intuitive sample list of networks includes (1) cities connected with roads, (2) oil wells connected with pipelines, (3) reservoirs connected with water canals, and (4) switching stations connected with telephone lines. There are a number of predefined network model problems, of which the following three are the most frequent:

1. **Shortest path problem.** What is the shortest (or cheapest, or least time-requiring) path through a network in between a specific pair of nodes? There are many situations in which it is important to be able to reach certain locations at a minimum cost or minimum time. Some exemplary classic situations include firefighters responding to an alarm or an ambulance responding to a traffic accident. For such situations, it is important to know ahead of time what the fastest route is between the base and where emergencies occur.

2. **Minimal spanning tree problem.** How can the nodes be connected so that the total construction cost is minimized? Consider a town-planning decision with regard to building a new subdivision. Storm drains will be located at selected points within the subdivision, and we want to connect them to the existing system. We will let each of the storm drains be represented by a node. The location of the drains (the nodes of the network) is given; our problem is to choose the arcs of the network (drainage pipes in this example) at minimum cost. Other applications are: (a) to build a road network to connect cities, (b) to build a network of pipelines to connect oil wells, and (c) to build a network of cable to connect houses with a cable distribution center.

3. **Maximal flow problem.** In a network with capacity constraints, what is the maximal attainable flow between a selected
pair of nodes? A major problem in most large cities is how to
manage increasingly heavy traffic flows. Congestion on the road
network can cause commuters to spend hours driving to or from
work, instigating extra cost and discomfort. Thus, we would like
to be able to determine the capacity of an existing network and
the ways in which it can be expanded optimally.

All these models have their own specialized mathematical representations and algorithmic solutions, or procedures for finding the optimal
solution. What follows is a short description and an exemplary illustration of one of these network problems: the shortest path problem.

Hands-On Example: The Shortest Path Problem

Let us consider the network given in Figure 2.18 where the nodes
represent the physical locations and the number written on the arcs
represents the distance between the locations (Tulett, 2018). Suppose that we want to know the shortest path from node 1 to node 7.
Obviously, for such a small example, it is a trivial matter to find all
path alternatives, calculate the total distance of each, and determine
that the optimal solution is $1 \rightarrow 4 \rightarrow 6 \rightarrow 7$. However, we want to
develop an efficient solution procedure that can be used to optimally
solve problems of any size.

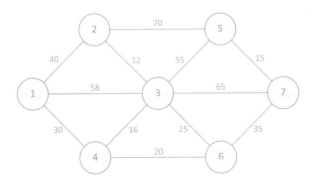

Figure 2.18 Graphical representation of the network model.

To illustrate the problem algebraically, we need to define and properly represent the decision variables. The goal is to find the shortest path, which is a sequence of paths from start to finish. Each arc in the network is either included in or excluded from the solution (the shortest path), so the decision variable becomes a 1-0 (one-zero) representation of the paths and can be written as follows:

X_{ij} : *Distance between node i and node j.*

$X_{ij} = 1$ *if arc between i and j is part of the shortest path*
     0 *otherwise*

all defined arcs i, j

Thus, the objective is to minimize the total travel distance on the path from the beginning to the end, and can be written as follows:

$$\begin{aligned}
\textit{Minimize } (40X_{1,2} &+ 58X_{1,3} + 30X_{1,4} + 40X_{2,1} + 12X_{3,2} \\
&+ 70X_{2,5} + 58X_{3,1} + 12X_{3,2} + 16X_{3,4} + 55X_{3,5} \\
&+ 25X_{3,6} + 65X_{3,7} + 30X_{4,1} + 16X_{4,3} + 20X_{4,6} \\
&+ 70X_{5,2} + 55X_{5,5} + 15X_{5,7} + 25X_{6,3} + 20X_{6,4} \\
&+ 36X_{6,7} + 65X_{7,3} + 15X_{7,5} + 35X_{7,6})
\end{aligned}$$

If we send one unit from the beginning node to the ending node (in this example, these are nodes 1 and 7, respectively), then the net flow at each node, or the total flow in minus the total flow out, must be –1 (negative 1) at the beginning, 1 at the end, and 0 at every other node. Therefore, the constraints can be written as follows:

    Beginning at

Node 1 $X_{2,1} + X_{3,1} + X_{4,1} - X_{1,2} - X_{1,3} - X_{1,4} = -1$

Node 2 $X_{1,2} + X_{3,2} + X_{5,2} - X_{2,1} - X_{2,3} - X_{2,5} = 0$

Node 3
$$X_{1,3} + X_{2,3} + X_{4,3} + X_{5,3} + X_{6,3} + X_{7,3} -$$
$$X_{3,1} - X_{3,2} - X_{3,4} - X_{3,5} - X_{3,6} - X_{3,7} = 0$$

Node 4
$$X_{1,4} + X_{3,4} + X_{6,4} - X_{4,1} - X_{4,3} - X_{4,6} = 0$$

Node 5
$$X_{2,5} + X_{3,5} + X_{7,5} - X_{5,2} - X_{5,3} - X_{5,7} = 0$$

Node 6
$$X_{3,6} + X_{4,6} + X_{7,6} - X_{6,3} - X_{6,4} - X_{6,7} = 0$$

Node 7
$$X_{3,7} + X_{5,7} + X_{6,7} - X_{7,3} - X_{7,5} - X_{7,6} = 1$$

To represent this algebraic formulation in an Excel sheet, we use square arrays for both the variables and the distances. As shown in Figure 2.20, on the main diagonal of the distance matrix, all the numbers are set to zero, and everywhere else the actual distance is used for all defined arcs. (The arc between nodes 1 and 3 has a distance of 40 meters.) For the undefined arcs, an arbitrarily large distance such as 999 is entered. The purpose of this high number is to discourage the algorithm from ever selecting the arc as part of the solution. In the flow matrix, the rows are summed in column I and the columns are summed in row 10. The net flow formulations are entered in column J. The Solver specification is shown in Figure 2.19. The objective function in cell K14 is computed by using the SUMPRODUCT function to multiply the two square matrixes (cells in B3:H9 and the corresponding cells in B13:H19). Solver minimizes cell K14 by changing variable cells B3:H9, subject to K3:K9 = M3:M9. The Excel representation of the network model and its optimal solution obtained using Excel Solver is shown in Figure 2.20.

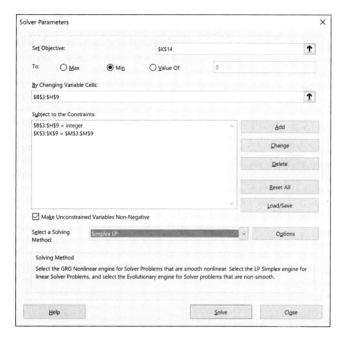

Figure 2.19 Excel Solver definitions for the network problem.

	A	B	C	D	E	F	G	H	I	J	K	L	M
1	Flow between nodes										Net		
2	From \ To	1	2	3	4	5	6	7	Out		Flow		RHS
3	1	0	0	0	1	0	0	0	1	Node 1	-1	=	-1
4	2	0	0	0	0	0	0	0	0	Node 2	0	=	0
5	3	0	0	0	0	0	0	0	0	Node 3	0	=	0
6	4	0	0	0	0	0	1	0	1	Node 4	0	=	0
7	5	0	0	0	0	0	0	0	0	Node 5	0	=	0
8	6	0	0	0	0	0	0	1	1	Node 6	0	=	0
9	7	0	0	0	0	0	0	0	0	Node 7	1	=	1
10	In	0	0	0	1	0	1	1					
11	Distance in between nodes												
12	From \ To	1	2	3	4	5	6	7			Shortest		
13	1	0	40	58	30	999	999	999			distance		
14	2	40	0	12	999	70	999	999		O.F.V. =	85		
15	3	58	12	0	16	55	25	65					
16	4	30	999	16	0	999	20	999					
17	5	999	70	55	999	0	999	15					
18	6	999	999	25	20	999	0	35					
19	7	999	999	65	999	15	35	0					
20													

Figure 2.20 Description of the transportation model and optimal solution.

As shown in Figure 2.20, the shortest path has a distance of 85 meters. The shortest path itself is composed of the non-zero decision variables in the flow matrix, which are $X_{1,4}$, $X_{4,6}$, $X_{6,7}$. This is also the arcs $1 \rightarrow 4 \rightarrow 6 \rightarrow 7$. If we want to find the shortest path between a different pair of nodes, not much work needs to be done on the user's part. Suppose that we want to know the shortest path between nodes 4 and 5. There is no change to the objective function. In the constraints, node 4 rather than node 1 would have a -1 (minus 1) on the right-hand side, and node 5 rather than node 7 would have a 1 on the right-hand side.

Analytics Success Story: Boston Public Schools Use Optimization Modeling to Consolidate Stops, Improve Student Experience, and Save Money

With public school districts across the U.S. often underfunded, any money that can be redirected into core educational efforts is a boon for schools—and students. Cost savings can lead to more teachers, better facilities or new books, supplies, and technology.

Due to these pressures, Boston Public Schools (BPS) began to look for ways to reduce costs while improving educational outcomes. As part of this effort, the transportation department turned to its busing system to examine how it could make changes that could benefit the classroom, the traffic, and the budget. With an annual transportation budget of $120 million, compromising nearly 10 percent of the district's overall appropriation, any savings could have a significant effect.

BPS turned to SAS Analytics to optimize its bus routes, improving quality of service to students while using fewer buses. SAS used BPS data to optimize the best bus routes and stops to meet the needs of its students. As a result, the district has been able to redirect the money saved toward enhancing educational quality.

A Better Way to Get from Point A to B

The oldest public school system in America, BPS operates 125 schools serving 57,000 students from pre-K through 12th grade. In 2016, the district provided transportation for 25,000 students via 650 buses across 45,000 miles. This adds up to 20,200 unique stops at nearly 5,000 locations each day.

"We have a generous assignment process where students have a wide array of school choice," says John Hanlon, chief of operations for BPS. "Plus, because of the locations of special education programs or English as a Second Language programs, it adds to a complicated transportation system. Students are transported across the city in the morning and afternoon, close to an hour each way in some cases."

This effort can cause on-time performance challenges that affect students and their families, as well as an expensive transportation system for the school district to maintain. The district used the same legacy bus stops year after year.

The logistics behind these stops largely weren't adjusted over time, which was driving up costs. The district wanted to consolidate and streamline routes. The software used to plan bus routes required significant manual adjustments, making it impossible to rapidly evaluate the systemwide impacts of any changes.

"When assigning stops, the district had applied blanket rules to all students," says Will Eger, strategic project manager. "For example, every student should walk less than half a mile to his or her bus stop. In reality, individual students were walking a wide range of distances. Nor did the stops take into account important factors like the student's age or neighborhood safety. We needed a way to automatically account for all of those factors without dramatically increasing costs."

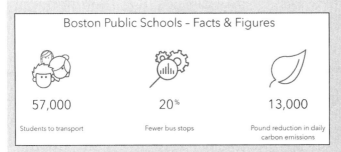

Figure 2.21 Summary of improvements. *(© 2019 SAS Institute Inc. All Rights Reserved.)*

Strategic Route Consolidation Quickly Yields Benefits

The district needed a method to more strategically designate bus stops. SAS Analytics analyzes numerous factors to reduce the number of bus stops to cut costs while better serving the needs of students. The transportation group can enter different sets of constraints into SAS Analytics and see the impact on the total number of stops across the entire system.

For example, the transportation group looked at how many stops it could cut under various route consolidation scenarios. "SAS enables us to understand the policy implications of various trade-offs throughout the system," Hanlon says. "Before, we didn't really control for the average distance that students walked by their grade or age, and we didn't control for neighborhood safety. Now, we can integrate that along with location and other information to better serve the students."

BPS has begun rolling out individualized walk-to-stop maximums for each student—all while reducing the number of bus stops. Strategic stop placement has been a big part of the story for a district that last year eliminated nearly 50 buses (about 8 percent of the total) for a long-term cost savings that's expected to top $5 million.

The reduction in force has also had significant environmental benefits. "We've saved about 13,000 pounds of carbon emissions a day, which is huge," Eger says.

"Because of SAS, we've found new ways to consolidate bus stops, which leads to savings for the school districts without putting students in unsafe situations, and keeping them close to home in terms of the distance to their bus stops," Hanlon says. "It also allows us to think differently about the power of analytics and what it can bring to the transportation system as a whole."

Optimizing bus routes helps funnel cost savings back to schools

SAS Analytics brings intelligence to student transportation.

$5M

Estimated savings from eliminating need for 50 buses

Figure 2.22 SAS Customer Success Story, 2018 *(© 2019 SAS Institute Inc. All Rights Reserved.)*

Optimization Modeling Terminology

As you may have already noticed, optimization modeling has its own language, special terms, and definitions. Following are the most common optimization-related terms and their brief definitions:

- **Decision variables** are the key components of any optimization modeling problem. The optimization modeling and analysis are conducted to identify the values of these variables. In a product mix problem, the decision variables are the optimal quantities of production quantities of all product types.

- **Objective function** is the mathematical representation of the objective of a given optimization problem. The goal of the optimization function is either to minimize or to maximize the objective function. It is usually represented using decision variables and numerical parameters.

- **Constraints** are the limitations imposed upon the solution of the optimization model. One of the key assumptions is the non-negativity constraint of the decision variables.

- **A feasible problem** is one for which there exists at least one set of values for the decision variables satisfying all the constraints.

- **A feasible solution** is any solution that complies with all the constraints and provides a solution to the given problem.

- **A feasible solution space** is the collection of all alternative solutions that comply with all the constraints. One of the solutions in this feasible solution space is the optimal solution.

- **An optimal solution** is one of the feasible solutions that optimizes (maximizes or minimizes) the objective function value.

- **An infeasible problem** is one for which no set of values for the decision variables satisfies all the constraints. That is, the constraints are mutually contradictory, and no solution exists; the feasible solution space is empty.

- **An unbounded problem** is a feasible problem for which the objective function goes to infinity—and can be better (smaller or larder) than any given finite value. Thus, there is no optimal solution because there is always a feasible solution that gives a better objective function value than does any given proposed solution.

- **Reduced cost** is a value identified in sensitivity analysis. If the value of a decision variable is found to be zero, this metric shows the increase (or decrease) that needs to take place in the respective objective function coefficient for that decision variable to assume a non-zero, positive value.

- **Objective coefficients** are the values of the objective function numerical parameters used to formulate the objective function.

- **Allowable increase**, in sensitivity analysis, is the value that shows the allowable increase in the respective objective function coefficients or right-hand-side values of the constraints to maintain the current optimal solution. That is, if the value is larger than the specified value, the optimal solution—the decision variable values—would change; therefore, a new optimal solution needs to be calculated.

- **Allowable decrease** is a similar measure in sensitivity analysis that shows the allowable decrease in the respective objective function coefficient or right-hand-side value of the constraints to maintain the current optimal solution.

- **Final value**, in a sensitivity analysis report, shows either the optimal values of the decision variables or the left-hand-side values of the constraints. The final values for constraints illustrate the consumption or utilization levels of the constraints. If, for a given constraint, this number is equal to the right-hand-side value, the constraint is said to be fully consumed or utilized.

- **A binding constraint** is a constraint that has the same value for the left and right-hand-side at the end of the optimization. That is, the constraint is fully consumed or utilized. Any increase in the right-hand-side value has the potential to improve the objective function value.

- **The shadow price** is the value, applying only to binding constraints, that shows the realizable increase in the objective function value when the right-hand-side value of this constraint is increased by one unit.

- **A non-binding constraint** is one that has different values for the left- and right-hand-side at the end of the optimization. That is, the constraint is not fully consumed or utilized.

- **Surplus** is the difference between the left- and right-hand-side values of a non-binding constraint, where the inequality between the left- and right-hand-side is greater-than or equal-to ($\geq$).

- **Slack** is the difference between the left- and right-hand-side values of a non-binding constraint where the inequality between the left- and right-hand-side is less-than or equal-to ($\leq$).

Heuristic Optimization with Genetic Algorithms

A majority of real-world optimization problems cannot be solved with mathematical programming because the underlying model is too complex to lend itself to be solved with the known linear, non-linear, or stochastic optimization techniques. Although the problem can be represented with mathematical/algebraic equations, because of the unsuitable characteristics of the model, an optimal solution cannot be obtained using any of the closed-form mathematical solution techniques. In such situations, because we cannot use the global optimization techniques, to find a satisfying solution to the optimization problem at hand, we can use a heuristic optimization technique. There are a number of heuristic optimization (also called metaheuristic) techniques in the literature. In heuristic optimization, a metaheuristic is a higher-level procedure, designed to find/generate/select a heuristic, or partial search algorithm, that can provide a sufficiently good solution to an optimization problem, especially with incomplete or imperfect information or limited computation capacity. The notable heuristic optimization techniques include Tabu search, simulated annealing, genetic algorithms, particle swarm optimization, and ant colony optimization. As can be noticed from their names, most of the heuristic optimization techniques are modeled after some natural phenomenon. In the following sections, we explain genetic algorithms, which are arguably the most commonly used heuristic optimization technique in practice.

Genetic algorithms are part of the family of nature-inspired global search techniques. They are typically used to find approximate solutions to optimization-type problems that are too complex to be solved with traditional optimization methods (which are guaranteed to produce the best solution to a specific problem, as discussed in the previous sections). Genetic algorithms are a part of the machine learning family of methods under artificial intelligence. Because they cannot guarantee the truly optimal solution, genetic algorithms are considered part of the heuristic methods—arguably the most famous one. Genetic algorithms are sets of computational procedures that conceptually follow the steps of the biological processes of evolution. That is, better and better solutions evolve from the previous generation of solutions until an optimal or near-optimal solution is obtained.

Genetic algorithms (also known as evolutionary algorithms) demonstrate self-organization and adaptation in much the same way that the biological organisms do by following the chief rule of evolution: *the survival of the fittest*. The method improves the solution by producing offspring—new collections of feasible solutions—using the best-fitted solutions of the current generation as "parents." The generation of offspring is achieved by a reproduction process modeled after the genetic reproductions where mutation and cross-over operators manipulate genes in constructing newer and "better" chromosomes. Notice that a simple analogy between the genes and decision variables and between the chromosomes and potential solutions underlies the genetic algorithms terminology. Genetic algorithms have been successfully applied to a range of highly complex real-world problems, including vehicle routing, bankruptcy prediction, and Web searching.

Terminology of Genetic Algorithms

A genetic algorithm is an iterative procedure that represents its candidate solutions as strings of genes called **chromosomes** and measures their viability with a fitness function. The fitness function is a measure of the objective to be obtained, whether maximum or minimum. As in biological systems, candidate solutions combine to produce offspring in each algorithmic iteration, called a **generation**. The offspring themselves can become candidate solutions. From the generation of parents and children, a set of the fittest survive to become parents that produce offspring in the next generation. Offspring are produced using a specific genetic reproduction process that involves the application of crossover and mutation operators. Along with the reproduction, some of the best solutions are migrated to the next generation—a concept called elitism—to preserve the best solution achieved up until the current iteration. Following are brief definitions of these key terms:

- **Reproduction.** Through reproduction, genetic algorithms produce new generations of potentially improved solutions by selecting parents with higher fitness ratings or by giving such parents a greater probability of being selected to contribute to the reproduction process.

- **Crossover.** Many genetic algorithms use a string of binary symbols (each corresponding to a decision variable) to represent chromosomes, or potential solutions. **Crossover** means choosing a random position in the string and exchanging the segments either to the right or to the left of that point with those of another string's segments that have been generated using the same splitting schema to produce two new offspring.

- **Mutation. Mutation** is an arbitrary (and minimal) change in the representation of a chromosome. It is often used to prevent the algorithm from getting stuck in a local optimum. The procedure randomly selects a chromosome (giving more probability to the ones with better fitness value) and randomly identifies a gene in the chromosome to inverse its value (from 0 to 1 or from 1 to 0) to generate one new chromosome for the next generation. The occurrence of mutation is usually set to a low probability (0.1 percent).

- **Elitism.** An important aspect in genetic algorithms is to preserve a few of the best solutions as they evolve through the generations. That way, you are guaranteed to end up with the best possible solution for the current application of the algorithm. In practice, a few of the best solutions are directly migrated to the next generation.

How Do Genetic Algorithms Work?

Figure 2.23 is a flow diagram of a typical genetic algorithm process. The problem to be solved must be described and represented in a manner amenable to a genetic algorithm. Typically, this means that a string of 1s and 0s (or other more recently proposed complex representations) are used to represent the decision variables, the collection of which represents a potential solution to the problem. Next, the decision variables are mathematically or symbolically pooled into a fitness function, or objective function. The fitness function can be one of two types: maximization (something that is more is better, such as profit) or minimization (something that is less is better, such as cost). Along with the fitness function, one should represent all the constraints on decision variables that collectively dictate whether a solution is feasible. Remember that only the feasible solutions can be part of solution population. Infeasible ones are filtered out before finalizing a generation of solutions in the iterations process. Once the representation is done, an initial set of solutions is generated (i.e., the initial population); all infeasible solutions are eliminated; and feasible ones' fitness functions are computed. The solutions are ranked ordered based on their fitness values so that the ones with better fitness values are given more probability (proportional to their relative fitness value) in the random selection process.

A few of the best solutions are migrated to the next generation. Using a random process, several sets of parents are identified to take part in the generation of offspring. Using the randomly selected parents and the genetic operators crossover and mutation, the offspring is generated. The number of potential solutions to generate is determined by the population size, an arbitrary parameter set prior to the evolution of solutions. Once the next generation is constructed, the solutions go through the evaluation and regenerations of new populations for a number of iterations. This iterative process continues until a good enough solution is obtained (an optimum is not guaranteed), no improvement occurs over several generations, or the time/iteration limit is reached.

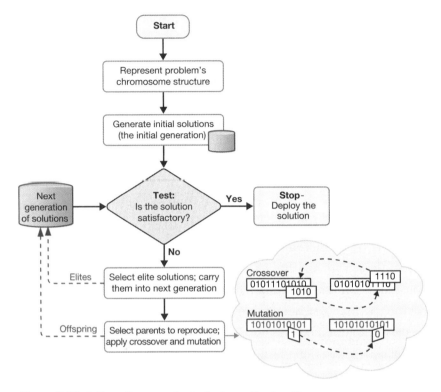

Figure 2.23 A flow diagram of a typical genetic algorithm process.

As briefly mentioned above, a few parameters must be set prior to the execution of the genetic algorithm. Their values are dependent on the problem being solved and are usually determined through trial and error:

- Number of initial solutions to generate (the initial population)
- Number of offspring to generate (the population size)
- Number of parents to keep for the next generation (elitism)
- Mutation probability (usually a low number, such as 0.1 percent)
- Probability distribution of crossover point occurrence (generally equally weighted)
- Stopping criteria (time-, iteration-, or improvement-based)
- The maximum number of iterations (if the stopping criteria are time/iteration based)

Sometimes these parameters are set and frozen beforehand, or they can be varied systematically while the algorithm is running for better performance.

Limitations of Genetic Algorithms

Following are among the most commonly identified limitations of genetic algorithms:

- Not all problems can be framed in the mathematical manner that genetic algorithms demand.

- Development of a genetic algorithm and interpretation of the results require an expert who has both the programming and the statistical/mathematical skills demanded by the genetic algorithm technology in use.

- In a few situations, the "genes" from a few comparatively highly fit (but not optimal) individuals may come to dominate the population, causing it to converge on a local maximum. When the population has converged, the ability of the genetic algorithm to continue to search for better solutions is effectively eliminated.

- Most genetic algorithms rely on random number generators that produce different results each time the model runs. Although there is likely to be a high degree of consistency among the runs, they may vary.

- Locating good variables that work for a particular problem is difficult. Obtaining the data to populate the variables is equally demanding.

- Selecting methods by which to evolve the system requires thought and evaluation. If the range of possible solutions is small, a genetic algorithm will converge too quickly on a solution. When evolution proceeds too quickly, thereby altering good solutions too quickly, the results may miss the optimum solution.

Genetic Algorithm Applications

Genetic algorithms are a type of machine learning for representing and solving complex problems. They provide efficient, domain-independent search heuristics for a broad spectrum of applications, including the following:

- Dynamic process control
- Induction of optimization of rules
- Discovery of new connectivity topologies, such as neural computing connections
- Simulation of biological models of behavior and evolution
- Complex design of engineering structures
- Pattern recognition
- Scheduling
- Transportation and routing
- Layout and circuit design
- Telecommunication
- Graph-based problems

A genetic algorithm interprets information that enables it to reject inferior solutions and accumulate good ones. Thus, it learns about its universe. Genetic algorithms are also suitable for parallel processing.

Conclusion

This chapter provided a summary of optimization modeling—arguably the most popular enabler of prescriptive analytics. As described earlier, optimization is the process of finding "the best" solution for a given problem situation. It is the part of the decision-making where the best of all feasible alternatives/choices is identified—the best in terms of optimizing the stated objective function. Depending on the nature of decision variables and alternatives, different types of optimization modeling techniques must be employed. For instance, if all the variables are deterministic, and the relations are linearly defined, a linear programming or an integer programming method is used. In contrast, if some or all of the variables are stochastic/probabilistic, a stochastic programming technique is more appropriate. For complex optimization problems where a mathematical model cannot be formulated or solved, a heuristic search type of solution such as genetic algorithms is usually used.

Numerous methods and tools have been developed to model and solve optimization problems. In this chapter, we explained a graphical solution for simple LP problems and then showed how more complex problems can be solved using the Excel Solver add-in. Highly complex real-world optimization problems are often solved with specialized software packages like LINDO, SAS/OR, AMPL, CPLEX, and AIMMS. Because these tools are readily available to solve optimization problems, the challenge and creativity of the process lie in the way we characterize and properly represent the real-world situation into an optimization problem formulation, which is often referred to as "the art" of the prescriptive analytics process.

References

SAS Customer Success Story, "Boston Public Schools Uses SAS Analytics to Consolidate Stops, Improve Student Experience and Save Money," available at https://www.sas.com/en_us/customers/boston-public-schools.html (accessed November 2018).

Tulett, D. M. (2018). *Decision Modeling*, available at linney.mun.ca/pages/view.php?ref=36808 (accessed November 2018).

3

Simulation Modeling for Decision-Making

Generally speaking, simulation is an imitation of reality within a computer environment. That is, a simulation is the computerized representation of a given real-world situation. To simulate, a model of the real-world scenario needs to be developed. Such a model is designed to represent the key characteristics, behaviors, and functions of the physical or abstract world, system, or process. Although simulation is usually developed to mimic the reality, sometimes it is developed for situations beyond reality—imaginary, surreal, "future" worlds. Perhaps the best example of the simulation of surreal worlds is video games. Many would agree that video games represent the most advanced, the leading edge of computer simulations in terms of functionality, randomness, and visual effects.

In this chapter, the type of simulation we are interested in is used to analyze and solve complex business problems and situations. Since the beginning of the analytics era, simulation has been one of the most popular enablers for advanced analytics. In 2010, Gartner, a leading provider of technical research and consultancy for business (see www.gartner.com), identified advanced analytics, which includes predictive and prescriptive analytics, including simulation, as one of the top ten strategic technologies. Since then, Gartner (2017) continuously has reemphasized the value of advanced analytics and simulation: "Because analytics is the 'combustion engine of business,' organizations invest in business intelligence even when times are tough. Gartner predicts the next big phase for business intelligence will be a move toward more simulation and extrapolation to provide more informed decisions." Relying on the early success of analytics, Gartner (2013) also states: "With the improvement of performance and costs, IT leaders can afford to perform analytics and simulation for every action taken in the business. The mobile client linked to cloud-based analytic engines and big data repositories potentially enables use of optimization and simulation everywhere and every time. This new step provides simulation, prediction, optimization and other analytics, to empower even more decision flexibility at the time and place of every business process action."

As has been the case for many other trends in analytics, the increased popularity of simulation can be, at least in part, attributed to the advancements in computer hardware and software, which have been rather impressive in recent years. Computers nowadays can provide storage and processing capabilities unimaginable to us even just a few short years ago. Improved user interfaces, 3D and immersive visualizations/animations, and massively parallel fast processing capabilities of computers have made simulation software much easier and naturally friendly to use, thereby lowering the level of expertise required to build and use simulation models. Breakthroughs in programming technologies continue to improve the modeling proficiencies to allow rich, realistic, and highly accurate modeling of complex real-world business systems. Hardware, software, and publicly available graphical widgets make it possible for even novice modelers to design and develop simulation models with compelling visualizations and animation to support better model validation and communication between domain experts and analytics practitioners. Due to these advancements and the proven power and expressiveness of simulation, there is no doubt that simulation will be one of the key enablers of the future of analytics and managerial decision-making.

Analytics Success Story—Vancouver Airport Case Study: Optimizing Airport Processes

As the second busiest airport in Canada, Vancouver International Airport (YVR) has daily nonstop flights throughout North America, Europe, Oceania, and Asia. In 2014, there were more than 310,000 takeoffs and 19,360,000 visitors. Vancouver has won the *Skytrax Best North American Airport Award* on multiple occasions, and in 2013 and 2014, YVR was the only airport to be in the top 10 airports in North America.

Simio, a leading simulation software tool, is used to assess and improve a variety of the airport processes (see Figure 3.1).

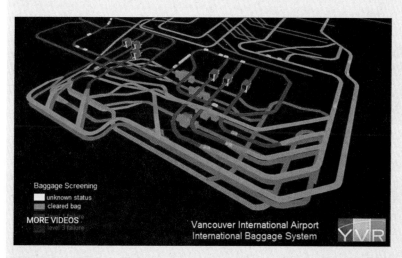

Figure 3.1 Simio model of Vancouver International Airport International baggage system. *(Courtesy of Simio LLC)*

The following Vancouver Airport Authority corporate values were the key drivers at the heart of this project:

- **Collaboration and Teamwork.** The Airport Authority sought input and ideas from appropriate stakeholders over the years. These included customs officials, security screeners, baggage handlers, and, of course, airline carriers. YVR recognized the importance of obtaining buy-in from all stakeholders, both internal and external, to make this project successful.

- **Creativity.** Alternative solutions were sought to improve upon the status quo. The airport business is constantly changing with market demand, and adapting to it is the key to maintaining an excellent reputation. Striving for originality and creativity, issues were analyzed, technology was leveraged, and most importantly stakeholders showed adaptability in managing change.

- **Accountability.** A commitment to achieving results by optimizing airport operations was stated from the beginning. Allowing stakeholders to take ownership of various aspects of the project has led to a natural path of self-motivation. Accordingly, stakeholder feedback was engaged to establish trust, build realistic expectations, manage execution of the project, and of course provide the ability to make sound decisions. Performance measures and targets were published in the corporate business plan. These served as targets by which the simulation results are measured.

- **Passion for Results.** All stakeholders shared a common desire and passion to achieving results. At stake is the profitability of the business while maintaining or improving service levels at world-class levels. Successful projects rarely occur by accident and without a great deal of passion. Rather, passion is the fuel that motivates one to keep striving for solutions to a problem.

The Approach

Simio modeling software was used to create the model, while Excel along with VBA automation was used for reporting the results. Auto-CAD drawings of the various termination levels were imported into Simio as bitmap images to provide working backgrounds for the model. Images were then scaled and calibrated appropriately for walking distances to be accurately calculated.

Key processes such as check-in, security screening, customs declaration, and baggage claim were modeled for all arriving and departing flights. Simulation results were rated against performance targets established in the annual Vancouver Airport Authority Business Plan. These results allow management to track its business plan progress against a number of measurable targets.

The Results

While the Vancouver Airport simulation model was quite complex and took time to build, it provided invaluable insight in the planning and operations of its terminals. When deciding to build new terminals or to expand new ones, simulation models, like Vancouver Airport's, can determine the capacity requirements and provide guidance in scoping a project.

When increased capacity is required, simulation models can be used to re-engineer processes to make them more efficient. In such cases, the refining of airport processes can lead to millions of dollars in savings as a result of deferred capital costs. One such example at Vancouver Airport has been the introduction of kiosks for the customs declaration of returning residents. The problem facing the Vancouver Airport was the need for more capacity in the customs hall. This problem was initially leading the airport down the path to expand the terminal, which would have created a ripple effect throughout, including the relocation of aircraft gates. With the aid of their Simio Simulation Model, Vancouver was able to see that the simple introduction of kiosks for the customs declaration of returning residents was all it needed to increase capacity and reduce strain on the facility. Doing that saved the airport close to $100 million.

Simulation models are not one-time use tools. Instead, once created, they can be used over and over to help a company save money. Now that the Vancouver Airport has its entire operations modeled within Simio, it can easily use it to improve day-to-day operations at the airport based on its established levels of service and save time and money.

Source: Simio, Customer Case Study, "Vancouver," 2018; Lazzaroni, 2012.

Simulation Is Based on a Model of the System

As mentioned earlier, to simulate, we first need to create a model of the specific situation. A model is an abstraction or simplification of the real situation. Building a model requires characterization and structuring of the real-world situation from a system perspective. A system is a set of interrelated components or parts that work together in a logical manner toward a common purpose (or outcome). A system can be as simple as a waiting line at a fast-food restaurant or as complex as a complete supply-chain of a worldwide retail giant. A system is often composed of a number of subsystems. The level at which a given system is defined and studied depends on the decision problem being analyzed. Selecting the right level of system definition (the scope of the problem situation) is critical to a successful and thorough analysis.

Modeling and simulation require analytics professionals to conceptualize and visualize the real or abstract situations as systems. This ability is often referred to as **systems thinking** or **systems view**, which applies systems theory to the analysis of complex situations to achieve the desired outcomes. It offers a unique approach to problem-solving and decision-making that views symptoms and problems as part of an overall system. Whereas traditional problem-solving approaches tend to focus on one or a few parts of a system, believing that changes to those parts offer a solution, the systems-thinking approach focuses on interactions and root causes among all components as the core dynamics of solving complex problems. The fundamental beliefs for systems thinking, regardless of the type and size of the system, include the following:

- A system is composed of a collection of interacting parts and components.
- There is logic and a common purpose behind the interactions among the parts.
- The behavior of an individual part is affected by the behavior of the other parts in the system.
- A system boundary defines the set of parts that comprise a system—what is included in and what is excluded from the system.
- Having a system boundary improves the analytics focus on what matters the most.
- Through its boundary, a system, or some parts of the system, may interact with parts of other systems.
- External interactions are meticulously defined so that they are less influential on system behavior than internal interaction.
- The behavior of a system is judged by examining the entire system, not individual parts.

The main point of systems and system thinking is that such an approach makes it possible for us to focus, understand, conceptualize, design, and develop a model of the reality so that it is rich enough to capture enough of the details of the situation but simple enough to be critically analyzed and reasoned with. Systems, especially simple systems, can also be studied by careful observations and direct manipulations. The main drawback of this approach is (1) you may need to watch the real system for an extended period of time to observe the particular conditions of the event or interest even once, let alone making enough observations to reach a reliable characterization of the phenomenon, and (2) it may not be feasible or possible to directly manipulate the actual system to see all the potential reactions. Including "what matters" and leaving out "what doesn't" is the process of abstraction/simplification that transforms real or imaginary systems into models for further experimentation, studying, understanding, and potentially improving. Figure 3.2 shows the process of creating models for real-word situations.

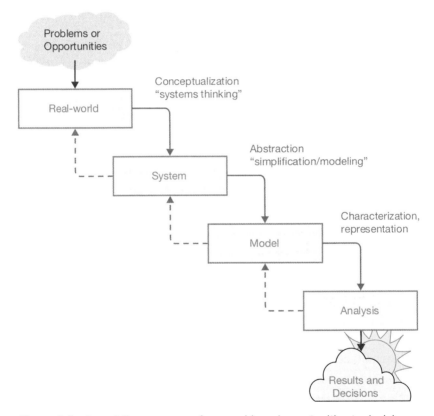

Figure 3.2   A modeling process—from problems/opportunities to decision.

As shown in Figure 3.2, to study/analyze the complexities arising from real-world situations—frequently occurring problems, continuously emerging opportunities—analysts and decision-makers ought to structure and simplify the reality into a manageable model. As mentioned earlier, construction of a model requires observation and characterization of the reality from a system perspective, which is the conceptualization process that converts a real-world situation into a collection of interacting components/agents working toward a common purpose within a well-defined boundary. Such a system view makes it possible to focus on a restricted/limited section of the reality where the problem/opportunity-related components and their inter-relationships are more transparent and easily observable. The next step in the process is to simplify the system through abstractions—simplifying assumptions—toward building a model of the reality. Some models are more abstract than others. As the level of abstraction increases, so does the distance from reality. Although it is desirable to limit the level of abstraction so that the model would be a close representation of the real-world situation, some analysis techniques can be used only with highly abstracted mathematical models. For instance, linear programming models require a significantly higher level of abstraction than simulation models. Once the model (at an optimal level of abstraction) of the system is constructed, through a systematic set of experimentation, the model is analyzed to solve a pressing problem, to take advantage of an emergent opportunity, or to discover new and innovative ways to improve the underlying real-world system toward perfection, a process that is often called **continuous process improvement**.

For the chief reasons of simplification of the reality and the magnification of the relationships among system components, we use models to analyze complex systems and their decision demanding situations. There are many types of models, each with its own advantages and limitations. Physical models, such as a scaled model of a car, airplane, bridge, or skyscraper, can provide both a sense of reality as well as interaction with the physical environment. Analytical models, also called closed-form, symbolic, representational models, use mathematical representations. These representations can be quite useful in providing solutions to specific problem domains, but their applicable domains are rather limited. Simulation is a modeling approach with much broader applicability.

What Is a Good Simulation Application?

Discrete event simulation (DES) has been applied to the analysis of a large number of complex systems. The systems that have complex logic and stochastics time are especially suitable to DES-type analytics methods. Successful applications of DES can be found in many industries, including manufacturing, healthcare, finance, mining, aerospace, telecommunication, tourism and entertainment, government, homeland security, defense, and military. Here are some high-level characteristics of the systems and situations that warrant development of a DES application[1]:

- Systems where it is too expensive, too risky, or impossible to do live experimentations. In such situations, simulation provides an inexpensive, risk-free way to test and study the changes incurred in the system.

- Complex systems for which a significant change/improvement is being considered. A guess is usually a poor substitute for an objective analysis of the system. Simulation can help in accurately predicting system behavior under projected condition changes and reduce the risk of making a poor decision.

- Systems where predicting process variability is important. A spreadsheet analysis cannot capture the dynamic aspects of a system—aspects that can have a major impact on system performance. Simulation can help you understand how various components interact with each other and how they affect overall system performance.

---

1. https://www.simio.com/applications (Accessed January 2019).

- Systems where you have incomplete data. Simulation cannot invent data where it does not exist, but simulation does well at determining sensitivity to unknowns. A high-level model can help you explore alternatives. A more detailed model can help you identify the most important missing data.

- Systems where you need to communicate ideas. Development of a simulation helps participants better understand the system. Modern 2D and 3D animations and other visual tools promote communication and understanding across a variety of stakeholders.

Applications of Simulation Modeling

Simulation modeling has been successfully applied to various business and nonbusiness settings. The following are just a few domains where simulation has been used to understand and improve system effectiveness.

- **Ecology.** Assessment of the natural changes in environment and their impact on organizations, industries, and human life.

- **Business process improvement.** Workforce optimization, capacity planning, inventory control, assessment of process alternatives, bottleneck identification, analysis.

- **Military.** Assessment of battle readiness, scenario analysis, risk assessment and mitigation, deployment, retrieval planning.

- **Public safety.** Spread of infectious diseases, containment and quarantine planning, disaster management, planning of first responders, assessment of evacuation alternatives.

- **Airports.** Parking-lot shuttles, ticketing, security, terminal transportation, food court traffic, baggage handling, gate assignments, airplane de-icing.

- **Hospitals.** Emergency department operation, disaster planning, ambulance dispatching, regional service strategies, resource allocation.
- **Ports.** Truck and train traffic, vessel traffic, port management, container storage, capital investments, crane operations.
- **Mining.** Material transfer, labor transportation, equipment allocation, bulk material mixing.
- **Amusement parks.** Guest transportation, ride design/startup, waiting line management, ride staffing, crowd management.
- **Call centers.** Staffing, skill-level assessment, service improvement, training plans, scheduling algorithms.
- **Supply chains.** Risk reduction, reorder points, production allocation, inventory positioning, transportation, growth management, contingency planning.
- **Manufacturing.** Capital-investment analysis, line optimization, product-mix changes, productivity improvement, transportation, labor reduction.
- **Military.** Logistics, maintenance, combat, counterinsurgency, search and detection, humanitarian relief.
- **Telecommunications.** Message transfer, routing, reliability, network security against outages or attacks.
- **Criminal-justice system.** Probation and parole operations, prison utilization and capacity.
- **Emergency-response system.** Response time, station location, equipment levels, staffing.
- **Public sector.** Allocation of voting machines to precincts.
- **Customer service.** Direct-service improvement, back-office operations, resource allocation, capacity planning.

Far from being a tool for manufacturing only, the domains and applications of simulation are wide ranging and virtually limitless.

Simulation Development Process

Designing, developing, and executing a computer simulation is a major undertaking. Although the new developments in software and hardware make simulation modeling a more approachable endeavor, accurate and actionable simulation modeling of complex real-world situations still demands considerable expertise in simulation modeling and application domain, attention to detail, and thorough analysis of the simulation outputs. A basic and high-level process of developing a simulation model is shown in Figure 3.3. As demonstrated, the simulation design, development, and execution process includes both sequential and iterative activities. In the following section, we briefly discuss each of these major components (Smith, Sturrock, and Kelton, 2018).

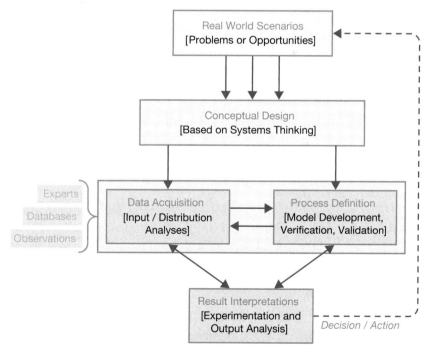

Figure 3.3 A high-level depiction of the simulation process.

Conceptual Design

A thorough understanding of the real-world situation being modeled is a must for any simulation modeling project (or any modeling project, for that matter). Conceptual design is the manifestation of the detailed understanding of the system being modeled. Conceptual design can be performed with pen and paper, on a whiteboard, or on some computer-mediated environment, individually or collectively as a group that promotes creative and rational thinking. The conceptual design process benefits from being performed outside of the simulation software environment being used, free of limitations and constraints posed by the software. Conceptual design requires system thinking to appropriately scope and characterize the real-world situation/scenario into a structured and manageable form. In practice, simulation modelers spend less time than required in the conceptual design, which is often the least exciting and laborious phase in the whole process. Instead, they tend to jump in and start the model development process. Allocating less time than required for conceptual design leads to inaccurate representation of the system and too many retractions in the modeling process; therefore, it usually increases the overall time required to complete the project.

Input Analysis

Input analysis involves collecting, analyzing, and characterizing all the inputs to the system. The sources of inputs include secondary databases such as an enterprise resource planning (ERP) system, expert opinions as to how long it takes to complete a specific task, and direct observations. The inputs are usually represented with probability distributions as opposed to deterministic numbers such as single averages. For instance, when an expert provides an opinion on how long it takes to complete a task, this person is asked to provide it in terms of optimistic, pessimistic, and most likely estimates so that these three estimates can then be converted to a triangular distribution for the simulation model. The data collected via direct observations and from secondary databases is then converted to random-number distributions using distribution-fitting software tools, which are included in most simulation software products. Virtually all commercial simulation software (including Simio) has built-in features for generating the input observations from specified random distributions. Therefore, the primary input-analysis task for the analyst is to access and collect the data, characterize the input random variables, and specify corresponding distributions and processes to the simulation software. If we do not have access to real-world data on inputs (because the system may not exist, where the purpose of the simulation is to come up with the specification of this future system), we can use projections, best estimates, similarity to other systems, and experimental design sensitivity analysis to perform the input-analysis task. Although not ideal, in the absence of past data or an existing system in-place, this is the best that anyone can do.

Model Development, Verification, and Validation

Model development is the translation process by which the conceptual model is converted into an executable simulation model. Whereas the conceptual model captures the inner-structure and inter-relationships of the components defining the underlying real-world phenomenon at a relatively high, "conceptual" level, the simulation model development task dives deeper to capture the most detailed description of the system specifications. Often, a more detailed reexamination of the system's components and underlying logic is needed. Most modern simulation packages provide sophisticated graphical user interfaces to support a model-building process, which generally involves dragging and dropping model components and filling in specific characteristics of each element via dialog boxes and property windows. That said, effective model development does require a detailed understanding of the general simulation methodology employed and the specific software being used. The verification and validation steps ensure that the model is accurate both syntactically and semantically. **Verification** is the process that ensures that the model behaves as the developer intended, and the **validation** component ensures that the model is accurate relative to the actual system being modeled.

Output Analysis and Experimentation

Once the model is developed, verified, and validated, it is executed to obtain detailed information about the underlying system. If one is interested in assessing performance metrics like the average time a patient waits in the emergency room before seeing a caregiver, the average number of patients in the waiting room, or the average time spent in the system by a specific class of patients, the related observational values captured during the simulation run need to be converted to those metrics. One may also be interested in making design-level decisions such as the number of doctors or nurses required to ensure that the average patient waits no more than 45 minutes. Assessing performance metrics and making design decisions using a simulation model involves output analysis and experimentation. Output analysis takes the individual observations generated by the simulation, characterizes the underlying random variables in a statistically valid way, and draws inferences about the system being modeled. Experimentation involves systematically varying the model inputs and model structure to investigate alternative system configurations (Smith et al. 2018).

Different Types of Simulation

Computer simulation imitates the behavior, functionality, and operation of a system as it relates to its internal processes, usually over time, often capturing the probabilistic/stochastic nature of the happenings, at an appropriate level of detail, to build intimate understanding and useful insight about the system's current and potential performance. Simulation models are created using software tools designed to capture and represent the system components and their interrelationships and calculate/record their behavioral outcomes over time. Simulation is used for predicting both the effect of changes to existing systems and the projected performance of an imaginary, futuristic, planned new system. Simulations are frequently used in the assessment of alternative designs, testing and validation of operations, and calculation of risk propensity of current and future systems.

Simulations can be categorized based on several dimensions. The most common categorizations of simulations are based on (1) whether they include time into their representation of the underlying system (that is, static versus dynamic simulation), (2) whether they handle the probabilistic nature of the system variables (that is, deterministic versus stochastic simulation), and (3) whether they perceive and represent the underlying phenomenon as a continuous system (that is, discrete versus continuous simulation). What follows is a short description of these categorizations of simulation types.

Simulation May Be Dynamic (Time-Dependent) or Static (Time-Independent)

Time is a crucial element of most systems; the systems change and evolve over time. Although it seems like time is an indispensable part of any system and simulation model, sometimes time can be excluded from a simulation-based analysis. If the time-varying nature of the system is not a primary component of the analysis, performing time-independent simulation analysis could be an acceptable approach, can save time, produce simpler and more understandable models, and result in better insights and solutions. One of the prime examples of time-independent simulation modeling is the Monte Carlo simulation, which will be explained in detail in the following sections.

Simulations May Be Stochastic or Deterministic

In a stochastic simulation, which is the most common type of simulation model, randomness is explicitly captured to better represent the variation found in most real-world systems. Activities involving people, such as the time it takes to complete a task or the quality outcome of performance, always vary. External inputs, such as the behavior of customers and the acceptability of incoming materials, vary also. Finally, exceptions, or infrequent failures, occur. Deterministic models have no variation. They are rare in simulation modeling but more common in optimization modeling such as linear programming.

Simulations May Be Discrete and Continuous

The terms **discrete** and **continuous** generally refer to the nature in which the states change within the system. A **state** in this context is a snapshot of the system as it is defined by all its parameters and their respective values. Some states, such as the length of a waiting queue and the status of a worker or a machine, can change only at discrete points in time (often called event times). Other states, such as pressure in a tank, changes in population dynamics, and temperature in an oven, can change gradually and continuously over time. Some systems are purely discrete or purely continuous, whereas others have both types of states present. Continuous systems are usually defined by differential equations that specify the rate at which the system state parameters change. System dynamics, a graphical approach for creating a simple causal simulation model of a given system using a set of differential equations, is often used for continuous simulations.

Figure 3.4 shows a simple typology of simulation model types. Using three layers of discerning characteristics, it shows the placement of the most popular simulation modeling types, which are also the ones we cover in detail in the following sections, namely Monte Carlo simulation (stochastic + discrete + static), discrete-event simulation (stochastic + discrete + dynamic), and system dynamics (stochastic + continuous + dynamics).

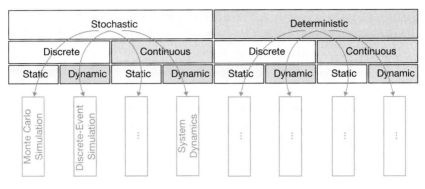

Figure 3.4 A typology for simulation models.

Monte Carlo Simulation

In the broadest sense of the term, Monte Carlo simulation refers to any simulation, manual or computer-based, that utilizes random numbers to represent one or more of the variables in the simulation model. Monte Carlo simulation is known to be named after the famous Mediterranean city of Monte Carlo in Monaco—more formally, an administrative area of the Principality of Monaco, which is a sovereign state/country on the French Riviera in Western Europe bordering France and the Mediterranean Sea. In addition to its natural beauty, Monte Carlo is famous for its casinos, chance gaming, and gambling. Because the simulation process involves generating random (or chance) variables to represent and illustrate random collective behavior, it has been called Monte Carlo simulation. Although Monte Carlo simulations and stochastic simulation are two synonymous terms, and frankly, stochastic simulation is a more descriptive and technical term for it, because of its name appeal, this type of simulation is commonly called Monte Carlo simulation.

Monte Carlo simulation is a simple, yet powerful, stochastic analysis tool commonly used to analyze random events and processes in physical sciences, engineering, natural sciences (e.g., climate change), computational biology (e.g., genetic evolution), computer graphics, operations research, applied statistics, computer games, finance, and business. Historically, it was first used for the Manhattan Project to solve the neutron diffusion problem in the development of the atomic bomb at Los Alamos National Laboratory, in New Mexico, USA, in the early 1940s. The Rand Corporation, an American nonprofit global policy think tank created in 1948 to offer research and analysis to the United States Armed Forces, and the U.S. Air Force were two of the major organizations responsible for funding and disseminating information on Monte Carlo simulation methods during that time, which has found a wide range of applications in many different fields. Monte Carlo simulation has been applied to diverse problems ranging from the simulation of complex physical phenomena such as atom collisions to traffic flow analysis, from project planning to risk assessment of financial portfolios and stock market movements.

Simulating Two-Dice Rolls

Because Monte Carlo is a gaming town, what better way to explain Monte Carlo simulation than with a dice-rolling game? Assume that we have two unbiased fair dice. The goal is to calculate the probability of getting a total of 7 while rolling two dice. When we look at all the permutations, we realize that there are six different ways to get a score of 7 with two dice. There are 36 (6×6) different combinations of numbers (each ranging from 1 to 6) that can happen with two dice. Therefore, the probability of rolling a 7 is 6/30 = 0.167. Because we use only two dice, the permutations are limited and easily countable, and the probability of getting a specific number on each dice is equal (uniform distribution between 1 and 6), we managed to calculate the probability of getting a certain total. (In this case, it was 7.) Figure 3.5 shows all the permutations of numeric sums that we can obtain from rolling two dice and the probability of getting each sum (between 2 and 12).

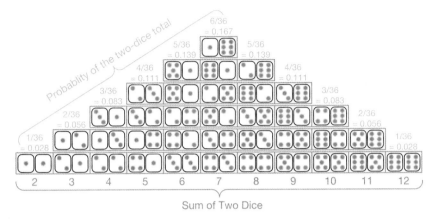

Figure 3.5 Probability of getting specific numbers of two-dice rolling sums.

Now let's try to do the same evaluation with a Monte Carlo simulation. As was the case before, in this simulation, we are to calculate the probability of $Y = 7$, where the value of Y is the sum of X_1 and X_2, as shown is the following simple equation:

$$Y = X_1 + X_2$$

where, $1 \leq X_1 \leq 6$ and $1 \leq X_2 \leq 6$.

We can execute this simulation by generating a large enough number of data rows using three columns. The first two columns would generate integer random numbers between 1 and 6, and the third column would sum the values of the first two columns. Then, using this data, we can calculate the proportion of the number of 7s obtained in the third column. If the data (number of rows) is large enough, we should get a value close to 0.167. Another way to execute the same simulation experiment in Excel is by using a simple macro. The Visual Basic for Applications (VBA) code to carry out this specific task is shown in Figure 3.6. As can be seen, in this experiment, we used 100,000 rolls/replications. It is worth noting that the larger the number of replications, the closer the value gets to the actual one. In this case, 100,000 replications produced the expected value.

Figure 3.6 An Excel macro for getting a 7 in two dice rolls with a Monte Carlo simulation.

Process of Developing a Monte Carlo Simulation

The step-by-step process of developing a Monte Carlo simulation solution to a real-world problem is illustrated in Figure 3.7 and further explained in the following section.

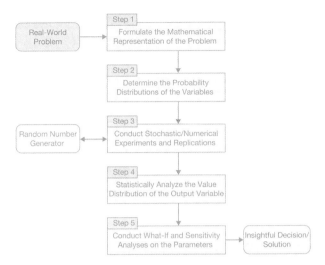

Figure 3.7 The process of developing a Monte Carlo simulation-based solution.

Step 1.   Formulate the mathematical representation of the problem, where some or all the variables are random.

Step 2.   Determine the proper random number distribution of each random variable.

  a. Determine the distributions based on observations/measurements, archival data, or subject matter experts.

  b. Based on the findings, decide to use either discrete/observational or theoretic random distribution. Figure 3.8 and Figure 3.9 show discrete and continuous probability distributions.

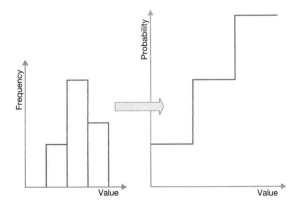

Figure 3.8 Discrete probability—discrete and cumulative distribution functions.

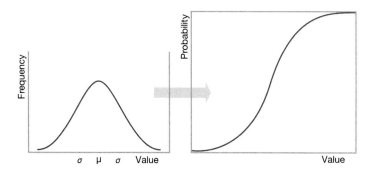

Figure 3.9 Continuous probability—frequency to cumulative distribution conversion.

Step 3.   Conduct the simulation for x number of iterations. For each iteration, do the following:

   a. For each random variable,

   i. Sample a random uniform number.

   ii. Convert/transform the uniform random numbers [0, 1] to proper random numbers that follow the given distribution.

   b. Execute the mathematical formula and record the results.

Step 4.   Once a large number of iterations are completed,

   a. Analyze the distribution of the resultant variable values. Such a distribution can provide the insight needed to assess the relative risk of obtaining certain values. Figure 3.10 shows a sample output variable value distribution (a histogram).

Step 5.   Conduct sensitivity analysis on coefficients and variable distributions and their parameters.

   Now let's illustrate this process with an overly simplified example.

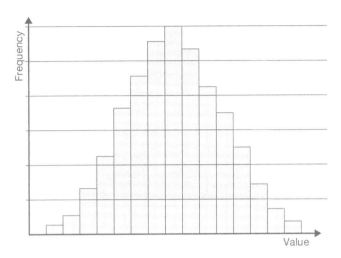

Figure 3.10 Distribution of values obtained for the output variable.

Illustrative Example—A Business Planning Scenario

The firm is contemplating introduction of a new product to the market. As the marketing manager of the firm, you are asked to assess the likelihood of financial success of this new product in the first year. Specifically, you are to estimate the first-year profit-loss profile of this product. Your assessment will be based on the following variables:

- Expected sales volume in units
- Estimated sales price per unit
- Expected cost
- Estimated fixed cost for the planning period
- Estimated variable cost per unit

Therefore, the simple profit equation can be written as follows:

$$Profit = Revenue - Total\ cost$$

$$Revenue = Sales\ volume \times Unit\ sales\ price$$

$$Total\ cost = Fixed\ cost + Variable\ cost$$

$$Variable\ cost = Sales\ volume \times Unit\ variable\ cost$$

$$Profit = (Sales\ volume \times Unit\ sales\ price) - \\ (Fixed\ cost + (Sales\ volume \times Unit\ variable\ cost))$$

Based on diligent information collection and consolidation efforts using expert opinions, archival data on similar products, and some market research, the following variable values are determined:

Variable	Value (Deterministic or Stochastic)
Sales volume	Normal (63,000, 5600)
Unit sales price	$12.50
Fixed cost	$220,000
Unit variable cost	Probability of 4: 20%, 5: 50%, 6: 30%)

As shown in the table, two of the four variables—namely, unit sales price and fixed cost—have deterministic, or fixed, values. The other two—namely, sales volume and unit variable cost—have stochastic/ probabilistic values. For instance, as per the intelligence gathering using the inputs from market research and archival data on similar products from the previous new product launch events, the annual sales volume for this new product is determined to follow a normal distribution with a mean of 63,000 and a standard deviation of 5,600. Similarly, based on operations analytics, it is determined that the unit variable cost will follow a discrete distribution with probability of 20% for $4, 50% for $5, and 30% for $6.

If we were to use the simple averages for all variables, we would have calculated the following to be the total profit.

$$Profit = (63,000 \times 12.50) - (220,000 + (63,000 \times 5))$$

$$Profit = \$252,500$$

Now let's do the same analysis with Monte Carlo simulation using Microsoft Excel. Using the first numerical row, we need to create the probabilistic variables in separate columns. Then we can apply the simple mathematical formula to calculate the value of the output in the first row. Once the definition of probabilistic variables is completed and verified, we replicate the first row for an arbitrarily large number of times, such as 10,000. After that, we draw a vertical bar chart or a histogram to illustrate the distribution of the 10,000 values calculated for the output variable (shown in the last row). Figure 3.11 shows the Excel screenshot of these calculations.

A2			f_x	=(B2*C2)-(D2+B2*E2)		
	A	B	C	D	E	F
1	Annual Total Profit	Annual Sales Volume	Unit Sales Price	Annual Fixed Cost	Unit Variable Cost	=RAND()
2	237202.9397	53788.58114	12.5	220000	4	0.049995607
3	248467.2757	55113.79715	12.5	220000	4	0.079528452
4	243158.5129	61754.46839	12.5	220000	5	0.411994889
5	264517.6226	64602.34968	12.5	220000	5	0.612612205
6	266572.8146	64876.37528	12.5	220000	5	0.631212733
7	213092.5519	66629.62337	12.5	220000	6	0.741555071
8	229166.8228	59888.90971	12.5	220000	5	0.289258632
9	252354.3005	62980.5734	12.5	220000	5	0.498616058
10	213425.678	66680.87354	12.5	220000	6	0.744505611
11	239641.4906	61285.53208	12.5	220000	5	0.379743322
12	247445.7772	71914.73495	12.5	220000	6	0.944298317
13	261683.0527	64224.40703	12.5	220000	5	0.586536356
14	220594.2218	58745.89624	12.5	220000	5	0.223728508
15	215166.091	51196.0107	12.5	220000	4	0.017521757
16	269343.8567	57569.86549	12.5	220000	4	0.166106283
17	264340.4251	64578.72335	12.5	220000	5	0.610995612

Figure 3.11 Monte Carlo simulation of the business planning scenario.

Using this distribution of values for the output variable, we can calculate the percentiles, and we can calculate the likelihood of obtaining a value or a range of values for the output variable. These calculations help us in assessing the level of uncertainty and risk associated with different values of the output variable. Figure 3.12 shows the distribution of the output variable. Figure 3.13 shows the distribution of the two stochastic variable values used in the simulation. The distributions closely follow the original definitional parameters.

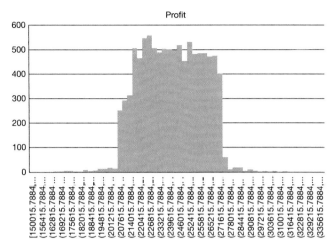

Figure 3.12 A histogram for the output variable value distribution.

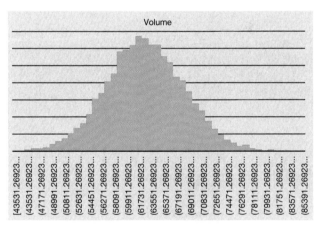

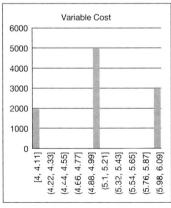

Figure 3.13 Distribution of the two stochastic variables.

Advantages of Using Monte Carlo Simulation

The following are the most prevalent advantages of using Monte Carlo simulation:

- It is founded on a solid theory.
- It is a simple and straightforward method to analyze stochastic variables.
- It allows for combining stochastic and deterministic variables.
- It provides a distribution of values for the output variables for better risk assessment.
- For simple optimization problems, it often provides the global optimum.
- It can be easily implemented in spreadsheet problems.

Disadvantages of Monte Carlo Simulation

The disadvantages of Monte Carlo simulation include the following:

- It requires large enough replications to get close to the optimal solution.
- It relies heavily on the randomness of the random number generator.
- It evaluates the function in a timeless manner; it ignores the time dimension.
- It does not provide a single number as the result; instead, it produces a distribution of values.
- It cannot handle complex logical interactions; it often needs oversimplification of the reality.

Discrete Event Simulation

Among the various types of simulation modeling paradigms, DES is undoubtedly the most popular and the most commonly employed modeling paradigm to study business processes and related business problems. The methodology behind DES lends itself quite nicely in modeling and analyzing complex processes governed by a logical sequence of events that are often found in real-world decision situations. Essentially, DES models the functionality of a given system as a collection of discrete events logically sequenced over time. Each event occurs at a particular instance in time, resulting in changes on certain system parameters and causing a transformation of the system state. Outside of events, the state of the system remains unchanged. In other words, between two consecutive events, nothing noteworthy happens; there's no change on the system variables/parameters or on the system state. That is why the execution of simulation can advance/jump from one event to the next in a time-ordered manner.

This event-driven progression of the simulation execution is the most significant difference between DES and continuous simulation where the simulation execution continuously tracks the system dynamics and functionality over time. Instead of being event-based, continuous simulation is called an activity-based simulation, where the time is broken up into small time slices and the system state is updated according to the set of activities happening in these time slices. Because discrete-event simulations do not have to simulate every time slice, they can usually run much faster than the corresponding continuous simulation.

At first, understanding and internalizing the event-driven functionality of DES modeling may be somewhat overwhelming. One may ask what an event is, what types of events need to be tracked, how the events are created, and how the events are executed. The best way to understand this event-driven functionality is to consider an example of a simple system.

DES Modeling of a Simple System

The most logical example in learning the functionality of a DES is to model a simple system—such as a single-line (single waiting queue) single-server system—where customers randomly arrive at a small neighborhood branch of a commercial bank to be served by a teller. In this scenario, there is a line where the customers build a queue and a server can service one customer at a time. The main events in this system are the arrival and the departure of a customer. But how about a server beginning to serve the next customer? Why is that not another event? Well, because the event of the teller starting to service a customer can be combined with either the arrival or the departure of a customer event, it does not need to be treated as a separate event; it can be combined into the logic of the arrival and departure events. To elaborate, if the system is empty and there are no customers in the queue, the customer arrival and the start of the service happen at the same time. Because there is no time difference, these two happenings can and should be combined into a single execution logic under the customer arrival event. In the case of a customer waiting in the queue, the beginning of the service can be combined with the customer departure event. In other words, when the previous customer departs, the next customer from the top of the queue moves into the service station. Because these two things happen at the same time, the execution logic behind the departure event handles them together, collectively. The system states that are changed by these events include *number of customers in the queue* (an integer number from zero to *n*) and *teller status* (busy or idle). The random variables that need to be characterized using probability distributions to model the stochastic nature of the system include *customer interarrival times* and *teller service times*. After running the simulation long enough, the collected data and statistics can be used to determine system performance–related metrics such as *average queue length*, *average service time*, and *average time spent in the system*, among others. The simulation-generated data is rich enough to go beyond simple averages by providing distributions of these performance metrics to calculate the best- and worst-case scenarios.

If the averages are all that is needed for the performance metrics, for a simple waiting-line system like this, perhaps queueing theory would be a more optimal solution approach. Queueing theory uses close-form, noniterative, mathematical formulas to quickly calculate these simple performance metrics. When the system gets complicated, the queuing theory falls short of properly representing and accurately solving the underlying waiting-line problem with simple mathematical formulas. Instead of queueing theory, for such situations, DES modeling should be used. In fact, most of the waiting-line type of complex real-world systems are analyzed and solved using DES modeling. Following is a brief description of the waiting-line systems.

Waiting-Line Systems and Queuing Theory

Queueing theory is the mathematical study of waiting lines, or queues. A queueing model of a given waiting-line system is constructed to calculate/estimate some of the system-related performance metrics such as queue lengths and waiting time. Like DES, queueing theory is generally considered a branch of operations research because the results are often used when making business decisions about the resources needed to provide a service. Historically speaking, queueing theory is known to have originated from Agner Krarup Erlang's earlier work on modeling the Copenhagen telephone exchange network in the early 1900s. The ideas behind queueing theory have since been applied to a variety of application domains, including design of systems for manufacturing, traffic flow, wireless networks, computing, and the Internet.

The simplest queuing model includes a single queue and a server. Usually called an M/M/1 queue, in this simple waiting-line system, the arrivals are assumed to follow a Poisson process, and the service times are assumed to be exponentially distributed. M/M/1, the most basic of the queueing models, allows for closed-form expressions to calculate the exact performance metrics of the underlying system. Its extensions include more than one server (such as M/M/c) and relaxation of the distributing assumption for random interarrival and service times (G/G/1).

An M/M/1 queue is a stochastic process whose state space is defined by the integer number of customers in the system, including any currently in service. The key parameters of an M/M/1 queue follow:

- Arrivals occur at rate λ according to a Poisson process. The first M in the M/M/1 is an illustration of the properly called Markovian (memoryless), denoting that the interarrivals are completely independent of each other. When a customer arrives, the system status changes, and the number of customers in the system increases by one.

- Service times have an exponential distribution with a rate parameter μ in the M/M/1 queue, where $1/\mu$ is the mean service time. Like the first M, the second M in the M/M/1 is an illustration of the properly called Markovian (memoryless), denoting that the service times are completely independent of each other.

- A single server serves customers one at a time from the front of the queue, according to a first-come-first-served queue discipline. When the service is completed, the customer leaves the queue, the system status changes, and the number of customers in the system reduces by one.

- In an M/M/1 queue, the capacity (the buffer) of the queue is assumed to be infinite in size, so there is no limit on the number of customers it can accommodate.

Although it seems to be rather simplistic, the exact calculations of the M/M/1 queue lays the foundation of more complex waiting-line systems, including many related subsystems (queuing network models). Figure 3.14a shows a graphical depiction of a single M/M/1 queue, whereas Figure 3.14b shows a graphical depiction of a queuing network.

(a) M/M/1 Queue

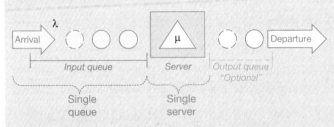

(b) Queuing Network

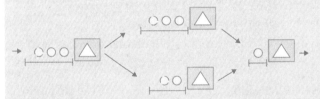

Figure 3.14 A simple depiction of queuing models.

The computational foundation of the modern-day queueing theory is based on Little's Law. Little's Law, developed by John Little in 1954, states that the long-term average number of customers (L) in a stationary (steady state) system is equal to the long-term average effective arrival rate (λ) multiplied by the average time that a customer spends in the system (W). Expressed algebraically, the law is

$$L = \lambda W$$

Although this formula looks simple and rather intuitive, it is quite remarkable because it shows that the relationship is not influenced by the arrival process distribution, the service distribution, the service order, or practically anything else. That means the formula applies to any system, and particularly, it applies to systems within systems. So, in a bank, the customer line might be one subsystem, and each of the tellers another subsystem, and the result of Little's Law applies to each system and to the whole—the system of the systems. The only requirements are that the system be stable and nonpreemptive, which rules out transition states such as the beginning (initial startup) or the ending (winding down to shutdown) of the system.

How Does DES Work?

Once the model is built, verified, and validated, the simulation is run using an experimental design process to test and assess the outcomes of a number of what-if analyses and hypothetical scenarios. The main activities of a DES can be grouped into three main phases: *start* (which is composed of the initialization of the simulation), run (which is the iterative process of enacting the underlying system for an extended period of time), and *end* (summarizing and reporting the simulation results). Figure 3.15 shows a high-level depiction of the logical flow of the DES execution process.

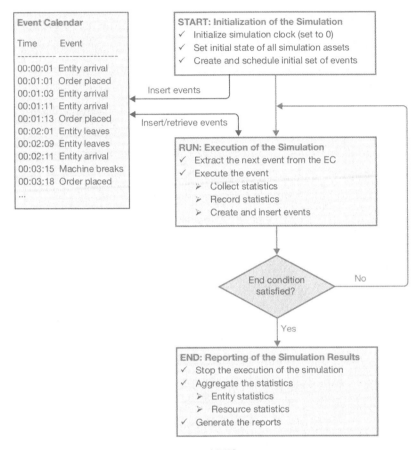

Figure 3.15 The execution process of DES.

Step 1: START—Initialization of the Simulation Model Parameters

At the start phase of the simulation execution, the event calendar is naturally empty, with no events to execute. To get the simulation execution started, we need to set the simulation clock to zero, set the system variable and statistics collection parameters to their initial state, insert the initial set of events into the event calendar, and decide on and record the simulation ending condition.

Once the initialization of the simulation model parameters is completed, the execution moves into the iterative process of removal and execution of events from the event calendar. This simulation run continues until the simulation ending condition is reached. The simulation ending condition can be based on a prespecified duration of simulation time, a certain number of customer arrivals or departures, or the actual execution time of the simulation itself. Following is the list of typical tasks performed during this phase.

- Initialize simulation clock—set it to zero.
- Initialize system variables.
- Schedule the initial set of events.
- Establish and record the simulation ending condition.

Step 2: RUN the Simulation Model

During the run phase of the DES, the events are removed and executed one by one from the event calendar in the order of event times. Figure 3.16 shows a graphical depiction of the event times $(e_2$ thru $e_n)$ and corresponding simulation time advances $(TA_1$ to $TA_n)$. As can be seen, the time between scheduled events is anything but uniform, resulting in an uneven progression of the simulation time.

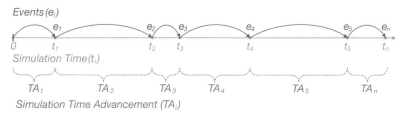

Figure 3.16 Advancement of simulation time at discrete events in the process.

Once an event is removed from the event calendar, it is "executed" as per the prescribed set of activities. Each event type would have a different set and order of activities. For instance, the customer arrival would typically include the following activities: (1) advance the simulation time to the current event time, (2) create the next customer arrival event, (3) update the customer arrival statistics, and (4) if the simulation completion condition is based on the number of customer arrivals, check for the simulation completion condition. Following is the list of typical tasks performed during this phase.

- Remove the nest event from the event calendar.
- Set the simulation clock to the current event time.
- Update variable values (change the system status).
- Collect relevant data and statistics.
- Check for the simulation ending condition.

Step 3: END the Simulation Run

Once the simulation-ending completing is reached, the logic of the model jumps to the simulation ending phase. In this phase, the data and statistics collected during the simulation run are aggregated, organized, and presented (in tabular and graphical forms) for the decision-maker to consume. Based on the insights obtained from these results, the decision-maker may conduct a what-if analysis (manipulate system parameters) to assess the insights' impact on the system output, thereby reaching the best possible solution to the problem at hand:

- Aggregate data/statistics on entities and resources.
- Generate simulation report.

DES Terminology

DES modeling has its own language. Following are the brief definitions of the specific terminology used in DES.

Entity

The objects that flow through the system are usually called **entity** in simulation terminology. While a physical widget in a manufacturing system simulation is modeled as an entity, a patient who shows up in a hospital emergency room or a customer who shows up at a fast-food restaurant is modeled as an entity for a DES. As entities move through the model, being subject to a number of activities, their time spent at different stations and time between different events are recorded as statistics for calculating the entity-related metrics at the end of the simulation run.

Resource

Resources are the individual or collective objects needed to complete the processing of the entities in a simulation model. For instance, in a hospital emergency room simulation model, nurses, doctors and receptionists are all resources, as are examination rooms and x-ray or MRI machines. The simulation model keeps track of the usage statistics of these resources to assess their capacity limitations. A type of resource that has a busy status over 90% of the time can be labeled a bottleneck and can be expedited or parallelized to increase the process flow and resultant throughput (number of patients seen in a 24-hour day shift).

Queue

As mentioned before, a majority of business process simulations are modeled using the characterization of waiting lines. In a waiting line depiction of a business process, each station-resource combination—collectively called a server—has a waiting line, or **queue**, in front of it for the incoming entities to wait when the server is busy. Once the server becomes idle, one of the waiting entities, if there are any, advances into the server for processing. If there are multiple entities waiting to be processed, which entity to advance is determined by the queue discipline or entity removal logic. The queue discipline would be as simple as first-come-first-serve or as complex as minimum-late-delivery-cost (service the entity that is part of the order that has the earliest delivery date to minimize the likelihood of late delivery penalties).

Server

A **server** in a DES model is a combination of resources at a specific location or logical step in the process, where the entities are processed and transformed. Once an entity goes through a server, its state changes. (One or more of the defining parameter values are updated.) Although, by definition, a server is similar to a resource, it differs from a resource by encapsulating one or more resources coming together to transform entities at a particular physical or logical point in the simulated process.

Event

In a DES model, an **event** is the depiction of all activities, the execution of which collectively changes the system status at a specific point in time. An event may contain one of more than one activity. These activities may or may not be interrelated. What brings these activities together within an event is the time at which they occur. In waiting-line-type simulation models, typical events include customer arrival, machine breakdown, and customer departure. Each of these events, as explained before, contains a number of activities/tasks that take place to mimic the happenings of the actual system being modeled.

Events List

The simulation model maintains a list of simulation events. This is sometimes called the pending **events list** or events calendar because it lists events that are created as a result of the previously simulated/ executed events but have yet to be simulated/executed themselves. An event is described by the time at which it occurs and a type, indicating the functionality (one of more activities that will result in changing the system state) that will be performed to simulate that event. It is common for the event code to include paraments for differentiation and specific execution of similar events under different conditions. The pending event set is typically organized as a priority queue, sorted by event time. In other words, regardless of the order in which events are added to the event set, they are removed in strictly chronological order. Typically, events are scheduled dynamically as the simulation proceeds. For example, in the bank example mentioned earlier, the customer arrival event at a specific time would include the creation of the subsequent customer departure event and whether the customer queue is empty and the teller is idle.

State

A system **state** is the value of all system variables that collectively capture and represent the salient properties of the system being studied. As one or more of the variable values changes, so does the system state. The change of the states over time can be mathematically represented by a step function. The state of the system changes whenever an event occurs that causes system variable values to change.

Simulation Clock

The **simulation clock** must keep track of the current simulation time in whatever measurement units are suitable for the system being modeled. In discrete-event simulations, simulation time jumps from one event time to the next chronologically, as opposed to continuous simulations, where the simulation clock advances continuously.

Random-Number Generators

The simulation needs to generate random variables of various kinds, depending on the system model. This is accomplished by one or more **pseudo-random number generators**. The use of pseudo-random numbers as opposed to true random numbers is a benefit should a simulation need a rerun with the same behavior.

Parameters

Entities and resources usually have specific characteristics that the simulation model must define and properly manage. In a DES model, these characteristics are captured using parameters. For instance, a patient arriving at a hospital emergency room can have a parameter that defines her condition or severity level. During the simulation run, this condition parameter can determine the patient's priority in the waiting queues and different sequence diagnostic and treatment regiments. Similarly, a widget in the manufacturing process can have a parameter to keep track of the customer order it belongs to, which can then be used to execute sophisticated queue disciplines.

Statistics

The simulation typically keeps track of the system's statistics, which at the end of the simulation run helps to quantify the performance metrics of interest. In the bank example, it is of interest to track the customer waiting times. In a simulation model, performance metrics can be driven from collected data or from the averages over replications (different runs of the model).

Ending Condition

Because events are interconnected to create new future events, theoretically speaking, a DES could run forever. Therefore, the simulation modeler must decide when the simulation needs to end. Typical choices are (1) after a certain amount of time (for example, after 8 hours or after seven days), (2) after processing a certain number of entities (for example, creating or departing a certain number of customers), and (3) when enough data is collected to reliably calculate the desired statistical measures.

System Dynamics

Simulation of continuous systems is usually defined by a series of differential equations that collectively specify the rate at which the system state changes. Simulation software uses numerical integration to generate a solution to the system of differential equations over time. System dynamics, which is a graphical approach to creating causal models of the complex systems, is often used to evaluate continuous simulations.

System dynamics (SD) modeling, originally called industrial dynamics, was introduced by Jay Forrester (1958) at the Sloan School of Management at Massachusetts Institute of Technology. Forrester used this new approach to study the causal relationships and collective behavior of industrial system dynamics, principles of complex systems, the nature of urban settings, and large-scale world dynamics. In SD, Forrester emphasized the importance of behavioral change in complex systems, the action-reaction continuums, and the eventual improvements.

In terms of the underlying philosophy and the theory, Forrester drew attention to the multitude of variables in complex systems that are causally connected in feedback loops that themselves interact with each other systematically. These systemic links among feedback loops establish the structure of the system and its collective behavior. To accurately represent the structure of the complex system, the modeler should perform a thorough analysis of the real-world system to identify (1) the system boundary (considering and including all the significant interacting elements and excluding the elements that do not affect the intended system behavior), (2) the feedback loops (discovering the causal loops within the defined boundary, characterizing their nature as positive or negative, and mapping their interactions), (3) the rates or flows and stocks or levels (where rates and flows are used to represent the relationships between elements, and stocks and levels are used to represent the accumulated quantity of the element), and (4) the simulation environment (which is used to discover the dominant feedback loops, predict the effect of time delays, and take action to add new loops or break or refine existing links/loops).

In SD-based simulation modeling, system structure is usually represented using four key features, altogether constituting the principles of this employed approach: (1) order, which refers to the number of levels, (2) direction, which refers to the feedback being either positive or negative, (3) nonlinearity, which refers to nonlinear relationships between loops leading to dominance shifts, and (4) loop multiplicity, which refers to the appropriate representation of the managerial, economic, or social situations and the complexities the modeler face to identify the relevant variables that make simulation model realistic for the underlying real process. Forrester defined the high-level methodology of SD using the following sequential stages:

1. Identify the complex relationships and related key variables that affect the system.

2. Construct a feedback loop that reveals connections between variables.

3. Transform the feedback loop into a mathematical model by considering rates and levels that capture the inter-relationships within the system.

4. Verify the loop and relationship definitions, and validate the model by comparing its structure and behavior with the existing real-world situation.

5. Design a set of experiments to discover alternative courses of action that potentially improve the performance of the system.

6. Conduct sensitivity analysis to assess the level of sensitivity and robustness of the individual components within the model of the system.

7. Make recommendations based on the findings of the SD-based simulation modeling.

In this SD methodology, it is implied and expected that human creativity plays a key role in problem identification and structuring, designing the feedback loops, and modeling the underlying key variables. SD simulation, if performed properly, helps in unearthing unknown and unexpected outcomes derived from the dynamic behavior of the underlying system. Forrester's methodology, outlined earlier, can be simplified at a higher conceptual level using only five stages:

1. Problem structuring

2. Causal loop modeling

3. Dynamic modeling

4. Scenario planning and modeling

5. Implementation and organizational learning

The first three stages aim to identify the problem specifics, the positive and negative loops, and the effect of the feedback process. The last two stages aim to test various strategies under different scenarios to find answers to the pressing problem of improving the performance of the modeled system. The same iterative SD-based simulation modeling process can also be described by the following stages:

1. **Problem Articulation.** This stage includes tasks like theme selection, key variables identification, time horizon consideration, and dynamic problem definition.

2. **Dynamic Hypothesis Formulation.** This stage is concerned with initial hypothesis generation, endogenous focus design, and mapping.

3. **A Simulation Model Formulation.** This stage includes tasks like structure specification, parameters estimation, and consistency testing.

4. **Testing.** This stage includes comparing reference modes, verification and validation of the model, and measuring its robustness under extreme conditions.

5. **Policy Design and Evaluation.** This stage includes tasks like scenario specification, policy design, what-if analysis, sensitivity analysis, and interaction of policies.

SD modeling of complex continuous systems is not a simple sequential process; it is often nonlinear in nature, and it involves numerous feedback loops. Thus, during modeling, it is necessary to question, test, and refine the proposed model iteratively to reach the desired modeling state. The initial steps of modeling—structuring of the problem, and defining the boundary and scope of the problem space—can change later as the specific feedback loops are learned and implemented during the modeling process. The necessity for iterations and refinements can be initiated from any step to any other earlier steps. These iterations need to be executed as many times as necessary until the model matures and stabilizes.

SD-based simulation modeling has enriched system theory, information science, organizational theory, control theory, tactical decision-making, cybernetics, and military games. SD also offers a new way of thinking that can be defined as a wholistic system thinking approach. It intrinsically handles imperceptible complexities, ambiguities, and imperfections by modeling the system at a high-level dynamic representation. SD provides the means to better understand, study, visualize, and analyze systems defined by large-scale, complex, dynamic feedbacks. SD does all these as an analytics tool or language that is capable of investigating and making deductions about the complexities and dynamic cause and effect relationships.

This SD language is visual and diagram based, has its special rules (syntax), translates perceptions into explicit pictures (diagrammatic representation), and clarifies the closed interdependencies. By doing so, it offers the modeling and learning capabilities to unfold the system behavior and the underlying structure. The SD approach is commonly used in a structured and hierarchical manner to investigate the interaction between systems and policies across time and space.

Application Case—Analyzing Airline MRO Operations Using a System Dynamics Approach

This case begins with a statement of the problem.

Problem

The life span of an aircraft is usually around 30 years in the commercial aviation industry. During this time span, an aircraft needs maintenance to stay in service. The cost of maintenance, repair, and overhaul (MRO) activities in its pure nature is a significant portion of the lifetime cost of the underlying system, accounting for around 10% of the total cost. The purpose of this application case study is to design/develop and critically assess a comprehensive model of the operations at Turkish Technic—the MRO department of Turkish Airlines. One of the largest and most successful air carriers in the world, Turkish Airlines has been increasing its capacity in terms of the number of passengers served, the number of domestic and international destinations flown, and the size of its airplane fleet. The increase in the capacity led to strained/overutilized resources and created significant challenges for its MRO operations.

Proposed Solution

A comprehensive system dynamics model was designed and developed to holistically represent and critically assess the different facets of MRO operations to help in analyzing various decision scenarios and what-if analyses at Turkish Airlines. In this model development effort, subject matter experts' opinions, experiences, and judgments were used to identify the key variables and their interrelationships and to establish the initial conditions of the model parameters. Individuals' mental models, even when well-intended, offer only a limited viewpoint on the causal processes of the MRO operations. Therefore, in this case, a group-based collective model–building approach was employed. As is the case in most multi-expert knowledge elicitation processes, in this study we have also faced some knowledge elicitation challenges. Specifically, a few conflicts about the provided knowledge arose, and they were handled via consultation and compromising among the domain experts. The high-level causal model developed for this case study is shown in Figure 3.17.

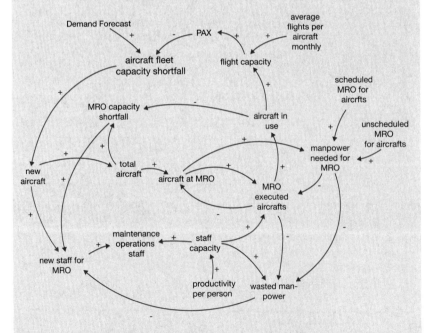

Figure 3.17 High-level SD model structure and boundary.

Findings

The developed system dynamics model presented unique opportunities by laying the foundation to thoroughly and realistically test various MRO operations' workload and aircraft fleet expansion policy alternatives. The developed model can also be used as a "learning laboratory" by allowing the assessment of the impact and boundaries (sensitivity) of various low-level system parameters and the testing of the value and viability of different high-level operational policies. The case study results suggested that MRO operations have direct impact on the available number of airworthy aircrafts and hence the usable fleet seat capacity. To sustain a profitable airline fleet, the airline companies should take into account the unique characteristics/needs of MRO operations for both existing and new/prospective aircrafts.

More details about this application case study can be found in the paper published by the book author and his colleagues from Turkey (Tokgöz et al., 2018).

Other Varieties of Simulation Models

Other varieties of simulation models include lookahead, visual interactive, and agent-based.

Lookahead Simulation

Simulation models are usually developed to identify root causes of problems and to improve performance of existing systems. Sometimes simulation models can also be developed to study nonexisting systems. Such a model can help to conduct what-if analysis to optimize the system parameters for an ideal actual system. For instance, NASA uses simulation to assess a complex set of parameters to mitigate potential risks. Sometimes simulation models are developed to foresee future states of a given complex system. These simulation models are usually called **lookahead simulators**. Using currently available data, information, and knowledge about an existing system, a model is developed to study the future risks. For instance, in a nuclear reactor, a simulation model can be used to assess what the system status will be a few hours or a few days later. Such an assessment would help identify and prevent undesirable system outcomes.

Visual Interactive Simulation Modeling

Visual interactive simulation (VIS), also known as visual interactive modeling (VIM) and visual interactive problem-solving, is a simulation method that lets decision-makers see what the model is doing and how it interacts with the decisions made, as they are being made. The technique has been used with great success in operations management DSS. The user can employ his knowledge to determine and try different decision strategies while interacting with the model. Enhanced learning, about both the problem and the impact of the alternatives tested, can and does occur. Decision-makers also contribute to model validation. Decision-makers who use VIS generally support and trust their results.

VIS uses animated computer graphics displays to present the impact of different managerial decisions. It differs from regular graphics in that the user can adjust the decision-making process and see the results of the intervention. A visual model is a graphic used as an integral part of decision-making or problem-solving, not just as a communication device. Some people respond better than others to graphical displays, and this type of interaction can help managers learn about the decision-making situation.

VIS can represent static or dynamic systems. Static models display a visual image of the result of one decision alternative at a time. Dynamic models display systems that evolve over time, and the evolution is represented by animation. The latest visual-simulation technology has been coupled with the concept of virtual reality, where an artificial world is created for a number of purposes, from training to entertainment to viewing data in an artificial landscape. For example, the U.S. military uses VIS systems so that ground troops can gain familiarity with terrain or a city to quickly orient themselves. Pilots also use VIS to gain familiarity with targets by simulating attack runs. The VIS software can also include GIS coordinates.

Agent-Based Simulation

Agent-based simulation is founded on top of agent-based modeling, where the elements of a given system are modeled using autonomous agents. An agent is the encapsulation of a real-world object/element with its properties and behavioral characteristics. An agent can represent a single atomic object or a composite object that is composed of a collection of atomic objects/elements. Once a variety of related agents (atomic and composite) are brought together, they constitute a complex structure that is often called a multi-agent system. Usually, individual agents are modeled with simple properties and behavior so that the collective intelligent behavior emerges when they get together as a collective system, portraying wisdom of the crowd. That said, the individual agents, in the general sense of modeling, can have and partially show behavior of learning/intelligence and can move between different systems over the Internet (the mobile agent). In simulation modeling, the individual agents are usually modeled as simple elements, whereas the collective system of agents is modeled to be a rich representation of the underlying complex, evolving, learning/intelligent system.

Agent-based simulation (ABS) modeling is relatively new to the world of simulation. Although the idea of modeling a complex system using agents dates back to the 1940s, its manifestation into the simulation world started to happen in the mid-to-late 1990s. ABS is a class of sophisticated computational models for simulating the actions and interactions of autonomous agents (both individual or collective entities such as organizations or groups) with the purpose of assessing their effects on the system as a whole. The fundamentals of ABS are based on game theory, complex systems, computational sociology, multi-agent systems, and evolutionary programming. Traditionally, ABS models are used on noncomputing-related scientific domains including biology, ecology and social science. These types of ABS models search for explanatory insight into the collective behavior of agents that are individually following simple rules, typically in natural and ecological systems. ABS models are now being used for complex systems outside of their initial ecology-limited domain, successfully being applied to specific business and engineering problems.

ABS models are a kind of microscale model that simulates the simultaneous operations and interactions of multiple agents in an attempt to re-create and predict the collective behavior of complex systems. The process is one of emergence from the lower (micro) level of elements (agents) to a higher (macro) level of systems (the complex phenomenon). As such, a key notion of ABS modeling is that simple behavioral rules governing the agents generate complex behavior at the system level. This principle is extensively adopted in the modeling community. Another central tenet is that the whole is greater than the sum of the parts. Individual agents are typically characterized as boundedly rational, presumed to be acting in what they perceive as their own interests—such as reproduction, economic benefit, or social status—using heuristics or simple decision-making rules. ABS modeling agents may also portray learning, adaptation, and reproduction.

Most ABS models are composed of: (1) numerous agents specified at various levels and scales (typically referred to as agent-granularity); (2) decision-making heuristics at the individual agent level; (3) learning rules or adaptive processes; (4) an interaction topology; and (5) an environment. ABS models are typically implemented on computers either as custom software or via ABS development toolkits. This software can then be used to conduct what-if analysis on how certain changes in individual behaviors will affect the system's emerging overall behavior.

Applications of ABS can be found in many domains, including these:

- Natural sciences
- Business, engineering and technology (characterization of the changes in organizational behavior, team dynamics, consumer behavior, social networks, Internet of Things (IoT)/wireless sensor networks, and so on)
- Economics and social science (gradual changes in economics and social dynamics)
- Public safety and security (evolution of infectious diseases, epidemics, natural disaster planning, biowarfare, and so on)

Advantages of Simulation Modeling

Simulation is used in decision support modeling for the following reasons:

- The theory is well defined and fairly straightforward.
- A great amount of time compression can be attained, quickly giving a manager some feel as to the long-term (1- to 10-year) effects of many policies.
- Simulation is descriptive rather than normative. This allows the manager to pose what-if questions. Managers can use a trial-and-error approach to problem-solving and can do so faster, at less expense, more accurately, and with less risk.
- A manager can experiment to determine which decision variables and which parts of the environment are really important, and with different alternatives.

- An accurate simulation model requires intimate knowledge of the problem, thus forcing the MSS builder to constantly interact with the manager. This is desirable for DSS development because the developer and manager both gain a better understanding of the problem and the potential decisions available.

- The model is built from the manager's perspective.

- The simulation model is built for one particular problem and typically cannot solve any other problem. Thus, no generalized understanding is required of the manager; every component in the model corresponds to part of the real system.

- Simulation can handle an extremely wide variety of problem types, such as inventory and staffing, as well as higher-level managerial functions, such as long-range planning.

- Simulation generally can include the real complexities of problems; simplifications are not necessary. For example, simulation can use real probability distributions rather than approximate theoretical distributions.

- Simulation automatically produces many important performance measures.

- Simulation is often the only DSS modeling method that can readily handle relatively unstructured problems.

- Some relatively easy-to-use simulation packages, including Monte Carlo simulation, are available. Find add-in spreadsheet packages such as @RISK, influence-diagram software, Java-based (and other Web development) packages, and the visual interactive simulation systems to be discussed shortly.

Disadvantages of Simulation Modeling

The primary disadvantages of simulation are as follows:

- An optimal solution cannot be guaranteed, but relatively good ones generally are found.

- Simulation model construction can be a slow and costly process, although newer modeling systems are easier to use than ever.

- Solutions and inferences from a simulation study are usually not transferable to other problems because the model incorporates unique problem factors.

- Simulation is sometimes so easy to explain to managers that analytic methods are often overlooked.

- Simulation software sometimes requires special skills because of the complexity of the formal solution method.

Simulation Software

Numerous simulation software packages are available for a variety of modeling and decision-making situations. Many run as Web-based systems. ORMS Today publishes a periodic review of simulation software (https://pubsonline.informs.org/magazine/orms-today). Some of the notable software packages include Analytica (Lumina Decision Systems, lumina.com) and the Excel add-ins Crystal Ball (now sold by Oracle as Oracle Crystal Ball, oracle.com) and @RISK (Palisade Corp., palisade.com). Two major commercial software packages for discrete event simulation have been Simio (sold by Simio, LLC., simio.com) and Arena (sold by Rockwell Intl., arenasimulation.com). Another popular discrete event VIS software application is ExtendSim (extendsim.com). SAS has simulation software as part of the OR offerings called Simulation Studio (www.sas.com/en_us/software/simulation-studio.html). For more information about simulation software, see the Society for Modeling and Simulation International (scs.org).

Analytic Success Story—Shell Optimizing Transport Systems in the Gulf of Mexico with Simulation Modeling

The Challenge

To devise a strategy in Shell where utilization of ship vessels was redefined from dedicated support vessels for each installation to a model where most installations share the same vessel ("Strategy"). Shell contracts with multiple suppliers of vessels to support logistic requirements for its global assets. With multiple offshore locations needing supply from multiple port facilities, vessel demand can be irregular yet very high. Port facilities have limited storage capacity, and coordinating the scheduled arrival of material at base with the expected loading times can be challenging.

Improving the utilization of vessel capacity, eliminating idle time, and coordinating and optimizing the demand through an IT tool were found to be imperative for the success of the strategy.

The Approach

To identify the components and the required inputs for Shell to create simulation models using the SIMIO tool ("SIMIO"), a probabilistic vessel scheduling software. Use of SIMIO enabled predictive analysis for expected operations by optimizing voyages, proactively sharing vessels transiting to a common field area and enabling the business to maximize the vessel's capacity for offshore asset material movements.

Modelers are able to use the simulation aspect of the tool to ascertain the validity of the model configuration and identify further opportunities to align to operational variances. Further, it helps to identify parameters that may be exposed for schedulers to adjust settings to better reflect "typical" operating conditions (for example, lift rates or bulk loading times and vessel transit speeds).

Using the models and iteratively updated information helps create schedules that allow for in-depth operational planning involving vendors, vessels, and offshore locations. Using the latest weather, demand requirements, and vessel information, the IT tool optimizes the use of the vessel fleet and improves efficiency of port operations. Schedule data shows when materials need to arrive at the port, which vessels are to be loaded, expected load times, vessel transit routing, and offloading times.

Resulting schedules need broad visibility by Shell internal resources and third-party external partners. This has been accomplished by periodic updating of the current schedule to the Simio portal (Web-facing software as a service), where users can view their scheduled voyages for planning or confirmation purposes. The complete simulation process is conceptually illustrated in Figure 3.18.

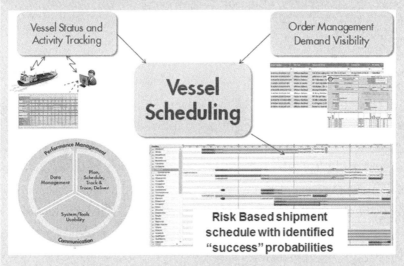

Figure 3.18 Conceptual depiction of the simulation modeling process.

The Results

Outputs from the SIMIO are both varied and comprehensive. Summary statistics allow the user to quickly gauge the quality of a schedule based on metrics that drive operations. Gantt charts visually display details of each asset, slip, vessel, and demand item, enabling the user to view the schedule from various perspectives. Exportable dashboards and detailed reports promote simple interpretation and constraint analysis. All outputs are customizable, which allows the user to react to changing business objectives. When the schedule is finalized, it is published to a secure web portal.

Use of SIMIO assisted Shell in achieving a fit for purpose fleet size and contributed significantly to its ability to optimize vessel utilization.

Source: Simio, Customer Case Study, "Shell," 2018.

Conclusion

This chapter provided an overview of simulation modeling—one of the most popular enablers of prescriptive analytics, only second to optimization. Simply stated, simulation is the art and science of imitating and replicating the real-world systems and processes in computers for the purpose of conducting experiments and what-if scenarios. Whereas Monte Carlo simulation is a simple yet useful technique to address stochastic/probabilistic business and scientific problems, discrete event simulation is a technique to model and study highly complex stochastic business processes. Because simulation allows for rich representation of the reality, including the imprecise/stochastic/probabilistic nature of the actual systems, it is suitable for complex systems that do not lend themselves to optimization-type prescriptive analytics methods. Compared to optimization, simulation is more descriptive than prescriptive; it is not a tool capable of providing the optimal solution. However, simulation is an excellent technique to describe the nature of the real-world systems, capable of producing much-needed information at a granular level to support timely and accurate decisions. Simulation is often used when an optimization (mathematical programming type) solution is not feasible.

Due to its versatility, demand for simulation software products has been increasing, resulting in a rich collection of tools and service/consultancy-providing companies. In the analytics market, one can find narrowly defined simulation tools (specific to an industry or a problem type) as well as generalized broad-spectrum software tools that claim to have the capability to address the situation. Common software tools include Simio, Arena, ProModel, AnyLogic, GoldSim, and SAS Simulation Studio, among others. Modern-day simulation modeling tools employ graphical and intuitive user interfaces that make it easy to model complex systems; however, as is the case in optimization, the secret sauce to great simulation modeling is in the way we characterize and represent the real system into a proper abstraction. Moving from a real system/subsystem/problem to an accurate and rich representation/abstraction as a computer simulation model is still more of an art than science. It's one that requires diligent studying and in-depth understanding of the underlying real-world system, acquisition/collection of all related data/information, and meticulous representation of the underlying components and their logical relationships.

References

Forrester, J. W. (1958). Industrial dynamics: a major breakthrough for decision makers. Harvard business review, 36(4), 37-66.

"Gartner Identifies the Top 10 Strategic Technologies for 2010," https://www.gartner.com/newsroom/id/1210613

"Gartner Identifies the Top 10 Strategic Technology Trends for 2013," https://www.gartner.com/newsroom/id/2209615

"Gartner Predicts Business Intelligence and Analytics Will Remain Top Focus for CIOs Through 2017," https://www.gartner.com/newsroom/id/2637615

Lazzaroni, M. (2012). "Modeling Passenger and Baggage Flow at Vancouver Airport," https://www.simio.com/newsletter-pdfs/Modeling-Passenger-and-Baggage-Flow-at-Vancouver-Airport.pdf (accessed November 2018).

Simio, Customer Case Study, "Shell—Optimizing Transport Systems in the Gulf of Mexico," available at https://www.simio.com/case-studies/Optimizing-transport-systems-in-the-gulf-of-mexico/full-case.php (accessed November 2018).

Simio, Customer Case Study, "Vancouver Airport Case Study—Optimizing Airport Processes," available at https://www.simio.com/case-studies/Vancouver-Airport/index.php (accessed November 2018).

Smith, Jeffrey S., Sturrock, David T., and Kelton, W. David (2018). *Simio and Simulation: Modeling, Analysis, Applications*, Fifth Edition, Published by Simio, LLC. (www.simio.com).

Tokgöz, A., Bulkan, S., Zaim, S., Delen, D., and Torlak, N. G. (2018). "Modeling Airline MRO Operations Using a Systems Dynamics Approach: A Case Study of Turkish Airlines." *Journal of Quality in Maintenance Engineering*, 24(3), 280–310.

4 Multi-Criteria Decision-Making

Decision-making is the foundation of any action, any reaction, or anything at all in our life. We humans are profoundly decision-makers. Everything we do is the result of some decision that we make, either consciously or unconsciously. The main ingredient for better decision-making is information. The quality, quantity, and timeliness of the information are among the key components of good decision-making. That said, not all information is useful. Unrelated or excess information may be detrimental to good decision-making. The concept of **information overload** is often used to emphasize the negative impact that too much information may play in decision-making in humans, especially if the decisions are being made without the help of computer-mediated decision-support systems. This does not suggest ignoring information while making decisions; rather, it stresses the importance of the right size and proper context of the information. Sometimes when the information is hard to obtain or merely does not exist, we make decisions based on intuitions, gut feelings, and personal preferences and biases, all of which may be founded through our life experiences—in such cases, longer and richer experiences make the decision-maker more proficient among the peers. As the data and information become readily available, the reliance on experience and gut-feelings-driven decision-making has lost its appeal and usefulness. The new trend of decision-making is now based on data, information, and scientific methods and methodologies.

Simon's decision theory clearly delineates the decision-making process into four consecutive phases: Intelligence > Design > Choice > Implementation. Chapter 1, "Introduction to Business Analytics and Decision-Making," discussed the importance of a flow-like structure in decision-making. Each consecutive phase relies on the output of the previous one. If the activities at a specific phase do not lead to desirable outcomes, the structure also allows for feedback and reactivation of the previous phase. This decision-making process starts with the Intelligence phase, where gathering of the relevant data and information and defining of the problem or opportunity happen. The quality of information at this phase lays the foundation for the quality of decisions made at the end. Beyond a clear definition of the problem (or opportunity), identification of solution alternatives and definition of proper criteria by which to compare these alternatives are important in decision-making. If you have oversimplified the problem situation, you may have to deal with a simple decision that is characterized by a single goal, clearly identified; a limited number of alternatives; and a single, easily measurable, quantifiable criterion. But in most situations, you will be faced with decision situations that are characterized by many goals, often conflicting with each other; sometimes virtually unlimited alternatives; and numerous criteria. Making rational decisions in such complex situations requires employment of a scientific method to identify the "optimal" decision without making unrealistic, overly simplifying assumptions. A family of scientific methods, commonly called multi-criteria decision-making methods, is proposed to help in addressing these complex decisions.

Multi-criteria decision methods (MCDMs), also referred to as multi-criteria decision analysis (MCDA), have been developed to support the decision-maker in the complex decision-making process. MCDMs provide sound methodologies and related scientific techniques for finding an uncompromising, rational solution to a given problem. MCDMs emphasize placing the decision-maker at the center of the decision-making process. They are not automatable methods that lead to the same solution for every decision-maker; rather, they incorporate subjective information for a customized and contextual solution. Subjective information, also known as preference information, is often provided by the decision-maker or a group of stakeholders, which ultimately leads to the customized and contextual solution.

MCDM, as a collection of decision-support mechanisms, has been around for a long time. Its methods' depth and breadth have improved significantly over the years, each new advancement making it more capable of handling complex situations with less or no compromise on the representational richness of the problem's situation. MCDM is a discipline of its own but relies on other disciplines such as mathematics, management, informatics, psychology, social science, and economics. Its application has been widening progressively and exponentially because it can now be used to solve any problem with any level of complexity where a significant decision needs to be made. In professional settings, these decisions can be operational, tactical, or strategic, depending on the time perspective of the decision.

A variety of methods have been developed to solve multi-criteria decisions. This development is ongoing both in academic and in industry, which is evident with the exponential increase in the number of MCDM-related publications. This expansion, among others, can be attributed to (1) ever-so-complex problems that require rational/optimal decisions, (2) availability of data/information and computational power, (3) effectiveness and efficiency of researchers due to increasing connections and collaboration opportunities, and (4) the interest and value realization in the development of specific methods for the different types of problems encountered in MCDM. The computational advancements coupled with the range of general-purpose and specialized software tools, including spreadsheets containing macros, off-the-shelf implementations, and Web or smartphone applications, have made MCDM methods more accessible to a wider audience for both usage and contributions/advancements.

Types of Decisions

People face a variety of personal and professional decision-making situations. At the highest level of conceptualization, these human-related decisions can be grouped into four types (Roy, 1981):

1. **The choice problem.** The goal is to select the single best option or reduce the group of options to a subset of equivalent or incomparable "good" options. For example, this type of decision might be a manager selecting the right person for a particular project.

2. **The sorting problem.** Options are sorted into ordered and predefined groups, called **categories**. The aim is to then regroup the options with similar behaviors or characteristics for descriptive, organizational, or predictive reasons. For instance, employees can be evaluated for classification into different categories such as outperforming employees, average-performing employees, and weak-performing employees. Based on these classifications, necessary measures can be taken. Sorting methods are useful for repetitive or automatic use. They can also be used as an initial screening to reduce the number of options to be considered in a subsequent step.

3. **The ranking problem.** Options are ordered from best to worst by means of scores or pairwise comparisons. The order can be partial if incomparable options are considered or complete. A typical example is the ranking of universities according to several criteria, such as teaching quality, research expertise, and career opportunities.

4. **The description problem.** The goal is to describe options and their consequences. This is usually done in the first step to understand the characteristics of the decision.

In addition to these four, the MCDM community proposed two other types of decisions: Costa (1996) proposed the elimination problem, a particular branch of the sorting problem, and Keeney (1992) proposed the design problem, where the goal is to identify or create a new action that will meet the goals and aspirations of the decision-maker.

A Taxonomy of MCDM Methods

Real-world decisions are usually complex. They tend to have multiple and conflicting objectives or attributes. The human brain is not capable of objectively solving such complex problems; therefore, we often make unrealistic assumptions to eliminate the majority of objectives or attributes/criteria so that the problem becomes simple enough to solve (an intrinsic outcome of the bounded rationality as it applies to humans). This leads to a solution that is often far from the "optimal" solution of the real problem, or we rely on scientific/ mathematical methods that help impose structure into the situation to better deal with the complexity posed by the problem. Numerous mathematical/scientific methods have been developed to better deal with complex decision problems. The fundamental reason for such a large collection of methods is the fact that each problem may have unique features that a specific method can address better than the others. Therefore, over time, each method is developed to address these unique situations better than the ones developed previously.

To better understand the landscape of these mathematical/ scientific solution methods developed to deal with complex decisions (usually named MCDM methods), herein we present a simple taxonomy. At the highest level, MCDM methods can be grouped into two main categories: multi-objective decision-making (MODM) and multi-attribute decision-making (MADM) (Hwang and Yoon, 1981). MODM methods study decisions whose space is continuous, where there can be numerous, often infinite, alternatives. A typical example of the problems that fall under MODM methods is mathematical-programming constraint-optimization problems potentially with multiple, conflicting objective functions. The first reference to this problem, also known as the vector-maximum problem, was defined in the early 1950s by Kuhn and Tucker (1951). Since then, MODM methods have been widely studied by various mathematical programming methods, including linear programming, with well-established theoretical foundations. (See Chapter 2, "Optimization and Optimal Decision-Making.") In general, MODM methods have decision variables whose values are determined within a continuous or integer domain presented as either an infinite or a large number of alternative choices, the best of which should satisfy the constraints while producing the best value for the decision-maker's objective function, or the goal.

MADM methods, on the other hand, have been used to solve problems with discrete decision spaces and a predetermined or a limited number of alternative choices (Pirdashti et al., 2011). The MADM methods require inter- and intra-attribute comparisons and often involve implicit or explicit trade-offs among the choices during this process. Figure 4.1 illustrates a simple taxonomy of the MCDM methods.

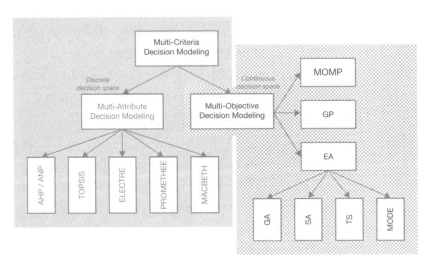

Figure 4.1 A simple taxonomy of MCDM methods.

In Figure 4.1, MODM methods include multi-objective mathematical programming (MOMP), goal programming (GP), and evolutionary algorithms (EA). In MOMP, one or more linear or nonlinear objective functions are optimized subject to several linear or nonlinear constraints. When objective functions and constraints are all linear, the problem is characterized as linear programming (see Chapter 2). When at least one objective function or constraint is nonlinear, the problem is called a multi-objective nonlinear programming problem. The MOMP becomes a convex problem when all the objective functions and the constraints are convex and nonconvex optimization problems or when at least one objective function or the constraint set is nonconvex. GP is an analytical method devised to tackle decision-making problems where goals are assigned to multiple, potentially conflicting attributes and where the decision-maker seeks a satisfactory and sufficient solution by minimizing the nonachievement of the corresponding goals. There are several classes of GP depending on the nature of the goal functions, decision variables, and coefficients. For example, goal functions may be linear or nonlinear; decision variables may be continuous, discrete, or mixed; and coefficients may be deterministic, stochastic, or fuzzy (Pirdashti et al., 2011).

Identifying the real global optimal solution for a majority of real-life MOMP problems is a difficult and often impossible undertaking. These problems often involve large—sometimes infinite, which is often characterized as nonpolynomial/NP-hard in computer science literature—and diverse solution spaces with several conflicting objective functions along with a number of nondeterministic, uncertain, fuzzy parameters. The EAs, such as genetic algorithms (GA), simulated annealing (SA), tabu search (TS), and multi-objective differential evolution (MODE), are potential candidates for solving these problems and are preferable to the MOMP methods because of their robust, simple, flexible, and easy-to-understand approach toward providing a solution to these overly complex decisions. Modeled after a real-world evolutionary process, the EA methods conduct a directed search on a population of potential/feasible solutions using two key principles: selection and variation. Whereas selection mimics the competitive nature of reproduction and resourcing in real-world phenomena, variation imitates the natural ability of creating different living beings by means of recombination and mutation. Because most real-world problems are too complex to be optimally solved with MOMP problems, EA methods have received tremendous attention in recent years. One should also keep in mind that EA methods do not optimize techniques like MOPS, and they do not guarantee finding an optimal solution; rather, they are search techniques inspired by real-world phenomena that are capable of finding a good/satisfying solution to a given complex problem. GA, arguably the most popular of all AE methods, is explained in detail in Chapter 2.

In this chapter, we focus on the MADM methods. Although there are several MADM methods and they are widely diverse in their logic and mathematical formulation, many of them share some common features. These structural features can be listed as the goal, alternatives, and attributes (or criteria), decision weights, and decision matrix, as briefly described here.

Alternatives represent the different feasible options for action available to the decision-maker. Usually the set of alternatives is assumed to be finite, ranging from several to hundreds. They are supposed to be screened, prioritized and eventually ranked. Each MADM problem contains multiple attributes.

Attributes are criteria by which the decision is to be made. Attributes represent the different dimensions from which the alternatives can be viewed. When the number of attributes is large, attributes may be arranged in hierarchical groups for better structuring and representation. In other words, some attributes may be major ones. Each major attribute may be associated with several subattributes. Similarly, each subattribute may be associated with several sub-subattributes, and so on. Although some MADM methods may explicitly consider a hierarchical structure in the attributes of a problem, most of them assume a single level of attributes, such as no hierarchical structure. Another issue arises with the incompatible attribute measures. Different attributes may be associated with different units of measure. For instance, in the case of buying a used car, the attributes cost and mileage may be measured in terms of dollars and thousands of miles, respectively. Having to consider different units makes MADM an intrinsically harder problem to formulate and solve without the help of a scientific or mathematical methodology.

The **goal** is to select the best alternative while collectively considering that all attributes exist in the problem space. Because different attributes represent different criteria dimensions of the collective nature of the alternatives, they may conflict with each other. For example, the cost of quality may conflict with the profit of sales.

Decision weights are the relative importance given to different problem attributes. Most of the MADM methods require that the attributes be assigned weights of importance. Usually these weights are normalized to add up to 1. These weights are usually determined by a specific procedure employed by the specific MADM method.

A **decision matrix** is a tabular representation of all decision parameters. An MADM problem can be easily expressed in a two-dimensional matrix. A decision matrix A is an (M × N) matrix, in which element a_{ij} indicates the performance of alternative A_i when it is evaluated in terms of decision criterion C_j, (for i = 1,2,3,..., M, and j = 1,2,3,..., N). It is also assumed that the decision-maker has determined the weights of relative performance of the decision criteria (denoted as W_j, for j = 1,2,3,..., N). This information can best be summarized as in Table 4.1. Given the previous definitions, the general MADM problem can be defined as follows:

Let $A = \{A_i,$ for $i = 1,2,3,\dots,M\}$ be a (finite) set of decision alternatives and $G = \{g_j,$ for $j = 1,2,3,\dots, N\}$ a (finite) set of goals according to which the desirability of an action is judged. Determine the optimal alternative A^* with the highest degree of desirability with respect to all relevant goals g_i.

Table 4.1 Matrix Representation of Typical MADM Problem Parameters

	Criteria				
	C1	C2	C3	...	CN
Alternatives	W_1	W_2	W_3	...	W_N
A1	a11	a12	a13	...	a1N
A2	a21	a22	a23	...	a2n
A3	a31	a32	a33	...	a3n
...				...	
AM	aM1	aM2	aM3	...	aMN

C: criteria, **A**: alternative, **W**: weight, **a**: waited value for an alternative for a given criteria.

Weighted Sum Model

To illustrate the utility of the decision matrix presented in Table 4.1, let's consider one of the simplest MADM methods, the weighted sum model. In some operations management literature, it is also called Factor Rating. Due largely to its simplicity and ease of operationalizability (often using a spreadsheet software like Microsoft Excel), the weighted sum model is probably the most commonly used approach for relatively small multi-criteria decision problems. Figure 4.2 shows the simple five-step process followed while executing factor-rating type decision-making.

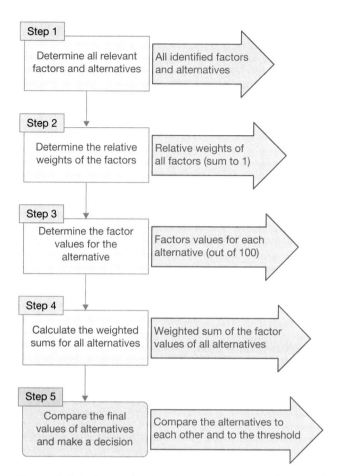

Figure 4.2 A simple step-by-step process for the factor rating method.

Under this method, if there are M alternatives and N criteria, the solution is the alternative that best satisfies the decision. The assumption that governs this model is the additive utility assumption. That is, the total value of each alternative is equal to the sum of products of all alternatives and weights. In single-dimensional cases, in which all the units are the same (such as dollars, feet, or seconds), this method can be used without difficulty. Difficulty with this method emerges when it is applied to multi-dimensional decision-making problems. Then, in combining different dimensions and consequently different units, a normalization mechanism needs to be used.

Hands-On Example: Which Location Is the Best for Our Next Retail Store?

As mentioned earlier, the weighted sum model or factor rating is a relatively simple technique that can be applied to a range of multi-criteria decision modeling situations, from personal to professional.

In operations management, this method can effectively be used to identify the best, or most rational, location option. A typical decision for a retail store location involves both qualitative and quantitative factors/attributes/criteria, which can vary drastically from situation to situation depending on the needs of the decision-maker and the organization.

The value of a factor rating method is that it provides a rational basis for objective, collective, and comparative evaluation of all alternatives by establishing a composite value—sum product between alternative weights and attribute values—for each alternative. The factor rating enables decision-makers to incorporate subjective measures, such as their personal opinions, and quantitative information into the decision-making process.

The steps involved in determining the best decision using factor rating are given here.

1. Determine which factors are relevant (for example, location of market, water supply, parking facilities, revenue potential).

2. Assign a weight to each factor that indicates its relative importance compared with all other factors.

3. Decide on a common scale for all factors (for example, 1 to 100), and set a minimum acceptable score if necessary.

4. Score each location alternative.

5. Multiply the factor weight by the score for each factor, and sum the results for each location alternative.

6. Choose the alternative that has the highest composite score unless it fails to meet the minimum acceptable score.

The results of this six-step decision modeling process are shown in Figure 4.3 as an Excel screenshot. In this illustration, the alternatives are shown in the columns along with their relative importance weights, and the criteria/factors are listed in the rows. The row/column combination shows the absolute value for each factor-alternative combination.

	A	B	C	D	E	F	G	H
1								
2				Alternatives			Weighted Sum	
3	Factors	Weight	Alt. #1	Alt #2	Alt. #3	Alt. #1	Alt #2	Alt. #3
4	Rental cost	0.30	90	80	50	27.0	24.0	15.0
5	Size	0.20	80	70	80	16.0	14.0	16.0
6	Shape/layout	0.10	85	60	90	8.5	6.0	9.0
7	Operating cost	0.10	45	50	40	4.5	5.0	4.0
8	Traffic volume	0.25	80	40	100	20.0	10.0	25.0
9	Distance to warehosue	0.05	40	30	50	2.0	1.5	2.5
10	Sum	1.00	*100: best; 0: worst			78.0	60.5	71.5

Figure 4.3 The results of the location alternative analysis with weighted sum model.

In the following section, we briefly cover some of the most popular methods shown on the left side of Figure 4.1, marked with a darker gray background.

Analytic Hierarchy Process

The analytic hierarchy process (AHP) is one of the most popular and most commonly used multi-criteria decision analysis techniques. AHP was developed by Professor Thomas L. Saaty in the 1970s and has been extensively studied and refined by many researchers since then. Essentially, AHP is a hierarchical problem–structured technique capable of organizing and analyzing complex (multi-attribute/multi-objective) decisions using mathematical theories and relatively simple algorithms.

Using a hierarchical structuring technique, AHP simplifies complex decisions into manageable smaller subdecisions and simple comparisons. In other words, AHP employs the divide-and-concur philosophy to bring order and simplicity to complicated multifaceted decisions. Because of its effectiveness and ease of use, AHP has been successfully deployed to address complex decision situations in various application domains including healthcare, energy, telecom, marketing, finance, science, government, and education. Instead of prescribing the best solutions to a decision situation (which is often the case in optimization methods such as linear programming), AHP helps decision-makers identify the solutions or decisions that best suit their goal based on their understanding of the specifics of the problem. AHP provides a holistic and rational framework for structuring a decision problem, for representing and quantifying its elements, for relating those elements to overall goals, for evaluating alternative solutions, and for identifying the best alternative under the current factors, comparison, or circumstances.

Use of AHP requires that the decision-maker first decompose the decision problem into a hierarchy of smaller, more easily understandable subcomponents/subproblems, each of which can then be analyzed easily and independently. The factors in the structured hierarchy can accommodate various imperfections related to the decision problem, including attributes/factors that can be characterized as quantitative or qualitative, tangible or intangible, carefully measured or roughly estimated, well understood or poorly assumed. One of the advantages of AHP is its ability to accommodate objective as well as subjective criteria in its decision analysis process.

A typical AHP hierarchy includes three layers: goal (of the decision-maker), criteria (of the decision situations, a mix of tangible/objective and intangible/subjective), and alternatives (potential choices for the decision). The hierarchy can be structured either individually by the decision-maker alone or collectively by the decision-maker and her collaborators. Once the hierarchy is built, the decision-maker systematically evaluates its various elements by comparing them to each other two at a time—pairwise comparison—with respect to their impact on the element immediately above them in the hierarchy. In making the pairwise comparisons, the decision-maker can use concrete/objective data about the elements, but she can also, and typically does, use her judgments about the elements' relative importance. It is the core attribute and the superior feature of the AHP that human judgments, not just the underlying data, can and should be used in performing the decision analysis, evaluation, and eventual decision.

In its analysis process, AHP converts objective and subjective evaluations of the decision-maker into numerical values, which can then be mathematically analyzed within and between the hierarchical layers and over the entire range of the problem. A numerical weight (or priority value) is derived for each element of each hierarchy, allowing diverse and often incomparable elements to be compared to one another in an objective, rational, and consistent manner. Then, in a similar manner, the numerical weights are calculated for each of the decision alternatives. These weights represent the alternatives' relative fit or superiority to achieve the decision goal; the one that assumes the highest numerical value is considered to be the best course of action. This capability is one of the most distinguishing features of AHP as it is compared to other decision analysis techniques.

Although it can be used by individuals working on straightforward decisions, AHP is shown to be the most useful decision analysis tool when stakeholders are working to address complex problems, especially those with high stakes involving human perceptions and judgments, whose resolutions have long-term repercussions. As mentioned before, AHP has unique advantages when important elements of the decision are subjective, opinion-driven, and difficult to quantify or compare, or where communication among stakeholders is impeded by their different personalities, experiences, specializations, or professional perspectives.

The decision situations that are most suitable to application of AHP include *choice* (the selection of one alternative from a given set of alternatives, usually with multiple decision criteria involved), *ranking* (placing a set of alternatives in a ranked order from most to least desirable), and *prioritization* (determining the relative superiority or merit of members of a set of alternatives, as opposed to selecting a single one or merely ranking them) AHP has also been used to perform decision tasks like *comparative intelligence* and *benchmarking* (comparing one's current process or capability to those of the other best-of-breed processes or capabilities), *resource allocation* (apportioning resources among a set of alternatives), *quality management* (dealing with the multi-dimensional aspects of quality and quality improvement), and *conflict resolution* (settling disputes between parties with apparently incompatible goals or positions).

How to Perform AHP: The Process of AHP

Performing AHP for a given multi-criteria decision involves a sequence of steps that results in a mathematical/numerical synthesis of judgments about the problem at hand. It is not uncommon for these factors to be at the level of dozens or even hundreds. Although for smaller problems the math can be done by hand or with a calculator, it is often necessary to use a spreadsheet program like Excel or one of several specialized software tools and cloud-based computerized environments for entering and synthesizing the judgments.

The general procedure—the step-by-step approach—for using the AHP for a given complex problem can be summarized graphically as in Figure 4.4.

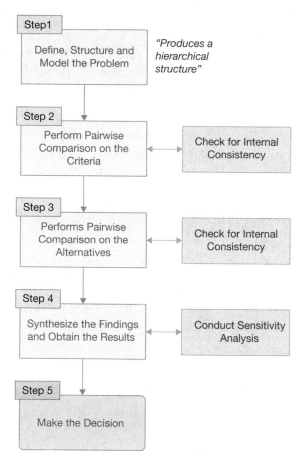

Figure 4.4 A graphical illustration of the AHP methodology.

Step 1: Define, Structure, and Model the Problem

The first step in executing an AHP method is to structure the problem and develop the hierarchical model of the problem as a hierarchy. In doing so, the decision-maker collects data and information to develop an in-depth understanding of the problem to properly decompose the problem—especially the criteria—into levels from general to detailed and then structure it into the multi-level hierarchy that the AHP method requires. As the decision-maker (and other stakeholders, if so needed) works to build the hierarchy, he increases his understanding of the problem, identifies mismatches and contextual deficiencies, and by collecting more data moves toward the ideal and complete hierarchical structure.

A **hierarchy** is a stratified system of ranking and organizing of things of a defined system in a number of distinct layers, where each element of the system, except for the top one, is the subordinate to one or more of the immediately above level elements. In AHP, a hierarchy is the structured way of modeling or simplifying the complex decision at hand. As shown in Figure 4.5, it consists of an overall goal at the top, a set of alternatives to select from at the bottom, and a set of factors in the middle that acts like a bridge between the goal and the alternatives. The criteria layer in the middle can be further broken down into additional sub-criteria layers as the complexity of the problem necessitates. When a criterion is too generic or high level for straightforward judgments and comparisons, it needs to be divided into sub-criteria where different aspects and intensities of the criterion can be captured and represented. When creating a hierarchical structure between criteria and sub-criteria, an optimal balance of specificity needs to be pursued because too many layers of sub-criteria can lead to exponentially increasing pairwise comparison and an impractically laborious comparison process.

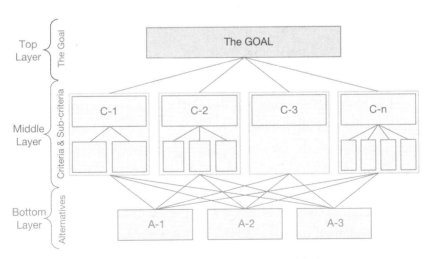

Figure 4.5 A generic representation of the AHP hierarchical structure.

The design of any AHP hierarchy depends not only on the complexity and the nature of the decision at hand, but on the available data as well as the knowledge, experience, judgments, values, needs, and wants of the stakeholders in the decision-making process. Constructing a hierarchy usually involves data collection, in-depth brainstorming and discussion, and research by those stakeholders involved in the process. Even after a laborious process of constructing the hierarchy, it can—and usually does—change to incorporate newly discovered elements.

Step 2: Perform Pairwise Comparison of the Criteria

Once the hierarchy has been constructed, the participants (a decision-maker or a number of stakeholders) analyze it through a series of pairwise comparisons to derive numerical scales and weights of measurement for the criteria. In this step, the criteria are pairwise compared against the goal for relative significance.

Priorities, or weights, are numbers associated with the criteria of an AHP hierarchy. They represent the relative importance of the criteria. Similar to probabilities or likelihoods, priorities are absolute numbers between 0 and 1, without units or dimensions. A criterion with a priority of 0.20 has twice the weight in reaching the goal as one with a priority of 0.10, ten times the weight of one with a priority of 0.02, and so forth. Depending on the problem at hand, weight can refer to importance, preference, likelihood, or whatever factor is being considered by the decision-makers.

Priorities are distributed over a hierarchy according to its architecture, and their values depend on the information entered by stakeholders of the decision process. In the overall structure of AHP, priorities of the goal, the criteria, and the alternatives are intimately related but need to be considered and calculated separately. By definition, the priority of the goal is 1.00. Therefore, the priorities of the alternatives should always add up to 1.00. Things can get somewhat complicated with multiple levels of criteria. If there is only one level, criteria priorities have to add to 1.00. If there are sub-criteria, the priority of the sub-criteria has to add up to the priority of its parent criterion (not to 1.00).

Pairwise Comparison   In most cases, AHP uses pairwise comparison to determine the relative importance of criteria under the goal and the priority of alternatives under each criterion. The rationale behind using pairwise comparisons is that it is easier to compare two things at a time than compare multiple things simultaneously. According to Saaty (1983), humans are more consistent and accurate in their judgments when they compare things in pairs. Psychologists often use this technique on humans and on animals for comparative analysis. For example, to evaluate the food preference of a cat, psychologists prefer presenting two dishes at a time. The cat indicates its preference by eating one dish. The use of pairwise comparisons, known as paired comparisons by psychologists, is generally evaluated on a scale of 1 to 9. The scale is often presented to the decision-makers in a domain-specific verbal context. The conversion from verbal to numerical scale is given in Table 4.2. As shown in Table 4.2, the main degrees of importance are represented and correspondingly defined using odd numbers, whereas even numbers are used to represent the compromises between the odd numbers. Psychologists suggest that a smaller scale, such as 1 to 5, would not provide the same level of detail, and the decision-maker could be indecisive in a larger scale. For example, on a scale of 1 to 100, it is difficult for the decision-maker to distinguish between a score of 62 and one of 63. Therefore, in practice, a 1 to 9 scale is assumed to be the optimal and is commonly used by academic researchers and by industrial practitioners.

Table 4.2 Mapping of the Verbal and Numerical Scales in Determining Decision-Maker Preferences

Degree of Importance	Definition
1	Equal importance
2	Weak
3	Moderate importance
4	Moderate plus
5	Strong importance
6	Strong plus
7	Very strong importance
8	Very, very strong
9	Extreme importance

Perform Consistency Checks   Check the consistency of the judgments. The quality of the decisions obtained from an AHP model depends on the consistency of the decision-maker's judgments on the pairwise comparisons. For instance, within the context of the goal, if criterion C_1 is more important than C_2, and C_2 is more important than C_3, then for a consistent judgment, C_1 is expected to be more important than C_3, not only in ordinal scale but in magnitude. In other words, in addition to the simple rank order of importance, the consistency of the criteria is judged using the degree of importance (the numerical representation of importance from 1 to 9). The consistency of all pairwise judgments at a given level in the AHP model is defined and calculated as a single measure called **consistency index** (CI). Then the CI is divided by a random index (RI), which is determined by a simulation of random numbers (for example, the average CI of 500 randomly filled matrices) to calculate the consistency ratio (CR). The CR is then used to conclude whether the evaluations or judgments are sufficiently consistent to move on to the next step in AHP. If the CR value exceeds a predetermined level—usually the value of 0.1—then the evaluation and judgments for one or more of the inconsistent pairwise comparisons need to be repeated until the needed CR level is achieved.

Step 3: Perform Pairwise Comparison of the Alternatives

This step is similar to the previous one, where the criteria are pairwise compared to each other within the context of the goal. The main difference is that instead of the criteria, herein the alternatives are pairwise compared to each other. Specifically, in this step, all the alternatives are pairwise compared to each other within the context of each criterion. In other words, the pairwise comparison of alternatives to each other is repeated for each criterion each time the context of the comparison is constrained by the specific criterion. Once all the comparisons are completed and the consistency ratios are calculated and validated, the priorities for each alternative are calculated.

Perform Consistency Checks   As was the case in Step 2, where the consistency of evaluations and judgments on the pairwise comparisons for the criteria are checked and validated, in this step, similar consistency checks are performed for the pairwise comparisons against the alternatives. Given a criterion, if alternative A_1 is more preferred than A_2, and A_2 is more preferred than A_3, then for a consistent judgment, A_1 is expected to be more preferred than A_3. The consistency of the alternatives is calculated using the degree of preference measures, or the numerical representation of preferences from 1 to 9. The consistency is calculated for each set of pairwise comparisons under each criterion, and then the overall consistency ratio is calculated. If the consistency ratio value exceeds a predetermined level—usually the value of 0.1—then the evaluations and judgments for one or more of the inconsistent pairwise comparisons need to be repeated until the required level of consistency ratio is achieved.

Step 4: Synthesize the Findings and Obtain the Results

In this step, the calculated and validated results of all levels in AHP are synthesized, and the alternatives are rank-ordered based on the priority values. Before making the final decision, to build confidence in the obtained results, the decision-maker is advised to conduct what-if analyses on the subjective parameters of the decision model, which is a process that is often called **sensitivity analysis**.

Perform Sensitivity Analysis   Sensitivity analysis is a common practice for a range of multi-criteria decision analysis techniques. The purpose behind performing the sensitivity analysis on an already built solution is to calculate and observe the strength and robustness of the identified outcome, and by doing so, build consensus and trust in the identified outcome for implementation. The sensitivity analysis is an experimentation technique that measures the observable changes in the output while systematically changing the model parameters. In AHP, this technique is often used to measure the sensitive nature of the found solution to the weights assigned to the criteria. Because the overall priorities of the alternatives are influenced by the weights given to the respective criteria, it would be useful to know how the final results would have changed if the weights of the criteria are changed. In AHP, sensitivity analysis allows us to understand how solid our solution is and what the main drivers for the solution are — which criteria influence the solution the most. Researchers as well as practitioners of AHP believe that this is an important part of the decision-making process, and the decision should not be finalized without performing a thorough sensitivity analysis.

Step 5: Make the Decision

Based on the synthesized findings and the final priority-based ranking of the alternatives, along with the observations from the sensitivity analysis (a deeper understanding of the significance of the trade-offs among the criteria and the alternatives), the decision-maker can make the final decision. While making the final decision, the decision-maker should look at the top choice and its priority distance from the runner-up. If the top alternatives are close to each other in priority ranking, perhaps a reevaluation of the criteria and one last critical rethinking of the AHP structure are worthwhile for an optimal solution.

Here is one last word of wisdom. Although it commonly is believed that AHP determines the decision that should be made, the reality is that the results should only be used as information—a blueprint of preferences and alternatives based on the level of importance obtained for the different criteria taking into consideration our comparative judgments—in making the final decision. In other words, AHP does not make the decision; the decision-maker does. The AHP methodology allows for the determination of which alternative is the most consistent with the criteria and the level of importance that is given them. In other words, AHP provides a structured, objective, and rational process to better understand the internal complexities of the problem so that the decision-maker can make an informed and holistic decision.

AHP for Group Decision-Making

Complex organizational decisions affect many people and can benefit from inputs coming from many if not all the stakeholders. The standard AHP can be adapted for such a group decision-making situation. The premise is that, by consulting various experts and other stakeholders, the biases originating from a single person's judgments can largely be mitigated or completely eliminated. There are many ways to combine the knowledge, experience, preferences, and judgments of participants into a consensus. In the most general form, the combination of opinions can start at the problem structuring step—all experts and stakeholders take part in the determination of the goal, criteria, and alternatives—using a brainstorming or Delphi-method as the collective knowledge elicitation technique. Once the structure of the problem is determined, the participants can individually work on the pairwise comparisons and then consolidate their results. When more than one person provides judgments, the conflicts are unavoidable. These conflicts can potentially be resolved through more discussions, justifications, and compromises. But this process can be time demanding and difficult. To simplify and potentially expedite the process, the consolidation can be delayed until the prioritization of the alternatives step. That is, the participants individually complete all pairwise comparisons and the finalization of the alternative priorities, and only then is the consolidation of the final results performed. No matter where in the AHP methodology the consolidations are performed, it is believed that the solution performed by multiple experts or participants produces better and more rational results with the caveat that it certainly would take more time and effort to perform.

The following is an illustrative example of this AHP process where the goal is to decide which car to purchase.

Hands-On Example: Buying a New Car/SUV

For most people, buying a new car is an exciting event, but it's a rather challenging decision. It requires thoughtful consideration of several criteria, some of which are contradicting. Maximizing on the appeal, performance, and safety of a car often means being willing to pay more. In this example, we assume that the buyer has already decided to purchase a sport utility vehicle and has the means to buy a mid-to-high price range vehicle. After considering a large number of criteria, the buyer has settled on four criteria: appeal, safety, performance, and cost. The appeal criterion is decomposed into two sub-criteria: (1) brand appeal and (2) "I just like it." Similarly, the cost criterion is decomposed into two sub-criteria: (1) purchase price and (2) operational cost. The alternatives are reduced to the following three: Lexus RX 350, Porsche Cayenne, and Tesla Model X. Figure 4.6 shows the graphical representation of the problem—the goal, two levels of criteria, and the three alternatives.

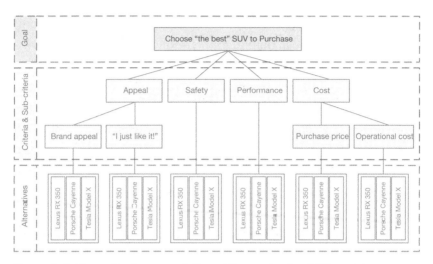

Figure 4.6 Hierarchical representation of the car-buying AHP model.

To find the optimal solution to the problem of which SUV brand to buy, we followed the AHP structured methodology. We decomposed the problem into smaller chunks—simple pairwise comparisons—from the goal to alternatives. Pairwise comparison of criteria followed by pairwise comparison of the alternatives produces the intermediate results that collectively establish the final/aggregated results. In this example, we used a Web-based AHP software environment called Transparent Choice, available at transparentchoice.com. The screenshot of the results is shown in Figure 4.7. As seen, based on the aggregation of the pairwise comparisons, considering all four criteria and sub-criteria, Tesla Model X came out to be the winner. The weight values of all criteria and sub-criteria are shown in two groups: Local and Global. Global shows the weight of criteria or sub-criteria at the highest level (contribution weight to the final decisions), whereas Local shows the weight of sub-criteria within a parent criterion. For criteria lacking sub-criteria, Global and Local weights would be the same.

Cars

Car	Score (0-100) Overall ▾
Tesla Model X	23.98
Porsche Cayenne	8.12
Lexus RX 350	4.46

Criteria weights

#	Criterion	Weight	
		Local	Global
1.	Appeal	24%	24%
1.1.	Brand appeal	83%	20%
1.2.	Just like it	17%	4%
2.	Cost	13%	13%
2.1.	Operational cost	20%	3%
2.2.	Purchase price	80%	10%
3.	Performance	6%	6%
4.	Safety	57%	57%

Figure 4.7 Solution to the AHP model using Transparent Choice (transparentchoice.com).

Application Case: Fuzzy AHP for Financial Portfolio Management

Although the ordinary AHP method provides reasonably good results when the decision-makers' preferences are consistent, it is often subject to the following shortcomings: (i) can only handle crisp/deterministic information in decision modeling; (ii) lacks in dealing with and consolidating the result obtained from an unbalanced scale of judgments; and (iii) ignores the uncertainty associated with the mapping of human judgment to the decision situation. Also, with the uncertainty of information and the vagueness of human feeling and recognition, the AHP is not effective in providing near-exact numerical values for the criteria. Therefore, experts often prefer intermediate judgments rather than certain judgments using the fuzzy set theory, which would make the comparison process more robust, flexible, and realistic. The following application case illustrates the superiority of fuzzification of the MCDA methods, in this case, using a fuzzy AHP methodology.

This illustrative application case was developed by the author of this book and his academic colleagues, and it is about industry selection for the challenging task of financial portfolio optimization. The 2008–2009 global financial crisis and its subsequent ramifications on capital markets have led to growing attention to the importance of cognitive and behavioral issues in finance and specifically in financial markets. The purpose of this application case study is to determine the ranked preference of the industry alternatives for investment portfolio optimization based on individual investors' perceptions. Accordingly, a hybrid analytic MCDA model—based on the Fuzzy Analytic Hierarchy Process (FAHP) and the Fuzzy Technique for the Order of Preference by Similarity to Ideal Solution (FTOPSIS) methods along with sensitivity analysis—was developed by the researchers to identify and rank-order the best performing industries. The proposed model was applied to Borsa Istanbul Stock Exchange 100 Index (*BIST 100*) in Turkey. The results indicated that (i) the investors' perception of market conditions and the global financial situation influences their industry selection on company stocks; (ii) the investors' perception of portfolio investments relies heavily on performance and risk levels of individual assets/stocks, and (iii) traded stocks of the financial industry (along with its subindustries) have greater performance expectations than those of the ones in other industries such as technology, services, and tourism.

A pictorial representation of the methodology employed in the case study is presented in Figure 4.8. The details of the methodology and the way in which it was executed in this case study can be found in Dincer et al. (2016).

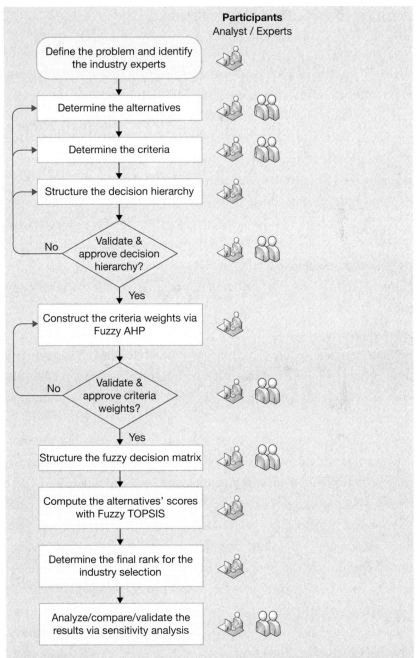

Figure 4.8 Graphical representation of the FAHP solution methodology.

Analytics Network Process

The analytic network process (ANP) is a more general form of the AHP. Both AHP and ANP are decision structuring and modeling techniques that were developed for the chief purpose of simplifying and measuring factors—especially intangible/subjective factors—by means of pairwise comparisons and judgments that represent the dominance of one element over another. Whereas AHP structures a complex decision problem into a unidirectional hierarchy with a goal, decision criteria, and alternatives, ANP structures the decision problem into a network of nodes, where nodes are the same elements in AHP—goal, decision criteria, and alternatives. Both ANP and AHP use a system of pairwise comparisons to measure the weights of the elements of the structure and rank the alternatives for the decision in the end.

As was the case for AHP, ANP was developed by Saaty (1996) to mitigate the independence requirement of AHP. In AHP, it's assumed that the criteria used in the problem structuring are independent of each other, are individually and independently pairwise compared against the goal, and are used as the context for the pairwise comparison of the alternatives. Although AHP is an excellent decision structuring method, many decisions cannot be structured hierarchically because they involve interactions and interdependencies of elements. Whereas the AHP represents a framework with unidirectional hierarchical relationships, the ANP allows for capturing complex interrelationships and interdependencies among elements represented within a cluster of elements (called **inner dependencies**) or between clusters of elements (called **outer dependencies**). To better understand the importance of interferences, consider the decision of buying a car, which was featured in the previous section. The decision-maker may want to decide among several moderately priced SUVs. He might choose to base his decision on only three factors: purchase price, safety, and prestige. Both the AHP and the

ANP would provide useful frameworks to use in making this decision. The AHP would assume that purchase price, safety, and prestige are independent of one another and would evaluate each of the SUVs independently on those criteria. The ANP would allow consideration of the interdependence of price, safety, and prestige. If one could get more safety or prestige by paying more for the car (or less safety by paying less), the ANP could explicitly take that into account. Similarly, the ANP could allow the decision criteria to be affected by the traits of the cars under consideration. If, for example, all the cars are safe, the importance of safety as a decision criterion could appropriately be reduced.

Essentially, ANP and AHP are founded on the same theory, except the dependencies within and among the decision clusters—goal, criteria, and alternatives—captured in ANP using what is commonly called a **supermatrix**. The influence of each node on other nodes within and between clusters in a network can be captured and represented in a supermatrix. Figure 4.9 shows a supermatrix schematic for a problem with three criteria and three alternatives.

Cluster Node Model		Goal	Alternatives			Criteria		
		G	A_1	A_2	A_3	C_1	C_2	C_3
Goal	G	0	Eigenvector of influence on each alternative (because of inner dependency in the alternative cluster)			Local priority of alternative A_i with regard to criteria C_i		
Alternatives	A_1	0						
	A_2	0						
	A_3	0						
Criteria	C_1	Weight of the Criteria	0	0	0	Eigenvector of influence on each criterion (because of inner dependency in the criteria cluster)		
	C_2		0	0	0			
	C_3		0	0	0			

Figure 4.9 A generic representation of the supermatrix.

The supermatrix in Figure 4.9 sets out the influence on the three clusters: goal, alternatives, and criteria. The order of these clusters within the matrix is irrelevant, which is not the case with the AHP, where a unidirectional hierarchy represents the structure of the problem. If dependencies do not exist between nodes, a 0 value is entered.

Figure 4.10 shows a comparative analysis of AHP and ANP in terms of their structural differences. As can be seen in Figure 4.10, the graphical depiction of AHP is a top-down, unidirectional hierarchy, whereas the depiction of ANP is a type of network characterized by interrelationships between and among all elements and clusters of elements.

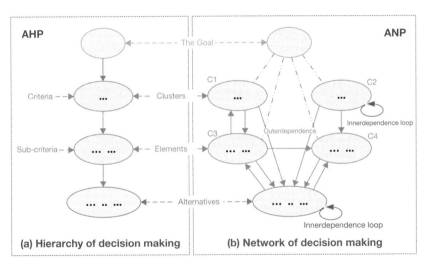

Figure 4.10 A graphical depiction of the structural differences between AHP and ANP.

In Figure 4.10, the interdependencies between two clusters (called outer dependence) are represented by a two-way arrow or by arcs that graphically represent the interdependencies among the different clusters of criteria. The interdependencies that are represented as a looped arc indicate the interdependencies within the same cluster of elements in ANP methodology.

The motivation for ANP is rather straightforward: most of the real-world MCDA problems are too complex—not suitable for a hierarchical structure unless the criteria interactions are ignored. That is why they need to be represented with a network-like structure. Incidentally, Saaty (1996), the original developer of AHP, proposed using the ANP for the problems that have dependence among the criteria or alternatives. To improve the richness of problem structuring so that it closely captures the complexities and imperfections in a real-world situation, in recent years, fuzzy-logic-based model representations have been popularized and widely used. In ANP, fuzzy logic is used to obtain priorities where there is uncertainty in the decision-makers' judgment while defining the interdependencies among the criteria or alternatives. Judgment with fuzziness is often expressed by fuzzy sets and is performed by linguistic methods.

A list of similarities and differences between ANP and AHP is shown in Table 4.3.

Table 4.3 Similarities and Differences Between AHP and ANP

Similarities	Applied to Both AHP and ANP
	They both aim to structure and simplify complex problems into smaller and better manageable subproblems.
	They both use pairwise comparison to simplify and objectify the determination of the preferences.
	They both provide a systematic, mathematical, well-founded methodology to derive the final priority ranking of the alternative.
	They both allow for sensitivity analysis to conduct what-if analysis and to build confidence in the obtained results.
	They both were proposed and initially developed by Thomas L. Saaty.
	They both are successfully applied to a range of MCDA problems.
	They both have plenty of software tools (commercially as well as free-of-charge) available for implementation.

Differences	AHP Versus	ANP
Problem structure	A unidirectional, multi-level, top-down hierarchy	An interconnected, multi-cluster network
Independence	Assumes the total independence of elements	Does not assume independence; can handle interdependencies
Simplicity	Simple to understand and implement the hierarchical model	Not as simple to structure and execute the network model
Comparisons	There are relatively fewer pairwise comparisons to make	There are more pairwise comparisons to make
Time Demand	Less time needed to design and develop the model	More time needed to design, develop, and execute the model
Accuracy	Decent level of accuracy for simpler problems	Better level of accuracy, especially for more complex problems
Reliability	Less reliable due to unrealistic independence assumption	More reliable due to richer representation of the problem

How to Conduct ANP: The Process of Performing ANP

The step-by-step process (or methodology) of conducting ANP for a given multi-criteria decision situation is shown in Figure 4.11. As shown in Figure 4.11, the ANP methodology parallels similarly those of the one for AHP and is composed of five steps.

ANP Process

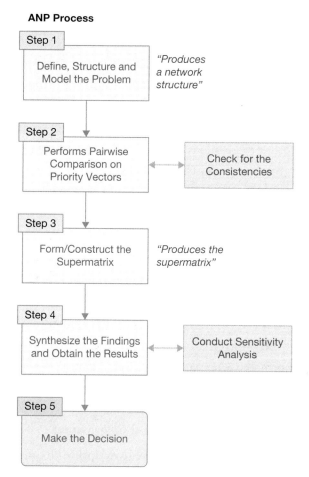

Figure 4.11 A graphical representation of the ANP methodology.

Step 1. In this step the model of problem is constructed. A thorough understanding of the problem with the goal, criteria, and alternatives leads to the representation of these elements (and clusters of elements) into a network-like model structure for the analysis of the specific decision. The output of this step is a validated and verified network structure that clearly and in detail represents the multi-criteria problem being addressed.

Step 2.   In this step, pairwise comparisons and priority vectors are constructed. Like AHP, in ANP, pairs of decision elements at each cluster are compared with respect to their importance within the context of the specific criteria. Furthermore, the interdependencies among criteria of a cluster are examined in a pairwise manner; the influence of each element on other elements is represented using an eigenvector. The relative importance values are determined with the scale originally proposed by Saaty. The pairwise comparison results are validated and confirmed with a thorough sensitivity analysis.

Step 3.   In this step, the supermatrix is constructed. The supermatrix concept is quite similar to the Markov chain process. To obtain global priorities in a system with interdependent influences, the local priority vectors are determined and entered into the appropriate columns of the matrix. The resultant supermatrix is actually a partitioned matrix, where each matrix segment represents a relationship between two clusters of elements for the modeled decision system. The output of this step is a normalized supermatrix.

Step 4.   In this step, the criteria and alternatives' priorities are synthesized, and based on the results the best alternative is determined. The priority weights of the criteria and alternatives, which are captured within the normalized supermatrix, are used to identify the preferred order of the alternatives for final decision. The results are validated and confirmed with a thorough sensitivity analysis.

Step 5.   Based on the obtained results, the specific needs, and the initial purpose of the problem situation, the final decision is made—the best alternative is selected for implementation.

Application Case—Development of a Hybrid MCDA Methodology for Energy Planning

Introduction

Energy is an indispensable resource for all human activities. Energy projections have shown that the need for energy has been growing steadily and is expected to maintain such an increasing pace. Because of its strategic value, energy has become one of the most important factors determining the balance of power in the global scale. Introduction of new and renewable energy sources and related technologies further complicates the strategic energy planning problem. At the country level, energy planning encompasses a continuous and tedious process of evaluating and reevaluating energy strategies that includes a fine mix of old- fossil-fuel-based and new-renewable energy sources. Authorities who are responsible for energy planning and management have to adjust their strategies with new and improved solutions based on the long-term sustainability criteria.

In recent years, Turkey has experienced a rapidly growing energy market because of the abundance of potential renewable energy sources both in type and magnitude. Further, the geopolitical and geostrategic position of Turkey creates a rather unique posture for it in the international arena. Turkey is a transit country in the field of energy, acting as a bridge between the world's crucial supply and demand regions. Additionally, Turkey is the seventeenth largest economy in the world and the sixth largest economy in Europe according to the World Bank in terms of gross domestic product. To increase its international effectiveness in this framework, Turkey has put forward several planning, implementation, investment projections, and related action plans about its long-term energy policy. Of them, the most significant global policy initiative was the Vision 2023, which is focused on the Turkish energy sector and renewable energy investment options until 2023. During these developments, the most pressing challenge that the administrators are facing is to have an objective and rational methodology to determine the most prominent strategies for the ever-more-dynamic energy planning. To address the need, in this study, researchers have proposed an integrated hybrid methodology for the analysis of Turkey's energy sector. They proposed to use a hybrid collection of MCDA methods that include the strengths, weaknesses, opportunities, and threats (SWOT) analysis, ANP, and technique for order performance by similarity to ideal solution (TOPSIS) method.

Methodology

The goal of the study was to formulate and collectively, holistically, and objectively analyze the energy strategy alternatives and priorities for the country. The hybrid methodology proposed in the study was capable of identifying the relevant criteria and sub-criteria using a SWOT analysis followed by the ANP approach to determine the weights of the SWOT factors and subfactors. Finally, the TOPSIS method was employed to prioritize the alternative energy strategies. The multi-stage, multi-method, hybrid methodology is graphically depicted in Figure 4.12.

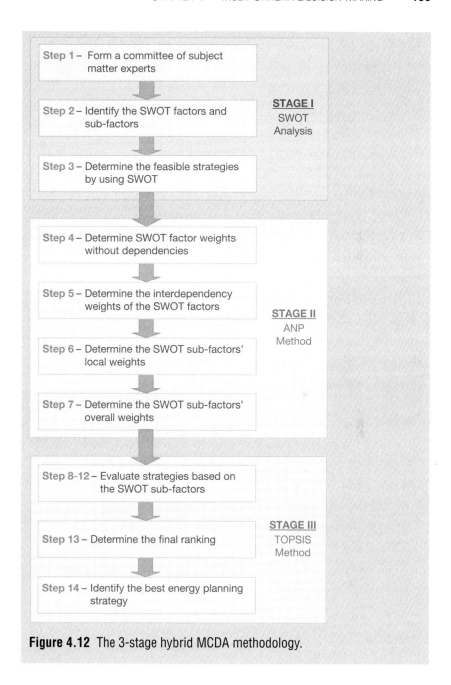

Figure 4.12 The 3-stage hybrid MCDA methodology.

The proposed methodology was applied to Turkey's energy sector to determine the national energy strategic plan. Initially, the researchers reviewed the literature to establish a comprehensive understanding of the strategic energy policy determinants. Then they identified a rich and diverse committee of experts from the energy sector (both government and commercial) in Turkey. In this way, they wanted to make sure that they included all factors and subfactors that may have an effect on the optimal energy planning outcome. They employed the SWOT analysis, which is known to be a powerful strategic planning tool capable of providing the means to identify and organize relevant information on the key issues that are important to achieving the determined objective. The SWOT analysis helped them identify the strengths and weaknesses of the planning situation, or the **internal factors**, and helped them uncover the opportunities and threats, which are called **external factors**. The details about the 14 steps that constitute the hybrid methodology can be found in Ervural et al. (2018).

Results

In the resultant paper (Ervural et al. 2018), the authors discuss the details of their study and the results obtained from applying the proposed integrated MCDA methodology for the determination and deployment of the long-term energy planning of Turkey. The final ranking of the results is shown in Figure 4.13. According to the obtained results, turning the country into an energy hub and an energy terminal by effectively using the geostrategic position within the framework of the regional cooperation processes emerged as the most important priority. Using the nuclear energy technologies within the energy supply strategies was found to be the least favored priority.

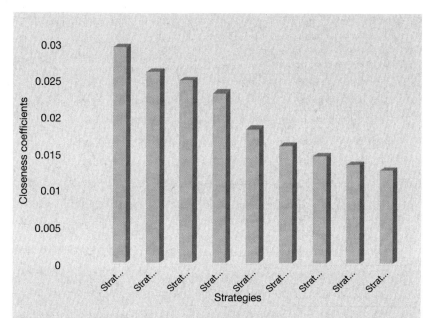

Figure 4.13 Ranked order of the strategies according to the proposed methodology.

The application case shows that MCDA techniques can be used collectively in a hybrid and tandem fashion to address complex decision-making situations. It is asserted by the researchers of the study that none of the employed tools—SWOT analysis, ANP method, or TOPSIS method—is capable of producing the level of accuracy, robustness, and objectivity obtained from the collective and systematic use of these tools.

Other MCDM Methods

Other popular MCDM methods include TOPSIS, ELECTRE, PROMETHEE, and MACBETH.

TOPSIS

TOPSIS is a multi-criteria decision analysis method originally developed by Ching-Lai Hwang and Yoon (1981) with further developments by Yoon (1987) and Hwang, Lai, and Liu (1993). TOPSIS has been shown to be one of the best MCDA methods in addressing the **rank reversal issue**, which is the change in the ranking of alternatives when a nonoptimal alternative is introduced. The philosophy of TOPSIS is based on the concept that the chosen alternative should have the shortest geometric distance from the positive ideal solution and the longest geometric distance from the negative ideal solution.

TOPSIS is an aggregation-based MCDM method that compares a set of alternatives by identifying weights for each criterion, normalizing scores for each criterion, and calculating the geometric distance between each alternative and the ideal alternative, which is the best score in each criterion. An assumption of TOPSIS is that the criteria are monotonically increasing or decreasing. Normalization is required because the parameters or criteria values can potentially produce incompatible or incomparable dimensions in multi-criteria decision problems. TOPSIS allows trade-offs between criteria, where a poor result in one criterion can be negated by a good result in another. This feature provides a more realistic form of modeling than other similar MCDA methods, which include or exclude alternative solutions based on hard cut-offs.

ELECTRE

ELECTRE is part of the family of outranking-based multi-criteria decision analysis methods that originated in Europe in the mid-1960s. The acronym ELECTRE stands for ELimination Et Choix Traduisant la REalité (ELimination and Choice Expressing REality). Bernard Roy is widely recognized as the father of the ELECTRE method, which was one of the earliest approaches in what is sometimes known as the French School of decision-making. It is usually classified as an "outranking method" of decision-making. The method was first proposed by Bernard Roy and his colleagues at SEMA consultancy company. A team at SEMA was working on the concrete, multiple criteria, real-world problem of how firms could decide on new activities and had encountered problems using a weighted sum technique. Bernard Roy was called in as a consultant, and the group devised the ELECTRE method. As it was first applied in 1965, the ELECTRE method was to identify the best action from a given set of actions, but it was soon after applied to all three main decision problems: choosing, ranking, and sorting. The method became more widely known when a paper by Bernard Roy appeared in a French operations research journal (Roy, 1968). With the efforts of a number of researchers working in the area, shortly after its introduction it evolved into ELECTRE I, and the evolutions have continued with ELECTRE II, ELECTRE III, ELECTRE IV, ELECTRE IS, and ELECTRE TRI. ELECTRE and its derivative methods were applied to the complex problems in a variety of fields including business, manufacturing, energy, marketing, and healthcare.

There are two main parts to the ELECTRE methodology. First is the construction of one or more outranking relations, which aims at comparing pairs of actions in a comprehensive way. Second is an exploitation procedure that elaborates on the recommendations obtained in the first phase. The nature of the recommendation depends on the type of decision problem being addressed: choosing, ranking, or sorting. Similar to other ranking-based MCDM methods such as PROMETHEE, in ELECTRE, numeric differences in attribute values are not considered explicitly; in other words, it does not matter how much an attribute value is better than that of another attribute. Instead, what matters is the ranking of the attributes.

Usually the ELECTRE methods are used in concert with other MCDA methods. For instance, ELECTRE methods are often used to identify and discard unacceptable alternatives from the pool of alternatives to the problem, and then another MCDA method is used to select the best alternative from the remaining ones. The advantage of using the ELECTRE methods before applying another MCDA method is that ELECTRE is shown to be effective in identifying and eliminating less likely alternatives, producing a smaller restricted set of alternate pools to be used by another MCDA method in finding the best solution.

PROMETHEE

The Preference Ranking Organization METHod for Enrichment of Evaluations (PROMETEE) is a popular MCDA technique developed at the beginning of the 1980s but extensively studied and refined since then. The basic elements of the PROMETHEE method were introduced by Professor Jean-Pierre Brans in 1982 (Brans, 1982) and further developed and implemented by Professor Jean-Pierre Brans and Professor Bertrand Mareschal. PROMETHEE has particular application in decision-making and is used around the world in a variety of decision scenarios, in fields such as business, governmental institutions, transportation, healthcare, and education.

Rather than pointing out a "right" decision, the PROMETHEE method helps decision-makers find the alternative that best suits their goal and their understanding of the problem. It provides a comprehensive and rational framework for structuring a decision problem, identifying and quantifying its conflicts and synergies and clusters of actions, and highlighting the main alternatives and the structured reasoning behind.

Although it can be used by individuals working on straightforward decisions, PROMETHEE is most useful when groups of people are working on complex problems, especially those with multi-criteria involving numerous human perceptions and judgments whose decisions have long-term impact. It has unique advantages when important elements of the decision are difficult to quantify or compare or when collaboration among departments or team members is constrained by their different specializations or perspectives.

Decision situations to which the PROMETHEE method can be applied include (1) choice—the selection of one alternative from a given set of alternatives, usually with multiple decision criteria involved, (2) prioritization—determining the relative merit of members of a set of alternatives, as opposed to selecting a single one or merely ranking them, (3) resource allocation—allocating resources among a set of alternatives, (4) ranking—putting a set of alternatives in order from most to least preferred, and (5) conflict resolution—settling disputes between parties with apparently incompatible objectives. The applications of PROMETHEE to complex multi-criteria decision scenarios have numbered in the thousands and have produced extensive results in problems involving planning, resource allocation, priority setting, and selection among alternatives. Other areas have included forecasting, talent selection, and tender analysis.

MACBETH

Measuring attractiveness through a categorical-based evaluation technique (MACBETH) is an MCDA approach that was developed by Carlos António Bana e Costa, from the University of Lisbon, in cooperation with Professor Jean-Claude Vansnick and Dr. Jean-Marie De Corte, from the Université de Mons (Bana e Costa et al. 2012). MACBETH has many similarities with AHP. Both methods are based on pairwise comparisons entered by the user, but MACBETH uses an interval scale, and AHP adopts a ratio scale.

Similar to the other MCDA methods, MACBETH has a goal of evaluating options/alternatives against multiple criteria within the scope of the goal defined for a given decision problem. The key distinction between MACBETH and other MCDA methods is that MACBETH needs only qualitative judgments about the difference of attractiveness between two elements at a time to generate numerical scores for the options in each criterion and to weight the criteria. MACBETH uses seven semantic categories—no, very weak, weak, moderate, strong, very strong, and extreme—to signify the attractiveness to differentiate between the alternatives.

MACBETH structures the decision problem into a tree-like hierarchy while making a distinction between criteria and noncriteria nodes on the tree. Noncriteria nodes are included in the tree to help with the evaluation of criteria nodes but are not directly influential in the decision. They act only as complements to the structure of the problem and therefore are not evaluated. Only one-criterion nodes can be set between the overall node (top of the tree) and the leaves (bottom of the tree). For example, in Figure 4.14 (Ishizaka and Nemery, 2013), only Quality is set as a criterion between the top of the tree (Caterer selection) and the leaf (Food). It would have been impossible to set another node (Consumables, Service, Drinks, or Food) as the criterion under the node Quality. Compared to AHP, this is rather unusual. Indeed, if there is only one criterion between the overall node and the leaf, the value tree is not equivalent to the AHP criteria tree. The structure can be reduced to one level with no sub-criteria.

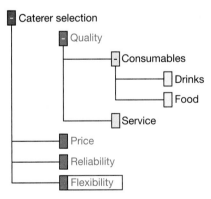

Figure 4.14 Tree-like representation of a decision situation.

Fuzzy Logic for Imprecise Reasoning

Most of the previously listed and explained MCDM methods use precise reasoning. In other words, the information and the subsequent reasoning are captured and calculated using single-valued deterministic measures. In the field of decision science, this is widely considered an oversimplification—a far-reaching assumption while modeling the complex uncertain real-world decision situation. To remedy the situation, decision scientists developed fuzzy derivatives of most, if not all, the MCDM techniques covered in the previous sections. A quick search on the Web would reveal numerous papers written on the technical details and comparative analysis of the fuzzy MCDM techniques. In this section, we provide a simple introduction to fuzzy logic and its application to decision modeling.

Fuzzy logic deals with reasoning that is approximate rather than precise, which intimately resembles the kind of uncertainty and partial information that today's decision-makers are constantly being exposed to in real-world situations. In contrast to **binary logic**, also known as crisp logic, the variables represented with fuzzy logic can have membership values other than just 0 or 1 (or true/false, yes/no, black/white, and so on). The term "fuzzy logic" emerged from development of the theory of fuzzy sets by Lotfi Zadeh. This technique, which uses the mathematical theory of **fuzzy sets**, simulates the process of human reasoning by allowing the computer to process information that is less precise, which is quite contrary to the foundation of conventional computer logic. The thinking behind this approach is that decision-making is not always a matter of "black or white" or "true or false"; it often involves tones of gray and varying degrees of truth. In fact, creative decision-making processes are usually unstructured, playful, contentious, and rambling.

Fuzzy logic can be useful because it is an effective way to describe human perceptions of many decision-making problems in situations that are not 100 percent true or false. Many control and decision-making problems do not easily fit into the strict true/false situation required by mathematical models, and when they are forced into such binary logic representation they tend to suffer from lack of representational integrity and inaccurate reasoning. A good description of fuzzy logic and its applications can be found on the *Stanford Encyclopedia of Philosophy* (http://plato.stanford.edu/entries/logic-fuzzy/).

Illustrative Example: Fuzzy Set for a Tall Person

Let's look at an example of a fuzzy set that describes a tall person. If we survey people to define the minimum height a person must attain before being considered tall, the answers could range from 5 to 7 feet (1 foot is about 30 cm, 1 inch is 2.54 cm). The distribution of answers might look like the following:

Height	Proportion Voted For
5'10"	0.05
5'11"	0.10
6'	0.60
6'1"	0.15
6'2"	0.10

Suppose that Jack's height is 6 feet. From probability theory, we can use the cumulative probability distribution and say there is a 75 percent chance that Jack is tall. In fuzzy logic, we say that Jack's degree of membership in the set of tall people is 0.75. The difference is that in probability terms, Jack is perceived as either tall or not tall, and we are not completely sure whether he is tall. In contrast, in fuzzy logic, we agree that Jack is more or less tall. Then we can assign a membership function to show the relationship of Jack to the set of tall people (the fuzzy logic set):

$$\{Jack,\ 0.75 = Tall\}$$

In contrast to certainty factors that include two values (such as the degrees of belief and disbelief; see Chapter 5, "Decisioning Systems," for details), fuzzy sets use a spectrum of possible values called belief functions. We express our belief that a particular item belongs to a set through a membership function, as shown in Figure 4.15.

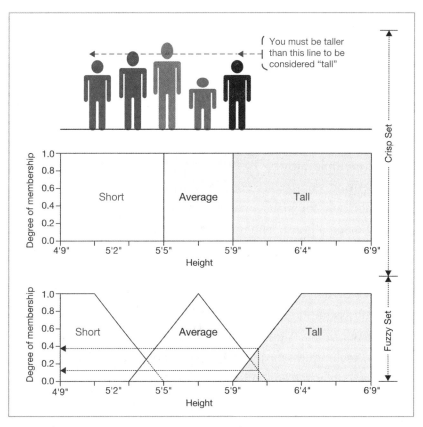

Figure 4.15 Degree of membership in fuzzy logic and in crisp logic.

At a height of 69 inches, a person starts to be considered tall, and at 74 inches, he or she is definitely tall. Between 69 and 74 inches, the person's membership function value varies from 0 to 1. Likewise, a person has a membership function value in the set of short people and medium-height people, depending on height. The medium range spans both the short and tall ranges, so a person has a belief of potentially being a member of more than one fuzzy set at a time. This is a critical strength of fuzzy sets: they lack crispness, yet they are consistent in their logic. The application of fuzzy logic to managerial decision support has recently been gaining momentum despite the fact that it is complex to develop, requires considerable computing power, and is difficult to explain to users. However, thanks to increasing computational power and software, this situation has been changing since the 1990s.

Conclusion

The majority of real-world decisions involve more than one objective and multiple factors. To further complicate the situation, these objectives and constraints conflict with each other. This situation is true not only for managerial decisions but for personal decisions such as buying a house, choosing a job, and deciding on which MBA program to pursue. Considering all the objectives and criteria while making decisions is not easy or even feasible for our brain. Therefore, regardless of our intellectual ability, we make overly simplified or unrealistic assumptions to cope with the complexity of the decision to maintain our sanity. Alternatively, we can choose to use computerized tools and techniques, most of which are explained in this chapter, to make more objective and rational decisions.

References

Bana e Costa, C. A., De Corte. J-M, Vansnick, J-C. (2012). "MACBETH." *International Journal of Information Technology & Decision Making*, 11(02):359–387.

Brans, J. P. (1982). L'Ingénierie de la Décision: Élaboration d'Instruments d'Aide à la décision. La méthode PROMETHEE. Presses de l'Université Laval.

Costa, B. A. C. (1996). "The Problems of Helping the Decision: Towards the Enrichment of the Trilogy Choice-Sorting-Selecting," *Operations Research*, 30(2), 191–216.

Dincer, H., Hacioglu, U., Tatoglu, E., and Delen, D. (2016). "A Fuzzy-Hybrid Analytic Model to Assess Investors' Perceptions for Industry Selection." *Decision Support Systems*, 86, 24–34.

Ervural, B. C., Zaim, S., Demirel, O. F., Aydin, Z., and Delen, D. (2018a). "An ANP and Fuzzy TOPSIS-Based SWOT Analysis for Turkey's Energy Planning." *Renewable and Sustainable Energy Reviews*, 82, 1538–1550.

Hwang, C. L., Lai, Y. J., and Liu, T. Y. (1993). "A New Approach for Multiple Objective Decision Making." *Computers and Operational Research*, 20: 889–899.

Hwang, C. L., and Yoon, K. (1981). *Multiple Attribute Decision Making: Methods and Applications*. New York: Springer-Verlag.

Ishizaka, A., and Nemery, P. (2013). "Multi-Criteria Decision Analysis: Methods and Software." Available at www.it-ebooks.info (accessed December 2018).

Keeney, R. (1992). *Value-Focused Thinking: A Path to Creative Decision Making*. Cambridge, MA: Harvard University Press.

Kuhn, Harold W., and Albert W. Tucker. (1951). "Nonlinear Programming," in (J. Neyman, ed.) Proceedings of the Second Berkeley Symposium on Mathematical Statistics and Probability, 481–492.

Pirdashti, M., Tavana, M., Hassim, M. H., Behzadian, M., and Karimi, I. A. (2011). "A Taxonomy and Review of the Multiple Criteria Decision-Making Literature in Chemical Engineering." *International Journal of Multicriteria Decision Making*, 1(4), 407–467.

Roy, B. (1968). "Classement et Choix en Présence de Points de Vue Multiples (la Méthode ELECTRE)." *La Revue d'Informatique et de Recherche Opérationelle (RIRO)* (8): 57–75.

Roy, B. (1981). "The Optimization Problem Formulation: Criticism and Overstepping." *Journal of the Operational Research Society*, 32(6), 427–436.

Saaty, T. L. (1996). *Decision Making with Dependence and Feedback: The Analytic Network Process*. Pittsburgh, Pennsylvania: RWS Publications.

Saaty, T. L. (1983). "Priority Setting in Complex Problems." *IEEE Transactions on Engineering Management*, (3), 140–155.

Yoon, K. (1987). "A Reconciliation Among Discrete Compromise Situations." *Journal of Operational Research Society*, 38: 277–286.

5

Decisioning Systems

During the past several decades, many AI applications have emerged to showcase the capabilities of computers in making decisions and solving complex problems in a somewhat similar manner to the way human beings are capable of doing. Even though the term **artificial intelligence (AI)** has many different definitions, most experts agree that it is concerned with two basic ideas. First, it involves studying the thought processes of humans to understand what intelligence is. Second, it deals with representing and duplicating those thought processes in computers and robots. One well-publicized, classic definition of AI is *the behavior by a machine that, if performed by a human being, would be called intelligent*. Figure 5.1 shows a figurative illustration of the most popular AI applications and the AI foundational disciplines.

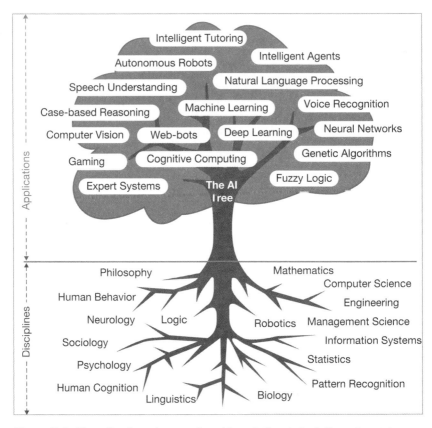

Figure 5.1 AI applications (outputs) and foundational disciplines (inputs).

Artificial Intelligence and Expert Systems for Decision-Making

With the reemergence and rapidly increasing popularity of the new generation of AI systems, some of the earlier AI-based decision-ing systems have been gaining popularity, having new and improved contextualization, and promising new use potentials and value propositions. In this chapter, we specifically describe and exemplify two of these systems: rule-based inferencing systems and condition-based reasoning systems. These systems have been around since the 1980s, helping to build intelligent computer systems to tackle expertise requiring problems. Some of the implementations of rules-based inferencing systems have been performing a critical role in tools and appliances that we use every day, such as automatic transmissions of cars and auto-focus mechanisms of video cameras, washing machines, toasters, and more. Because of the large and feature-rich digitized data sources along with tremendous advancements in computational forefronts both on hardware and software, the use of these AI systems is finding new and improved roles and use cases for themselves.

According to a recent survey conducted by Deloitte (2017), 49% of U.S. companies that work with AI are still using rule-based inferencing and expert systems, and they underlie and augment some other AI systems like robotic process automations, natural language generators, and marketing recommendation engines. Rule-based systems normally require human experts and knowledge engineers to construct production rules in a particular knowledge-intensive application domain. They have been commonly employed in insurance and banking for credit evaluation, approval, and underwriting (Davenport, 2018). They work well for narrowly defined systems and are easy to understand and explain. However, when the application domain has a broad scope, the number of rules can get extremely large, leading to slow execution and inferencing and often conflicting rules, all of which potentially render these AI systems impractical. That said, with the new advancements in computational technologies, these shortcomings are being addressed and mostly eliminated one by one. Following is a classic example of how expert systems can provide expert advice to wine consumers.

Application Case—A Web-Based Inferencing System for Wine Selection

MenuVino, Inc., a Web-based wine retailer, has developed several online knowledge automation expert systems to provide expert advice on wine selection. The system analyzes Website visitors' individual flavor preferences to determine their personal taste profile so it can recommend wines that they are more likely to enjoy. The system also matches wines to certain meals, including food-related details such as ingredients, preparation, and sauce. The expert knowledge embedded into the system allows gastronomic specification along with the combination of ingredients to be used collectively in determining detailed matching of specific wines to specific meals. The advising expert systems are part of a commercial site aimed at matching users with their ideal wines.

Problem

Selecting the right wine for a given situation is an expertise-demanding task. We often buy a wine without knowing the taste, without knowing if it suits us or if it is in harmony with the prepared meal or the occasion. We, the nonexperts, go by the price—higher is better!—and high-level classification of red for meat and white for fish. Beyond this simple classification schema, most people are clueless about what it is that they are buying. Everyone agrees that it is preferable to savor the wines we genuinely like and appreciate. It is difficult to form an opinion unless you have tasted all wines, which is an impossible proposition if you are buying them over the Web. Tastes are personal to individuals, and discovering yours may be difficult even if you did have the opportunity to try all of them. Tastes tend to change based on other factors such as the occasion, meal, and mood.

Solution

The solution is to provide the user with a Web-based expert system in which the knowledge and experience of wine experts is embedded into an interactive information system. MenuVino did just that. It built a Web-based expert system that is capable of not only advising the user on wine selection, but democratizing and facilitating the discovery of wine. As MenuVino says, "Here, you are home. Take a seat at our table. You may be surprised, even amazed. Do not hesitate to participate. We appreciate the interaction, and all your requests will be taken in consideration... MenuVino—Wine has never been so simple."

The MenuVino's expert advisor has two main functions. The first one is the **taste profile** subsystems that emulate the conversation a person would have with a wine expert, or sommelier. The taste profiler portion of the expert system aims to identify personal preferences of the user. Using the interactive features of the Corvid expert system shell, it asks expert questions to reveal characteristics that intrigue and amuse most users. Once the profile is established, the system recommends appropriate wines in different price ranges. The system also allows price limitation and feedback opportunities. The second function of the expert system aims to **pair wines with foods**, recommending the best wines for different flavor combinations. Finding a wine that will complement a meal is difficult unless you are a professional cook or a wine expert. The pairing subsystem incorporates many different types of food, their ingredients, and the cooking methods from the U.S., Canada, France, and Australia. Hundreds of ingredients, condiments, and styles of preparation cover most Western cuisine. Want to know the ideal wine to go with braised kangaroo marinated in Bourgogne mustard and rice wine vinegar? You'll find it here: Domaine André, Mireille et Stéphane Tissot En Barberon 2004—Red.

Maybe you prefer broiled sea bream in lime with coriander, salt, and gray pepper, which is paired best with Pétale de Rose côtes-de-provence rosé 2005—Rosé. This level of detail and granularity can recommend the ideal wines for most any type of meal.

Results

Using the knowledge of many wine experts, MenuVino developed an expert system that mimics the advising one would receive from a guru. In fact, because it encompasses the knowledge of many experts, it may provide even better recommendations than a single human expert. The MenuVino Web-based expert system was developed with ExSys Knowledge Automation systems that capture "deep" expert knowledge in a complex area and use Corvid's MetaBlock approach for probabilistic product selection. The user interface of the system is run with the Corvid Servlet Runtime, which builds graphical and attractive HTML screens to ask questions and interact with the users. The system runs in both French and English. As good as it sounds, do not take our word for it. Try it yourself at http://www.menuvino.tv/, register as a new user for free, run the system, and get expert wine advice.

With the help of expert systems (a popular member of the AI family of techniques), different types of specialized knowledge and experience can be extracted and represented in a computer for either nonexperts to use or automated decisioning. When the experts and identifiable expertise are hard to come by, such an automated AI system is useful.

The vine selection case presented here is a typical application of an expert system. The knowledge and experience of wine experts is captured and embedded into a Web-based information decision support system so that it can be readily used by someone who is not a wine expert. Making such specialized knowledge accessible to many users in an automated and interactive environment has the greatest potential to boost the utility and profitability of many business applications.

Source: ExSys Customer Success Stories and Case Studies, 2019.

The application case just summarized illustrates that in some expertise-requiring decision-making situations, the support that can be offered by data and data-driven analytics models alone may be insufficient. At wine selection, the needed support was provided by a rule-based expert system to substitute for human expertise and offer the necessary knowledge in the form of an automated and interactive information system. In addition to rule-based expert systems, there are several other intelligent technologies that can support decisions in which expertise is the most needed ingredient. Most of these technologies use qualitative or symbolic knowledge rather than numerical or mathematical models to provide the needed supports; therefore, they are referred to as **knowledge-based systems (KBS)**. The overarching field of study that encompasses these technologies and underlying applications is AI.

In addition to the functional systems that compete against humans in intelligence-requiring tasks and games (as described in the application case study "Man Versus Machine" in Chapter 1, "Introduction to Business Analytics and Decision-Making"), many scholars previously have attempted to develop, test, and measure systems to define, and characterize intelligence on the part of machines. For instance, Alan Turing, the famous English computer scientist, in 1950 designed an interesting test to determine whether a computer exhibits intelligent behavior. The test is later called with his name, the Turing test. According to this test, a computer can be considered smart only when a human interviewer cannot discern between the human and the computer while conversing with both within a completely blinded interaction environment. The graphical schematic of such a setup for a Turing test is shown in Figure 5.2. In this setup, the interviewer sits behind a wall and asks questions in written form to both a human and a computer and receives and evaluates the answers provided. If the interviewer cannot tell for sure the provider of the answers, the computer is deemed to be intelligent.

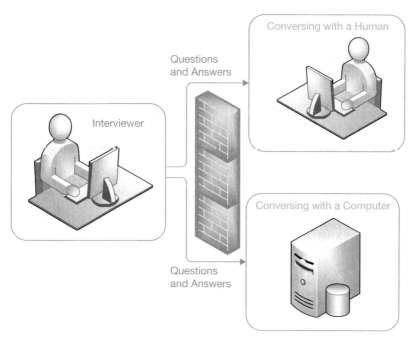

Figure 5.2 A pictorial representation of the Turing test.

These illustrative examples prime the question of "what are the key differences between artificial intelligence—presented by machines/computers—and natural intelligence—presented by humans?" Following are pointers that help in making such a distinction.

- **AI is more permanent.** Natural intelligence is perishable from a commercial standpoint in that workers can change their place of employment or forget information. However, AI is permanent as long as the computer systems and programs remain unchanged.

- **AI offers ease of duplication and dissemination.** Transferring a body of knowledge from one person to another usually requires a lengthy process of apprenticeship; even so, expertise can seldom be duplicated completely. However, when knowledge is embedded in a computer system, it can easily be transferred from that computer to any other computer on the Internet or over the organization's intranet.

- **AI can be less expensive than natural intelligence.** There are many circumstances in which buying computer services costs less than having a corresponding human resource carry out the same tasks. This is especially true when knowledge is disseminated over the Web.

- **AI, being a computer technology, is consistent and thorough.** Natural intelligence is erratic because people are erratic; they do not always perform consistently.

- **AI can be documented.** Decisions made by a computer can be easily documented by tracing the activities of the system. Natural intelligence is difficult to document. For example, a person may reach a conclusion but at some later date be unable to re-create the reasoning process that led to that conclusion or even to recall the assumptions that were part of the decision.

- **AI can execute certain tasks much faster than a human can.** Once the intelligence is embedded into machines, the execution of such intelligent behavior would be significantly faster compared to humans.

- **AI can perform certain tasks better than many or even most people.** When knowledge and intelligence are collected from multiple experts and other knowledge sources, AI systems have been shown to perform better than the best among the human experts.

Natural intelligence does have some advantages over AI, such as the following:

- Natural intelligence is truly creative, whereas AI is uninspired. The ability to acquire knowledge is inherent in human beings, but with AI, knowledge must be built into a carefully constructed system constrained by a large number of assumptions.

- Natural intelligence enables people to benefit from and use sensory experience directly in a synergistic way, whereas most AI systems must work with numerical or symbolic inputs in a sequential manner with predetermined, representational forms.

An Overview of Expert Systems

Expert systems (ES), or inferencing systems, are computer-based information systems that internalize expert knowledge to attain a high level of decision performance in a narrowly defined problem domain. MYCIN, developed at Stanford University in the early 1980s for medical diagnosis, is perhaps the most well-known early success story for ES applications. In addition to medical diagnosis, ES has been used in taxation, credit analysis, equipment maintenance, help desk automation, environmental monitoring, and fault diagnosis. ES has been popular in large- and medium-sized organizations as a sophisticated computer-based decisioning tool for improving productivity and quality.

The basic concepts of ES include how to determine who experts are, what expertise is, how expertise can be extracted and transferred from a person to a computer, and how the expert system should mimic the reasoning process of human experts. We describe these concepts in the following sections.

Experts

An **expert** is a person who has the special knowledge, judgment, experience, and skills to put her knowledge in action to provide sound advice and to solve complex problems in a narrowly defined area. It is an expert's job to provide knowledge about how she performs a task that a KBS will perform. An expert knows which facts are important but understands and explains the dependency relationships among those facts. In diagnosing a problem with an automobile's electrical system, for example, an expert mechanic knows that a broken fan belt can be the cause for the battery to discharge.

There is no standard definition of expert, but decision performance and the level of knowledge a person has are typical criteria we use to determine whether a person is an expert. Typically, experts must be able to solve a problem and achieve a performance level that is significantly better than average. In addition, experts are relative and not absolute. An expert at a time or in a region may not be an expert in another time or region. For example, an attorney in New York may not be a legal expert in Beijing, China. A medical student may be an expert compared to the general public but may not be considered an expert in brain surgery. Experts have expertise that can help solve problems and explain certain obscure phenomena within a specific problem domain. Typically, human experts are capable of doing the following:

- Recognizing and formulating a problem
- Solving a problem quickly and correctly
- Explaining a solution
- Learning from experience
- Restructuring knowledge
- Breaking rules if necessary
- Determining relevance and associations
- Degrading gracefully, or being aware of one's limitations

Expertise

Expertise is the extensive, task-specific knowledge that experts possess. The level of expertise determines the performance of a decision. Expertise is often acquired through training, reading, and experience in practice. It includes explicit knowledge, such as theories learned from a textbook or in a classroom, and implicit knowledge, gained from experience. The following is a list of possible knowledge types:

- Theories about the problem domain
- Rules and procedures regarding the general problem domain
- Heuristics about what to do in a given problem situation
- Global strategies for solving these types of problems
- Metaknowledge, or knowledge about knowledge
- Facts about the problem area

These types of knowledge enable experts to make better and faster decisions than nonexperts when solving complex problems. Expertise often includes the following characteristics:

- Expertise is usually associated with a high degree of intelligence, but it is not always associated with the smartest person.
- Expertise is usually associated with a vast quantity of knowledge.
- Expertise is based on learning from past successes and mistakes.
- Expertise is based on knowledge that is well stored, organized, and quickly retrievable from an expert who has excellent recall of patterns from previous experiences.

Common Characteristics of ES

ES must have the following features:

- **Expertise.** As described in the previous section, experts differ in their levels of expertise. An ES must possess expertise that enables it to make expert-level decisions. The system must exhibit expert performance with adequate robustness.
- **Symbolic reasoning.** The basic rationale of AI is to use symbolic reasoning rather than mathematical calculation. This is

also true for ES. In other words, knowledge must be represented symbolically, and the primary reasoning mechanism must be symbolic. Typical symbolic reasoning mechanisms include backward chaining and forward chaining, which are described later in this chapter.

- **Deep knowledge.** Deep knowledge concerns the level of expertise in a knowledge base. The knowledge base must contain complex knowledge not easily found among non-experts.

- **Self-knowledge.** ES must be able to examine their own reasoning, or self-knowledge, and provide proper explanations as to why a particular conclusion was reached. Most experts have strong learning capabilities to update their knowledge constantly. ES also need to be able to learn from their successes and failures and from other knowledge sources.

The development of ES is divided into two generations. Most first-generation ES use if-then rules to represent and store their knowledge. The second-generation ES are more flexible in adopting multiple knowledge representation and reasoning methods. They may integrate fuzzy logic, neural networks, or genetic algorithms with rule-based inference to achieve a higher level of decision performance. A comparison between conventional systems and ES is given in Table 5.1.

Table 5.1 Comparison of Conventional Information Systems and Expert Systems

Conventional Systems	Expert Systems
Information and its processing are usually combined in one sequential program.	The knowledge base is clearly separated from the processing (inference) mechanism. Knowledge rules are separated from the control.
The program does not make mistakes; programmers or users do.	The program may make mistakes.
Conventional systems do not usually explain why input data is needed or how conclusions are drawn.	Explanation is part of most ES.

Conventional Systems	Expert Systems
Conventional systems require all input data. They may not function properly with missing data unless planned for.	ES do not require all initial facts. ES can typically arrive at reasonable conclusions with missing facts.
Changes in the program are tedious except in DSS.	Changes in the rules are easy to make.
The system operates only when it is completed	The system can operate with only a few rules as the first prototype.
Execution is done on a step-by-step, algorithmic basis.	Execution is done by using heuristics and logic.
Large databases can be effectively manipulated.	Large knowledge bases can be effectively manipulated.
Conventional systems represent and use data.	ES represent and use knowledge.
Efficiency is usually a major goal. Effectiveness is important only for DSS.	Effectiveness is the major goal.
Conventional systems easily deal with quantitative data.	ES easily deal with qualitative data.
Conventional systems use numeric data representations.	ES use symbolic and numeric knowledge representations.
Conventional systems capture, magnify, and distribute access to numeric data or information.	ES capture, magnify, and distribute access to judgment and knowledge.

Application Case—Expert System Help in Identifying Sport Talents

In the world of sports, recruiters are constantly looking to discover new talents while the parents are looking to identify the sport that is the most appropriate for their children. Identifying the most plausible match between a person characterized with a large number of unique qualities and limitations and a specific sport is anything but trivial. Such a matching process requires adequate information about the specific person (values of certain characteristics), as well as the deep knowledge of what this information should include (the types of characteristics). In other words, particular expert knowledge is what is needed to accurately predict the sport with the highest success possibility for a specific individual.

It is hard to find the true experts for this difficult matchmaking problem. Because the domain of the specific knowledge is divided into various types of sports, the experts have in-depth knowledge of the relevant factors only for a specific sport, and beyond the limits of that sport they are not any better than an average speculator. In an ideal case, you would need experts from a range of sports brought together into a single room to collectively create a match-making decision. Because such a setting is not feasible in the real world, one might consider creating it in the computer world using expert systems. Expert systems are known to incorporate knowledge coming from multiple experts, so this situation seems to fit well with an expert-type solution. In a recent publication, Papic et al. (2009) reports on an expert system application for the identification of sports talents. Tapping into the knowledge of a large number of sports experts, they have built a knowledge base of a comprehensive set of rules that map the expert-driven factors of physical and cardiovascular measurement, performance test, skill assessments, and the like to different sport types. Taking advantage of the inexact representation capabilities of fuzzy logic, they managed to incorporate the exact natural reasoning of the expert knowledge into their advising system.

The whole system was built as a Web-based DSS using the ASP. NET development platform. Once the system development is completed, it is tested for verification and validation purposes. The prediction results of the system were evaluated by some of experts using real cases collected from the past. A comparison was done between the sport proposed by the expert system and the actual outcome of the person's sports career. Additionally, using a large number of test cases, the comparison between the expert system output and the human expert suggestions was done. All tests showed high reliability and accuracy of the developed system.

Source: Papic, Rogulj, and Pleština (2009) and Rogulj, Papic, and Pleština (2006).

Applications of Expert Systems

ES have been applied to many business and technological areas to support decision-making. Following are some interesting examples. Many more can be found with a simple search on the Internet.

Classical Applications of ES

Early ES applications, such as DENDRAL for molecular structure identification and MYCIN for medical diagnosis, were primarily in the science domain. XCON for configuration of the VAX computer system at Digital Equipment Corp., a major producer of minicomputers in the 1990s that was later taken over by Compaq, was a successful example in business.

The **DENDRAL** project was initiated by Edward Feigenbaum in 1965. It used a set of knowledge- or rule-based reasoning commands to deduce the likely molecular structure of organic chemical compounds from known chemical analyses and mass spectrometry data. DENDRAL proved to be fundamentally important in demonstrating how rule-based reasoning could be developed into powerful knowledge engineering tools and led to the development of other rule-based reasoning programs at the Stanford Artificial Intelligence Laboratory (SAIL). The most important of those programs was MYCIN.

MYCIN, developed by a group of researchers at Stanford University in the 1970s, is a rule-based ES that diagnoses bacterial blood infections. By asking questions and backward-chaining through a base of about 500 rules, MYCIN can recognize approximately 100 causes of bacterial infections, which allows the system to recommend effective drug prescriptions. In a controlled test, its performance was rated to be equal to that of human specialists. The reasoning and uncertainty processing methods used in MYCIN are pioneers in the area and have generated long-term impact in ES development.

XCON is a rule-based system developed at Digital Equipment Corp. This system uses rules to help determine the optimal system configuration that fits customer requirements. The system can handle a customer request within 1 minute that typically took the sales team 20 to 30 minutes. With the ES, the service accuracy has increased to 98 percent, from a manual approach with accuracy of 65 percent. XCON saves millions of dollars every year.

Newer Applications of ES

More recent applications of ES include risk management, pension fund advising, business rule automation, automated market surveillance, and homeland security.

- **Credit Analysis Systems.** ES are developed to support the needs of commercial lending institutions. They can help analyze the credit record of a customer and assess a proper credit line. Rules in the knowledge base can also help assess the risk and risk-management policies. These kinds of systems are used in more than one-third of the top 100 commercial banks in the United States and Canada.

- **Pension Fund Advisors.** Nestlé Foods Corporation has developed an ES that provides information on an employee's pension fund status. The system maintains an up-to-date knowledge base to give participants advice concerning the impact of regulation changes and conformance with new standards. A system offered on the Internet at the Pingtung Teacher's College in Southern Taiwan has functions that allow participants to plan their retirement through what-if analysis that calculates their pension benefits under different scenarios.

- **Automated Help Desks.** BMC Remedy (remedy.com) offers HelpDeskIQ, a rule-based help desk solution for small businesses. This browser-based tool enables small businesses to deal with customer requests more efficiently. Incoming emails automatically pass into HelpDeskIQ's business rule engine. The messages are sent to the proper technician based on defined priority and status. The solution assists help desk technicians in resolving problems and tracking issues more effectively.

- **Homeland Security Systems.** PortBlue Corp. (portblue. com/pub/solutions-homeland-security) has developed an ES for homeland security. It is designed for assessing terrorist threats and provides (1) an assessment of vulnerability to terrorist attack, (2) indicators of terrorist surveillance activity, and (3) guidance for managing interactions with potential terrorists. Similarly, the U.S. Internal Revenue Service uses intelligent systems to detect irregular international financial information and to block possible money laundering and terrorist financing.

- **Market Surveillance Systems.** The National Association of Security Dealers (NASD) has developed an intelligent surveillance system called Securities Observation, New Analysis, and Regulations (SONAR) that uses data mining, rule-based inference, knowledge-based data representation, and NLP to monitor the stock markets and futures markets for suspicious patterns. The system generates 50 to 60 alerts per day for review by several groups of regulatory analysts and investigators (Goldberg et al., 2003).

- **Business Process Reengineering Systems.** Reengineering involves the exploitation of information technology to improve business processes. KBS are used in analyzing the workflow for business process reengineering. For example, Gensym's System Performance Analysis Using Real-Time Knowledge-based Simulation (SPARKS) can help model the formal and informal knowledge, skills, and competencies that must be embedded in a reengineered system. SPARKS has three components: process flow model, resource model, and work volumes and descriptions.

- **Customer Support.** Logitech is one of the largest vendors of mouse devices and Web cameras in the world. Because the company offers many different models of these tools, customer support is a major challenge. To take advantage of the Internet and technologies in intelligent systems, Logitech deploys an interactive knowledge portal to provide Web-based self-help customer support to its QuickCam customers in North America. The noHold Knowledge Platform emulates the way a human would interact with a customer, allows the user to ask questions or describe problems in natural language, and carries on an intelligent conversation with the user until it has enough information to provide an accurate answer.

- **Allocation of Freight Trains System.** An ES was developed in China to allocate freight cars and determine what and how much to load on each car. The ES is integrated with the existing management information system (MIS), and the system is distributed to many users.

- **Forecaster Electricity Market.** EnvaPower developed an electricity market forecasting system, called MarketMonitor, that uses AI techniques to gather, synthesize, and analyze factors that may affect the consumption of electricity.

- **Designing Mobile Games.** In reaction to the rapid growth in mobile devices and entertainment needs, a group of researchers in the United Kingdom is creating a rule-based AI engine that can support the development of games on mobile devices. The system allows downloadable games to have AI components so that they can become more intelligent.

- **Financial Diagnosis System.** SEI Investment uses business rules management technologies to create an enabling platform for delivering financial wellness solutions to its client. The system includes rules for regulatory and application checks, transaction management governance, and automation of transactions without human interruption.

Now that we are familiar with a variety of different ES applications, it is time to look at the internal structure of an ES to understand how it does its tasks to achieve the decisioning goal for which it is designed and developed.

Structure of an Expert System

ES can be viewed as having two environments: the development environment and the consultation environment (see Figure 5.3). An ES builder uses the development environment to build the necessary components of the ES and populate the knowledge base with appropriate representation of the expert knowledge. A nonexpert uses the consultation environment to obtain advice and to solve problems using the expert knowledge embedded into the system. These two environments can be separated at the end of the system development process.

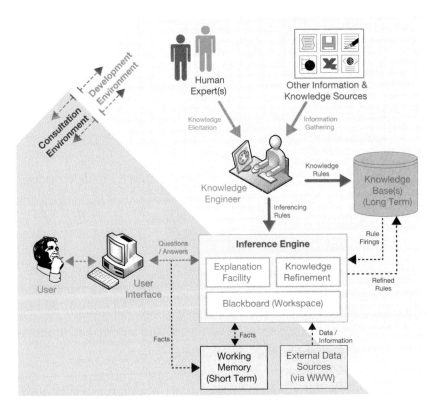

Figure 5.3 Structure/architecture of an expert system.

The three major components that appear in virtually every ES are the knowledge base, inference engine, and user interface. In general, though, an ES that interacts with the user can contain the following additional components: knowledge acquisition subsystem, blackboard (workplace), explanation subsystem (justifier), and knowledge refining system.

Knowledge Base

The **knowledge base** is the foundation of an ES. It contains the relevant knowledge necessary for understanding, formulating, and solving problems. A typical knowledge base may include two basic elements: (1) facts that describe the characteristics of a specific problem situation and the theory of the problem area, and (2) special heuristics or rules (knowledge nuggets) that represent the deep expert knowledge to solve specific problems in a particular domain. Additionally, the inference engine can include general-purpose problem-solving and decision-making rules, or meta-rules detailing how to process production rules. It is important to differentiate the knowledge base of an ES and the knowledge base of an organization. The knowledge stored in the knowledge base of an ES is often represented in a special format so that it can be used by a software program—an expert system shell—to help users solve a problem. The organizational knowledge base, however, contains various kinds of knowledge in different formats, most of which is represented in a way that it can be consumed by people and may be stored in different places. The knowledge base of an ES is a special case and only a small subset of an organization's knowledge base.

Inference Engine

The "brain" of an ES is the **inference engine**, also known as the control structure or the rule interpreter (in rule-based ES). This component is essentially a computer program that provides a methodology for reasoning about information in the knowledge base and on the blackboard to formulate appropriate conclusions. The inference engine provides directions about how to use the system's knowledge by developing the agenda that organizes and controls the steps taken to solve problems whenever a consultation takes place.

User Interface

An ES contains a language processor for friendly, problem-oriented communication between the user and the computer, known as the **user interface**. This communication can best be carried out in a natural language. Due to technological constraints, most existing systems use the graphical or textual question-and-answer approach to interact with the user.

Blackboard (Workplace)

The **blackboard** is an area of working memory set aside as a database for description of the current problem, as characterized by the input data. It is also used for recording intermediate results, hypotheses, and decisions. Three types of decisions can be recorded on the blackboard: a plan of how to attack the problem), an agenda offering potential actions awaiting execution, and a solution with candidate hypotheses and alternative courses of action that the system has generated thus far. Consider this example. When your car fails to start, you can enter the symptoms of the failure into a computer for storage in the blackboard. As the result of an intermediate hypothesis developed in the blackboard, the computer may then suggest that you do some additional checks, such as verifying whether your battery is connected properly, and ask you to report the results. This information is also recorded in the blackboard. Such an iterative process of populating the blackboard with values of hypotheses and facts continues until the reason of the failure is identified.

Explanation Subsystem (Justifier)

The ability to trace responsibility for conclusions to their sources is crucial both in the transfer of expertise and in problem-solving. The explanation subsystem can trace such responsibility and explain the ES behavior by interactively answering questions such as these:

- Why was a certain question asked by the ES?
- How was a certain conclusion reached?
- Why was a certain alternative rejected?
- What is the complete plan of decisions to be made in reaching the conclusion? For example, what remains to be known before a final diagnosis can be determined?

In most ES, the first two questions (why and how) are answered by showing the rule that required asking a specific question and showing the sequence of rules that were used to derive the specific recommendations, respectively.

Knowledge-Refining System

Human experts have a knowledge-refining system. In other words, they can analyze their own knowledge and its effectiveness, learn from it, and improve on it for future consultations. Similarly, such evaluation is necessary in expert systems so that a program can analyze the reasons for its success or failure, which can lead to improvements resulting in a more accurate knowledge base and more effective reasoning. The critical component of a knowledge refinement system is the self-learning mechanism that allows it to adjust its knowledge base and its processing of knowledge based on the evaluation of its recent past performances. Such an intelligent component is not yet mature enough to appear in many commercial ES tools at the moment, but it is being developed in experimental ES at several universities and research institutions.

Knowledge Engineering Process

The collection of intensive activities encompassing the acquisition of knowledge from human experts and other information sources and converting this knowledge into a repository, commonly named a knowledge base, is called the **knowledge engineering process**. The name *knowledge engineering* refers to the art of bringing the principles and tools of AI research to bear on difficult applications problems requiring the knowledge of experts for their solutions. Knowledge engineering requires the cooperation and close communication between the human experts and the knowledge engineer to successfully codify and explicitly represent the rules or other knowledge-based procedures that a human expert uses to solve problems within a specific application domain. The knowledge possessed by human experts is often unstructured and not explicitly expressed. A major goal of knowledge engineering is to help experts articulate how they do what they do and document this knowledge in a reusable form.

Figure 5.4 shows the process of knowledge engineering and the relationships among knowledge engineering activities. Knowledge engineers interact with human experts or collect documented knowledge from other sources in the knowledge acquisition stage. The acquired knowledge is then coded into a representation scheme to create a knowledge base. The knowledge engineer can collaborate with human experts or use test cases to verify and validate the knowledge base. The validated knowledge can be used in a knowledge-based system to solve new problems via machine inference and to explain the generated recommendation. Details of these activities are discussed in the following sections.

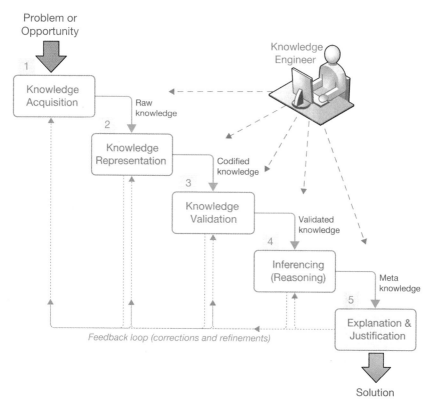

Figure 5.4 The process of knowledge engineering.

1. Knowledge Acquisition

Knowledge is a collection of specialized facts, procedures, and judgments usually expressed as rules. Knowledge may come from one or more sources, such as books, films, computer databases, pictures, maps, stories, news articles, sensors, and human experts. Acquisition of knowledge from human experts, often called **knowledge elicitation**, is arguably the most valuable and most challenging. The classical knowledge elicitation methods, which are also called manual methods, include interviewing, tracking the reasoning process, and observing. Because these manual methods are slow, expensive, and sometimes inaccurate, the ES community has been developing semi-automated and fully automated means to acquire knowledge. These techniques, which rely on computers and AI techniques, aim to minimize the involvement of the knowledge engineer and the human experts in the process. Despite its disadvantages, in real-world ES projects, the traditional knowledge elicitation techniques are still dominating.

Difficulties in Knowledge Acquisition

Acquiring knowledge from experts is not an easy task. The following are some factors that add to the complexity of knowledge acquisition from experts and its transfer to a computer:

- Experts may not know how to articulate their knowledge or may be unable to do so.
- Experts may lack the time or may be unwilling to cooperate.
- Testing and refining knowledge is complicated.
- Methods for knowledge elicitation may be poorly defined.
- System builders tend to collect knowledge from one source, but the relevant knowledge may be scattered across several sources.
- Builders may attempt to collect documented knowledge rather than use experts. The knowledge collected may be incomplete.
- It is difficult to recognize specific knowledge when it is mixed up with irrelevant data.
- Experts may change their behavior when they are observed or interviewed.
- Problematic interpersonal communication factors may affect the knowledge engineer and the expert.

A critical element in the development of an ES is the identification of experts. The usual approach to mitigate this problem is to build ES for a narrow application domain in which expertise is more clearly defined. Even then, there is a good chance that one might find more than one expert with a different, sometimes conflicting, composition of expertise. In such situations, one might choose to use multiple experts in the knowledge elicitation process. Some of the advantages and shortcomings of using multiple experts are listed in Table 5.2.

Table 5.2 Advantages and Shortcomings of Using Multiple Experts

Advantages	Shortcomings
On average, multiple experts make fewer mistakes than a single expert	Fear on the part of some domain experts or senior experts or a supervisor (lack of confidentiality)
Elimination of the need for finding and using the world-class expert	Compromising solutions generated by a group with conflicting opinions
Wider domain than a single expert's	Groupthink phenomenon
Synthesis of expertise	Dominating experts
Enhanced quality due to synergy among experts	Wasted time in group meetings and difficulties in scheduling the experts

2. Knowledge Verification and Validation

Knowledge acquired from experts needs to be evaluated for quality. The following terms are often used interchangeably, but here are our definitions:

- **Evaluation** is a broad concept. Its objective is to assess an ES's overall value. In addition to assessing acceptable performance levels, it analyzes whether the system would be usable, efficient, and cost-effective.

- **Validation** is the part of evaluation that deals with the performance of the system as it compares to the expert's. Simply stated, validation is building the right system.

- **Verification** is building the system right or substantiating that the system is correctly implemented to its specifications.

While developing ES, these activities are executed dynamically because they must be repeated each time the prototype is changed.

In terms of the knowledge base, it is necessary to ensure that the knowledge is valid. It is also essential to verify that the knowledge base was constructed properly.

3. Knowledge Representation

Once validated, the knowledge acquired from experts or induced from a set of data must be represented in a format that is both understandable by humans and executable on computers. There are many different methods for knowledge representation: production rules, semantic networks, frames, objects, decision tables, decision trees, and predicate logic. In the following section, we explain the most popular method: the production rules.

Production rules are the most popular form of knowledge representation for expert systems. Knowledge is represented in the form of condition/action pairs: IF this condition, premise, or antecedent occurs, THEN some action, result, conclusion, or consequence will or should occur. Consider these two examples:

- If the stop light is red AND you have stopped, THEN a right turn is okay.
- If the client uses purchase requisition forms AND the purchase orders are approved AND purchasing is separate from receiving AND accounts payable AND inventory records, THEN there is strongly suggestive evidence (90 percent probability) that controls to prevent unauthorized purchases are adequate. (This example from an internal control procedure includes a probability.)

Each production rule in a knowledge base implements an autonomous chunk of expertise that can be developed and modified independently of other rules. When combined and fed to the inference engine, the set of rules behaves synergistically, yielding better results than the sum of the results of the individual rules. In some sense, rules can be viewed as a simulation of the cognitive behavior of human experts. According to this view, rules are not just a neat formalism to represent knowledge in a computer; rather, they represent a model of actual human behavior.

4. Inferencing

Inferencing, or reasoning, is the process of using the rules in the knowledge base along with the known facts to draw conclusions. Inferencing requires some logic embedded in a computer program to access and manipulate the stored knowledge. This program is an algorithm that, with the guidance of the inferencing rules, controls the reasoning process and is usually called the inference engine. In rule-based systems, it is also called the rule interpreter.

The inference engine directs the search through the collection of rules in the knowledge base, a process commonly called **pattern matching**. In inferencing, when all the hypotheses (the "IF" parts) of a rule are satisfied, the rule is said to be fired. Once a rule is fired, the new knowledge generated by the rule (the conclusion or the validation of the THEN part) is inserted into the memory as a new fact. The inference engine checks every rule in the knowledge base to identify the ones that can be fired based on what is known at that point in time (the collection of known facts) and keeps doing so until the goal is achieved. The most popular inferencing mechanisms for rule-based systems, forward and backward chaining, are described in the next section.

- **Backward chaining** is a goal-driven approach in which you start from an expectation of what is going to happen, a hypothesis, and then seek evidence that supports or contradicts your expectation. Often, this entails formulating and testing intermediate hypotheses or subhypotheses.

- **Forward chaining** is a data-driven approach. We start from available information as it becomes available or from a basic idea, and then we try to draw conclusions. The ES analyzes the problem by looking for the facts that match the IF part of its IF-THEN rules. For example, if a certain machine is not working, the computer checks the electricity flow to the machine. As each rule is tested, the program works its way toward one or more conclusions.

Forward and Backward Chaining Example: Should I Invest in IBM Stock?

Here is an example involving an investment decision about whether to invest in IBM stock. The following variables are used:

A = Have $10,000

B = Younger than 30

C = Education at college level

D = Annual income of at least $40,000

E = Invest in securities

F = Invest in growth stocks

G = Invest in IBM stock (the potential goal)

Each of these variables can be answered as true (yes) or false (no).

The facts: We assume that an investor has $10,000 (that A is true) and that she is 25 years old (that B is true). She would like advice on investing in IBM stock (yes or no for the goal).

The rules: Our knowledge base includes these five rules:

R1: IF a person has $10,000 to invest and she has a college degree,

THEN she should invest in securities.

R2: IF a person's annual income is at least $40,000 and she has a college degree,

THEN she should invest in growth stocks.

R3: IF a person is younger than 30 and she is investing in securities,

THEN she should invest in growth stocks.

R4: IF a person is younger than 30 and older than 22,

THEN she has a college degree

R5: IF a person wants to invest in a growth stock,
THEN the stock should be IBM.

These rules can be written as follows:

R1: IF A and C, THEN E.

R2: IF D and C, THEN F.

R3: IF B and E, THEN F.

R4: IF B, THEN C.

R5: IF F, THEN G.

Our goal is to determine whether to invest in IBM stock. With **backward chaining**, we start by looking for a rule that includes the goal (G) in its conclusion (THEN) part. Because R5 is the only one that qualifies, we start with it. If several rules contain G, the inference engine dictates a procedure for handling the situation. This is what we do:

Step 1. Try to accept or reject G. The ES goes to the assertion base to see whether G is there. At present, all we have in the assertion base is that A is true. B is true. Therefore, the ES proceeds to step 2.

Step 2. R5 says that if it is true that we invest in growth stocks (F), we should invest in IBM (G). If we can conclude that the premise of R5 is either true or false, we have solved the problem. However, we do not know whether F is true. What shall we do now? Note that F, which is the premise of R5, is also the conclusion of R2 and R3. Therefore, to find out whether F is true, we must check either of these two rules.

Step 3.   We try R2 first (arbitrarily); if both D and C are true, then F is true. Now we have a problem. D is not a conclusion of any rule, nor is it a fact. The computer can either move to another rule or try to find out whether D is true by asking the investor for whom the consultation is given if her annual income is above $40,000. What the ES does depends on the search procedures used by the inference engine. Usually a user is asked for additional information only if the information is not available or cannot be deduced. We abandon R2 and return to the other rule, R3. This action of trying something else knowing that we are at a dead end is called **backtracking**. The computer must be preprogrammed to handle backtracking.

Step 4.   Go to R3; test B and E. We know that B is true because it is a given fact. To prove E, we go to R1, where E is the conclusion.

Step 5.   Examine R1. It is necessary to determine whether A and C are true.

Step 6.   A is true because it is a given fact. To test C, it is necessary to test R4, where C is the conclusion.

Step 7.   R4 tells us that C is true because B is true. Therefore, C becomes a fact and is added to the assertion base. Now E is true, which validates F and our goal (the advice is to invest in IBM).

Note that during the search, the ES moved from the THEN part to the IF part, back to the THEN part, and so on. (See Figure 5.5 for a graphical depiction of the backward chaining.)

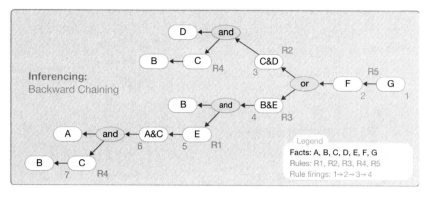

Figure 5.5 A graphical depiction of the backward chaining.

Let's use the same example we examined in backward chaining to illustrate the process of **forward chaining**. In forward chaining, we start with known facts and derive new ones by using rules on the IF side. The specific steps that forward chaining would follow in this example are as follows. (Also see Figure 5.6 for a graphical depiction of this process.)

Step 1. Because it is known that A and B are true, the ES starts deriving new facts by using rules that have A and B on the IF side. Using R4, the ES derives a new fact C and adds it to the assertion base as true.

Step 2. R1 fires (because A and C are true) and asserts E as true in the assertion base.

Step 3. Because B and E are both known to be true (they are in the assertion base), R3 fires and establishes F as true in the assertion base.

Step 4. R5 fires (because F is on its IF side), which establishes G as true. So the ES recommends an investment in IBM stock. If there is more than one conclusion, more rules may fire, depending on the inferencing procedure.

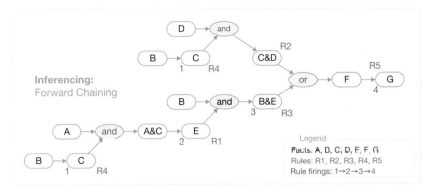

Figure 5.6 A graphical depiction of the forward chaining.

Inferencing with Uncertainty

Although uncertainty is widespread in the real world, its treatment in the practical world of AI is limited. One could argue that because the knowledge provided by experts is often inexact, to be comparable, the ES that mimics the reasoning process of experts should also be representative of such uncertainty. To incorporate uncertainty into the reasoning process, ES researchers proposed several methods including probability ratio, the Bayesian approach, fuzzy logic, and the theory of certainty factors. Following is a brief description of the theory of certainty factors, which is the most commonly used method to accommodate uncertainty in ES.

The theory of certainty factors is based on the concepts of belief and disbelief. The standard statistical methods are based on the assumption that an uncertainty is the probability that an event or fact is true or false, whereas certainty theory is based on the *degrees of belief* (not the calculated probability) that an event or fact is true or false.

Certainty theory relies on the use of certainty factors. **Certainty factors** (CF) express belief in an event, fact, or hypothesis based on the expert's assessment. Certainty factors can be represented with any numerical value ranges (for example, 0 to 100), where the smaller the value the less the probability that the event (or fact) is true or false. Because certainty factors are not probabilities, when we say that there is a certainty value of 90 for rain, we do not imply an opinion about no rain, which is not necessarily 10. Thus, certainty factors do not have to sum up to 100.

5. Explanation and Justification

A final feature of expert systems is the interactivity with the user and the capacity to provide an explanation consisting of the sequence of inferences that were made by the system in arriving at a conclusion. This feature offers a means of evaluating the integrity of the system when it is to be used by the experts. Two basic types of explanations are the why and the how. **Metaknowledge** is knowledge about knowledge; it is a structure within the system using the domain knowledge to accomplish the system's problem-solving strategy. This section deals with different methods used in ES for generating explanations.

Human experts are often asked to explain their views, recommendations, or decisions. If ES are to mimic humans in performing highly specialized tasks, they too need to justify and explain their actions. An explanation is an attempt by an ES to clarify its reasoning, recommendations, or other actions. The part of an ES that provides explanations is called an explanation facility (or justifier). The explanation facility has several purposes:

- Make the system more intelligible to the user.
- Uncover the shortcomings of the rules and knowledge base (debugging of the systems by the knowledge engineer).
- Explain situations that the user did not anticipate.
- Satisfy psychological and social needs by helping the user feel more assured about the actions of the ES.
- Clarify the assumptions underlying the system's operations to both the user and the builder.

- Conduct sensitivity analyses. Using the explanation facility as a guide, the user can predict and test the effects of changes on the system.

Explanation in rule-based ES is usually associated with a way of tracing the rules that are fired during the course of a problem-solving session. This is about the closest to a real explanation that today's systems come, given that their knowledge is usually represented almost exclusively as rules that do not include basic principles necessary for a human-type explanation. Although many explanations have been proposed, in the following section we provide a brief description of the two most common types: the why and the how explanations.

Why Explanations

A user poses a typical "why" question to a computer after the computer asks the user to provide some information. For example, using our earlier investment example, we might have the following dialogue:

Computer: What is your annual income?

Client: Why? (Why do you need to know?)

Computer: R2; meaning "In checking R2, I need to know whether your income is above $40,000. If this is true, I will conclude that because you have a college degree, you should invest in growth stocks."

How Explanations

A user poses a typical "how" question when he would like to know how a certain conclusion or recommendation was reached. Simple systems are limited to the final conclusion. More complex systems can handle intermediate conclusions as well. The system can explain why a certain rule was fired; that is, it shows the chain of rules used to reach the conclusion. In the investment problem, the how explanation might look like this:

Computer: Invest in IBM stocks.

Client: How? (How was the conclusion reached?)

Computer: R5–R3–R7–R4; meaning "Given that you have $10,000 to invest and you are younger than 30, then according to R4, you have a college degree. If this is the case, then according to R1, you should invest in securities. For a young investor like you, according to R3, you should invest in growth stocks if you are going to invest at all. Finally, according to R5, if you need to invest in growth stocks, then IBM is your best bet."

The *why* and *how* explanations often show the rules as they were programmed and not in a natural language. However, some systems have the capability to present these rules in natural language.

Benefits and Limitations of ES

The use of ES can create benefits and incur limitations. The following are some of those benefits and shortcomings commonly observed in the real-world application.

Benefits of Using ES

Benefits of using ES include the following:

- **Increased output and productivity.** ES can work faster than humans can. For example, the classic XCON enabled Digital Equipment Corp. to increase the throughput of its popular VAX minicomputers configuration orders fourfold.

- **Decreased decision-making time.** Using the recommendations of an ES, a human can make decisions much faster. For example, American Express authorities make charge approval decisions in less than 5 seconds, compared to about 3 minutes before implementation of an ES. This property is important in supporting frontline decision-makers who must make quick decisions while interacting with customers.

- **Increased process and product quality.** ES can increase quality by providing consistent advice and reducing the size and rate of errors. For example, XCON reduced the error rate of configuring computer orders from 35 percent to 2 percent and then even less, thus improving the quality of the minicomputers.

- **Reduced downtime.** Many operational ES are used for diagnosing malfunctions and prescribing repairs. By using ES, it is possible to reduce machine downtime significantly. For example, on an oil rig, one day of lost time can cost as much as $250,000. A system called DRILLING ADVISOR was developed to detect malfunctions in oil rigs. This system saved a considerable amount of money for the company by significantly reducing downtime.

- **Capture of scarce expertise.** The scarcity of expertise becomes evident in situations lacking enough experts for a task, when the expert is about to retire or leave the job, or when expertise is required over a broad geographic area. In the opening vignette, for example, more than 30 percent of all requests for authorization of benefits are approved automatically through eCare, enabling CIGNA Behavioral Health to handle more requests with its existing staff.

- **Flexibility.** ES can offer flexibility in both the service and the manufacturing industries.

- **Easier equipment operation.** An ES makes complex equipment easier to operate. For example, Steamer is an early ES intended to train inexperienced workers to operate complex ship engines. Another example is an ES developed for Shell Oil

Company to train people to use complex computer program routines.

- **Elimination of the need for expensive equipment.** Often, a human must rely on expensive instruments for monitoring and control. ES can perform the same tasks with lower-cost instruments because of their ability to investigate the information provided by instruments more thoroughly and quickly.

- **Operation in hazardous environments.** Many tasks require humans to operate in hazardous environments. An ES can allow humans to avoid such environments. They can enable workers to avoid hot, humid, or toxic environments, such as a nuclear power plant that has malfunctioned. This feature is extremely important in military conflicts.

- **Accessibility to knowledge and help desks.** ES make knowledge accessible, thus freeing experts from routine work. People can query systems and receive useful advice. One area of applicability is the support of help desks, such as the HelpDeskIQ system offered by BMC Remedy.

- **Ability to work with incomplete or uncertain information.** In contrast to conventional computer systems, ES can, like human experts, work with incomplete, imprecise, and uncertain data, information, or knowledge. The user can respond with "don't know" or "not sure" to one or more of the system's questions during a consultation, and the ES can produce an answer, although it may not be a certain one.

- **Provision of training**. ES can provide training. Novices who work with ES become more experienced. The explanation facility can also serve as a teaching device. So can notes and explanations that can be inserted into the knowledge base.

- **Enhancement of problem-solving and decision-making.** ES enhances problem-solving by allowing the integration of top experts' judgment into the analysis. For example, an ES called

Statistical Navigator was developed to help novices use complex statistical computer packages.

- **Improved decision-making processes.** ES provide rapid feedback on decision consequences, facilitate communication among decision-makers on a team, and allow rapid response to unforeseen changes in the environment, thus providing a better understanding of the decision-making situation.

- **Improved decision quality.** ES are reliable. They do not become tired or bored, call in sick, or go on strike, and they do not talk back to the boss. ES also consistently pay attention to all details and do not overlook relevant information and potential solutions, thereby making fewer errors. Finally, ES provide the same recommendations to repeated problems.

- **Ability to solve complex problems.** One day, ES may explain complex problems whose solution is beyond human ability. Some ES are already able to solve problems in which the required scope of knowledge exceeds that of any one individual. This allows decision-makers to gain control over complicated situations and improve the operation of complex systems.

- **Knowledge transfer to remote locations.** One of the greatest potential benefits of ES is its ease of transfer across international boundaries. An example of such a transfer is an eye care ES for diagnosis and recommended treatment, developed at Rutgers University in conjunction with the World Health Organization. The program has been implemented in Egypt and Algeria, where serious eye diseases are prevalent but eye specialists are rare. The PC program is rule based and can be operated by a nurse, a physician's assistant, or a general practitioner. The Web is used extensively to disseminate information to users in remote locations. The U.S. government, for example, places advisory systems about safety and other topics on its websites.

- **Enhancement of other information systems.** ES can often be found providing intelligent capabilities to other information systems. Many of these benefits lead to improved decision-making, improved products and customer service, and a sustainable strategic advantage. Some may even enhance an organization's image.

Limitations and Shortcomings of ES

Limitations and shortcomings of ES include the following:

- Knowledge is not always readily available.
- It can be difficult to extract expertise from humans.
- The approach of each expert to a situation assessment may be different, yet correct.
- It is difficult, even for a highly skilled expert, to abstract good situational assessments when under time pressure.
- Users of ES have natural cognitive limits.
- ES work well only within a narrow domain of knowledge.
- Most experts have no independent means of checking whether their conclusions are reasonable.
- The vocabulary, or jargon, that experts use to express facts and relations is often limited and not understood by others.
- Help is often required from knowledge engineers who are rare and expensive. This could make ES construction costly.
- Lack of trust on the part of end users may be a barrier to ES use.
- Knowledge transfer is subject to a host of perceptual and judgmental biases.
- ES may not be able to arrive at conclusions in some cases. For example, the initial fully developed XCON could not fulfill

about 2 percent of the orders presented to it. Human experts must step in to resolve these problems.

- ES, like human experts, sometimes produce incorrect recommendations.

Critical Success Factors for ES

As with any computer-mediated decision support systems, the level of managerial and user involvement in the development process directly affects the success or failure of the resultant ES. For success, the following issues should be considered:

- The level of knowledge must be sufficiently high.
- Expertise must be available from at least one cooperative expert.
- The problem to be solved must be mostly qualitative (fuzzy) and not purely quantitative; otherwise, a numeric approach should be used.
- The problem must be sufficiently narrow in scope.
- ES shell characteristics are important. The shell must be of high quality and naturally store and manipulate the knowledge.
- The user interface must be friendly for novice users.
- The problem must be important and difficult enough to warrant development of an ES (but it need not be a core function).
- Knowledgeable system developers with good people skills are needed.
- The impact of ES as a source of end-user job improvement must be considered.
- The impact should be favorable. End-user attitudes and expectations must be considered.
- Management support must be cultivated.

- End-user training programs are necessary.

- The organizational environment should favor adoption of new technology.

- The application must be well defined and structured, and it should be justified by strategic impact.

Managers attempting to introduce ES technology into the workplace should establish end-user education and training programs to demonstrate its potential as a business tool. For success, the organizational environment should also favor new technology adoption.

Case-Based Reasoning

The basic premise of AI and machine learning is that historical data preserve and delineate previous decision experiences. These experience-based records are usually called **cases**. They may be used as direct references to support similar decisions in the future or to induce rules or decision patterns (generalized decision models). The former, called **case-based reasoning (CBR)** or analogical reasoning, adapts solutions used to solve old problems for use in solving new problems. The latter, called **inductive learning**, allows the computer to examine historical cases and generate rules or other generalized knowledge representations that can solve new problems or can be deployed to automate the decision support process that repeatedly deals with a specific class of problems, such as evaluating loan applications. In this section, we describe the concept of CBR and its applications to intelligent management support systems.

The Basic Idea of CBR

CBR is based on the premise that new problems are often similar to old ones; therefore, past successful solutions may be of use in solving the current situation. Cases are often derived from legacy databases, converting existing organizational information assets into exploitable knowledge repositories. CBR is particularly applicable to problems in which the domain is not understood well enough to build a robust generalized-model-based prediction system using rules, equations, or other numeric or symbolic formulations. CBR is commonly used for diagnosis or for classification-type tasks, such as determining the nature of a machine failure from the observable attributes and prescribing a fix based on the successful solutions found in the history of similar occurrences.

The foundation of CBR is a repository (or library) of cases called a **case base** that contains a number of previous cases for decision-making. CBR has proven to be an extremely effective approach for problems in which existing rules are inadequate. In fact, because experience is an important ingredient in human expertise, CBR is thought to be a more psychologically plausible model of the reasoning of an expert than a rule-based model. A theoretical comparison of the two is summarized in Table 5.3. The use of the CBR approach is usually justified by the fact that human thinking does not use logic (or reasoning from first principles) but is basically a processing of the right information being retrieved at the right time. The central problem is the identification of pertinent information whenever needed.

Table 5.3 Comparison of CBR and Rule-Based Systems

Criterion	Rule-Based Reasoning	Case-Based Reasoning
Knowledge unit	Rule	Case
Granularity	Fine	Coarse
Knowledge acquisition units	Rules, hierarchies	Cases, hierarchies
Explanation mechanism	Backtrack of rule firings	Precedent cases
Characteristic output	Answer and confidence measure	Answer and precedent cases
Knowledge transfer across problems	High if backtracking; low if deterministic	Low
Speed as a function of knowledge base size	Exponential if backtracking; linear if deterministic	Logarithmic if index tree is balanced

Criterion	Rule-Based Reasoning	Case-Based Reasoning
Domain requirements	Domain vocabulary	Domain vocabulary
	Good set of inference rules	Database of sample cases
	Either few rules or rules apply sequentially	Stability (a modified good solution is probably still good)
	Domain mostly obeys rules	Many exceptions to rules
Advantages	Flexible use of knowledge	Rapid knowledge acquisition
	Potentially optimal answers	Explanation by examples
Disadvantages	Possible errors due to misfit rules and problem parameters	Suboptimal solutions
		Redundant knowledge base
	Black-box answers	Computationally expensive
		Long development time

The Concept of a Case in CBR

A case is the primary knowledge element in a CBR application. It is a combination of the problem features and proper business actions associated with each situation. These features and actions may be represented in natural language or in a specific structured format.

Cases can be classified into three categories—ossified cases, paradigmatic cases, and stories—based on their different characteristics and the different ways of handling them. **Ossified cases** appear often and are quite standard. They can be generalized into rules or other forms of knowledge through inductive learning. **Paradigmatic cases** contain certain unique features that cannot be generalized; they need to be stored and indexed in a case base for future reference. **Stories** are special cases that contain rich contents and special features with deep implications. Figure 5.7 shows the way the three types of cases can be handled. CBR is particularly designed for processing paradigmatic cases that cannot be properly handled by rule-based reasoning.

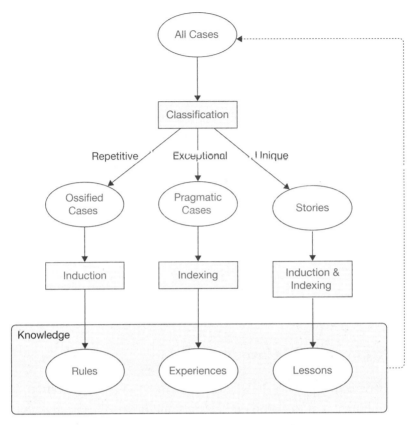

Figure 5.7 Deriving knowledge from different types of cases.

The Process of CBR

CBR can be formalized as a four-step process:

1. **Retrieve.** Given a target problem, retrieve from a library of past cases the most similar cases that are relevant to solving the current case.

2. **Reuse.** Map the solution from the previous case to the target problem. Reuse the best old solution to solve the current case.

3. **Revise.** Having mapped the previous solution to the target situation, test the new solution in the real world (or a simulation) and, if necessary, revise the case.

4. **Retain.** After the solution has been successfully adapted to the target problem, store the resulting experience as a new case in the case library.

The process of using CBR is shown graphically in Figure 5.8. Boxes represent processes, and ovals represent knowledge structure.

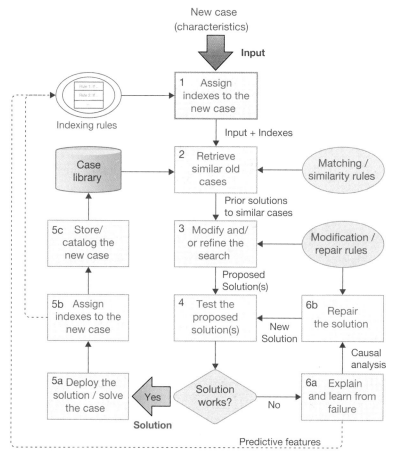

Figure 5.8 The process of case-based reasoning.

Example: Loan Evaluation Using CBR

Let's consider a possible scenario of CBR in loan evaluation. When a new case is received, the system builds a set of features to represent it. Let's assume that the applicant is a 40-year-old married man with a $50,000 annual income job in a midsize manufacturing company. The set of features is [age = 40, marriage = yes, salary = 50,000, employer = midsize, industry = manufacturing] The system goes to the case base to find similar cases. Suppose the system finds the following three similar cases:

> John = [age = 40, marriage = yes, salary = 50,000, employer = midsize, industry = bank]
>
> Ted = [age = 40, marriage = yes, salary = 45,000, employer = midsize, industry = manufacturing]
>
> Larry = [age = 40, marriage = yes, salary = 50,000, employer = small, industry = retailing]

If John and Ted performed well in paying their loans, and if Larry was unable to pay back due to company bankruptcy, then the system can recommend that the loan be approved because John and Ted, who are more similar to the new applicant (four of the five attributes are the same), were able to pay back without problems. Larry is considered less similar to the new applicant (only three of the five attributes are the same) and hence is less useful for reference.

Benefits and Usability of CBR

CBR makes learning easier and the recommendation more sensible. Many applications of CBR have been implemented. The following are the most commonly mentioned benefits of using CBR:

- Knowledge acquisition is improved. It is easier to build, simpler to maintain, and less expensive to develop and support knowledge acquisition.

- System development time is faster than when using manual knowledge acquisition.

- Existing data and knowledge are leveraged.

- Complete formalized domain knowledge (as required with rules) is not required.

- Experts feel better discussing concrete cases (not general rules).

- Explanation becomes easier. Rather than showing many rules, a logical sequence can be shown.

- Acquisition of new cases is easy because it can be automated.

- Learning can occur from both successes and failures.

Issues and Applications of CBR

CBR can be used on its own or can be combined with other reasoning paradigms. Several implementations of CBR systems combine rule-based reasoning (RBR) to address limitations such as accuracy in case indexing and adaptation. Table 5.4 lists and describes several CBR applications in different fields.

Table 5.4 Case-Based Reasoning Application Categories and Examples

Category	Examples
Electronic commerce	Intelligent product catalog searching, intelligent customer support, and sales support
Web and information search	Catalogs, case-based information retrieval in construction, and skill profiling in electronic recruitment
Planning and control	Conflict resolution in air traffic control and planning of bioprocess recipes in the brewing industry
Design	Conceptual building design aid, conceptual design aid for electromechanical devices, and very large-scale integration (VLSI) design
Reuse	Reuse of structural design calculation documents, reuse of object-oriented software, and reuse assistant for engineering designs

Category	Examples
Diagnosis	Prediction of blood alcohol content, online troubleshooting and customer support, and medical diagnosis
Reasoning	Heuristic retrieval of legal knowledge, reasoning in legal domains, and computer-supported conflict resolution through negotiation or mediation

Analysts must pay extra attention to the following questions regarding case-based reasoning systems implementation:

- What makes up a case? How can we represent case memory?

- How is memory organized? What are the indexing rules?

- How does memory function in relevant information retrieval?

- How can we perform efficient searching knowledge navigation of the cases?

- How can we organize, or cluster, the cases?

- How can we design the distributed storage of cases?

- How can we adapt old solutions to new problems? Can we simply adapt the memory for efficient querying, depending on context? What are the similarity metrics and the modification rules?

- How can we factor errors out of the original cases?

- How can we learn from mistakes? That is, how can we repair and update the case base?

- How can we integrate CBR with other knowledge representations and inferencing mechanisms?

- Are there better pattern-matching methods than the ones we currently use?

- Are there alternative retrieval systems that match the CBR schema?

Analysts should also pay attention to the following issues:

- Automatic case-adaptation rules can be complex.
- The quality of the results depends heavily on the indexes used.
- The case base may need to be expanded as the domain model evolves, yet much analysis of the domain may be postponed.

Application Case—A Case-Based Reasoning System for Optimal Selection and Sequencing of Songs

Although digital distribution of media over the Internet has revolutionized the way in which we buy and share music, the way we listen to songs in shared environments has not changed. Often, a large group of people with similar tastes listen to a unique stream of music in the virtual world without contributing feedback to the nature and sequence of selections. The same thing applies to the real-world situation. For instance, in a music club, a DJ can be too busy with selecting and mixing songs to check the feedback and reaction of the listeners. Similarly, on the radio, broadcasters have all kinds of difficulties assessing and meeting the needs and taste of listeners. Beyond the technical difficulties, there exist intrinsic representational challenges in developing recommendation and personalization techniques for music.

Whereas information retrieval systems such as search engines use keyword extraction to represent the subject matter — documents, customer comments or reviews, business transactions — for indexing and retrieval, the comparable process for audio artifacts is still a subject of much research. An alternative would be to rely on human input for content description, which can be a lengthy, knowledge-intensive process. The automated collaborative filtering (ACF) as part of a case-based reasoning (CBR) system is often proposed as a technique to ease the difficulties of knowledge elicitation (Hayes, 2003).

In an interesting research project, Baccigalupo and Plaza (2007) developed an interactive social framework to overcome the unidirectional music selection problem with the goal of improving the group satisfaction of an audience. They proposed a unique group-based Web radio architecture, called Poolcasting, whereby the music played on each channel was not preprogrammed, but influenced in real time by the current audience. In this architecture, users can submit explicit preferences via a Web interface, where they can request new songs to be played, evaluate the scheduled songs, and send feedback about recently played ones. The main issue in such a system is how to guarantee fairness to the members of the audience with respect to the songs that are being broadcast. For this purpose, they implemented a CBR system that schedules songs for each channel combining both musical requirements, such as variety and continuity, and listeners' preferences. To keep fairness in the presence of concurrent preferences, they used a strategy that favors those listeners who were less satisfied with the recently played songs.

The CBR system that they developed to accomplish the task of the song scheduler in the Poolcasting Web radio comprised the following three steps:

1. **Retrieving process.** In this process, a subset of songs, which are either recommended by someone in the audience via the Web interface or have not been played recently and are musically associated with the last song scheduled to play, are identified from the music pool of the specific channel.

2. **Reusing process.** This process takes the output of the retrieving process (the retrieved set) and ranks it by taking into account the preferences of the current listeners, giving more importance to those listeners who are less satisfied with the music recently played on that channel. The song that best matches the four properties (which are used as the similarity measures) is

to be scheduled to play in the channel after the song scheduled to play next. These four properties were:

   a. *Variety.* No song or artist should be repeated closely on a channel.

   b. *Continuity.* Each song should be musically associated with the song it follows.

   c. *Satisfaction.* Each song should match the musical preferences of the current listeners, or at least most of them.

   d. *Fairness.* The more a listener is unsatisfied with the songs recently streamed, the more her preferences should influence the selection of the next songs that will be played so that nobody in the audience will be left out.

3. **Revising process.** While a song is playing on a channel, the Web interface shows its title, artist, cover art, and remaining time, and it allows listeners to rate whether they like that song or not. Listeners can evaluate the songs played on the channel by giving positive or negative feedback, which in turn increases or decreases the degree of association of this song with the previous one played. The assumption is that if a user rates a song played on a channel positively, she likes that song or the song fits in the sequence of music programmed for that channel. Using this feedback, Poolcasting updates both the listeners' preference models and the musical knowledge about song associations.

Such a collective approach to music scheduling shifts the paradigm from a classical monolithic approach, where "one controls, many listeners," to a new decentralized scheduling approach, where "many controls, many listeners." The developers attest that the system generated satisfactory results for both passive users who provide nothing more than their implicit preferences and active users who provide constant feedback along with their preferences. Initial results of the system also showed that users enjoyed songs and discovered new music that was not included in their preference lists, crediting the success of the system that intelligently associates songs of similar flavor using a multi-dimensional similarity measure.

Case-based reasoning made it possible to overcome many of the surmountable obstacles in developing such an advanced music recommendation system where the composition of audience is dynamically changing. (New listeners are being added, while some are leaving the channel.) Using a fine balance between desirable properties for a radio channel and community preferences, the Poolcasting system seems to deliver on its promise. In fact, the article summarizing the system received the best application paper award at the Seventh International Conference on Case-Based Reasoning in Belfast, Ireland in 2007.

Source: Baccigalupo and Plaza (2007).

Conclusion

This chapter has been about artificial intelligence, expert systems, and case-based reasoning as the enablers of the new generation of prescriptive analytics techniques. Understanding and representing/formulating the human thought process (along with the logical reasoning that lay the foundation for the ability of making intelligent decision) in computers is advancing the boundaries of prescriptive analytics. Although artificial intelligence, expert systems, and case-based reasoning have been around for several decades and have had limited early success, because of the new trends and capabilities, these decisioning systems are regaining popularity more than ever, and promising new and innovative use cases and value propositions.

References

Baccigalupo, C., and Plaza, E. (2007). "A Case-Based Song Scheduler for Group Customized Radio." Proceedings of the Seventh International Conference on Case-Based Reasoning (ICCBR), Belfast, Northern Ireland, UK: Springer.

Davenport, T. H. (2018). "From Analytics to Artificial Intelligence." *Journal of Business Analytics*, 1(2), 73–80.

Deloitte. (2017). Deloitte State of Cognitive Survey. Retrieved from https://www2. deloitte.com/content/dam/Deloitte/us/Documents/deloitte-analytics/us-da-2017-deloitte-state-of-cognitive-survey.pdf (February 2019).

ExSys Customer Success Stories and Case Studies, "Menu Vino—Wine Advisor" available at http://www.exsys.com/winkPDFs/CommercialOnlineWineAdvisors. pdf (accessed January 2019).

Goldberg, H. G., Kirkland, J. D., Lee, D., Shyr, P., & Thakker, D. (2003, August). The NASD Securities Observation, New Analysis and Regulation System (SONAR). In *IAAI* (pp. 11–18).

Hayes, C. (2003). *Smart Radio: Building Community-Based Internet Music Radio*, Ph.D. thesis, University of Dublin, Ireland, UK.

Papic, V., Rogulj, N., and Pleština, V. (2009). "Identification of Sport Talents Using a Web-Oriented Expert System with a Fuzzy Module." *Expert Systems with Applications*, 36, 8830–8838.

Rogulj, N., Papic, V., and Pleština, V. (2006). "Development of the Expert System for Sport Talents Detection." *WSEAS Transactions on Information Science and Applications*, 9(3), 1752–1755.

6

The Future of Business Analytics

Adoption of business analytics is increasing, not only by companies in different industries and verticals, but in different sizes—penetrating downward from large and highly capable firms toward medium and small sizes. Many have successfully and rapidly evolved from descriptive to predictive, from predictive to prescriptive. Dr. Tom Davenport, a well-known business analytics guru, recently categorized business analytics into four eras of sophistication (Davenport, 2018). Figure 6.1 shows this progressive continuum of business analytics.

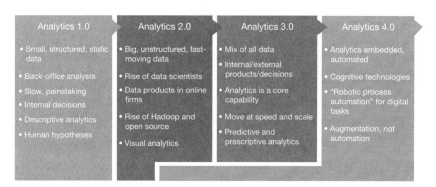

Figure 6.1 The four eras of business analytics sophistication.

The continuum that started with Analytics 1.0—essentially the era of business intelligence and data warehousing that summarized and contextualized the structured data collected within the organization and successfully produced insight for decision-makers—lasted nearly two decades. The evolution of analytics continued with Analytics

2.0—marked by predictive modeling, data, text, web mining, and the inclusion of unstructured and less structured data—producing foresight for better decision-making. Shortly after Analytics 2.0, with the emergence of Big Data, we embarked into Analytics 3.0. The last era of analytics, which has just started or is just about to be starting, is Analytics 4.0, also known as the emergence of artificial intelligence (AI) and cognitive computing. The current and future of analytics, as we know it, is defined by this era—the era of embedded and automated decisioning, robotic process automation, deep learning, and cognitive computing. In this chapter, we provide these topics with enough depth and breadth to paint a picture of the leading edge of analytics.

Big Data Analytics

Using data to better understand customers and business operations to sustain growth and profitability is an increasingly more challenging task for today's enterprises. As more and more data becomes available from within and outside the organization in various forms, effective and timely processing of the data with traditional means becomes impractical. This phenomenon is called **Big Data**, and it is receiving substantial press coverage and interest from both business users and academics. The result is that Big Data is becoming an overhyped and overused marketing buzzword.

Big Data means different things to people. Traditionally, the term has been used to describe the massive volumes of data analyzed by huge organizations like Google or research science projects at NASA. But for most businesses, it's a relative term: "big" depends on an organization's size and its data maturity. The point is more about finding new value within and outside conventional data sources. Pushing the boundaries of data analytics uncovers new insights and opportunities, and "big" depends on where you start and how you proceed. Consider, for instance, the popular description of Big Data: Big Data exceeds the reach of commonly used hardware environments and capabilities of software tools to capture, manage, and process it within a tolerable time span for its user population. Big Data has become a popular term to describe the exponential growth, availability, and use of information, both structured and unstructured. Much has been written on the Big Data trend and how it can serve as the basis for innovation, differentiation, and growth.

Where Does the Big Data Come From?

A simple answer nowadays is "Big Data comes from everywhere." Big Data may come from Web logs, RFID, GPS systems, sensor networks, social networks, Internet-based text documents, Internet search indexes, detailed call records, astronomy, atmospheric science, biology, genomics, nuclear physics, biochemical experiments, medical records, scientific research, military surveillance, photography archives, video archives, and large-scale ecommerce practices. Figure 6.2 illustrates the sources of Big Data in a three-level diagram. The traditional means of data sources—mainly the data generated as part of business transactions—are illustrated as the first echelon, where the volume, variety, and velocity of the data are moderate to low. The next echelon is the Internet- and social media–originated data sources. This human-generated data is perhaps the most complicated and potentially most valuable to understand collective ideas and perceptions of people. The volume, variety, and velocity of data at this echelon are moderate to high. The topmost echelon is the machine-generated data. With the automation of data collection systems on many fronts, coupled with the Internet of things (connecting everything to everything else), organizations are now able to collect data at the volume and richness they had never imagined possible. All three echelons of data sources create a wealth of information that can significantly improve an organization's capability of solving complex problems and taking advantage of opportunities—if recognized and leveraged properly.

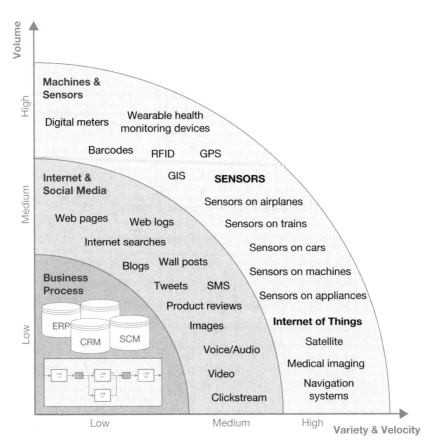

Figure 6.2 Wide range of sources for Big Data.

Big Data is not new. What is new is that the definition and the structure of Big Data constantly change. Companies have been storing and analyzing large volumes of data since the advent of the data warehouses in the early 1990s. While terabytes used to be synonymous with Big Data warehouses, now it's petabytes, and the rate of growth in data volumes continues to escalate as organizations seek to store and analyze greater levels of transaction details, as well as Web- and machine-generated data, to gain a better understanding of customer behavior and business drivers. Many academics and industry analysts alike think that Big Data is a misnomer. What it says and what it means are not exactly the same. Big Data is not just "big."

The sheer volume of the data is only one of many characteristics that are often associated with Big Data; others include variety, velocity, veracity, variability, and value proposition.

The Vs That Define Big Data

Big Data is typically defined by three Vs: volume, variety, and velocity. In addition to these three, we see some of the leading Big Data solution providers adding other Vs, such as veracity (IBM), variability (SAS), and value proposition.

Volume

Volume is obviously the most common trait of Big Data. Many factors contributed to the exponential increase in data volume, such as transaction-based data stored through the years, text data constantly streaming in from social media, increasing amounts of sensor data being collected, and automatically generated RFID and GPS data. In the past, excessive data volume created storage issues. But with today's advanced technologies coupled with decreasing storage costs, these issues are no longer significant; instead, other issues emerge, including how to determine relevance amidst the large volumes of data and how to create value from data that is deemed to be relevant.

As mentioned before, "big" is a relative term. It changes over time and is perceived differently by different organizations. With the staggering increase in data volume, even the naming of the next Big Data echelon has been a challenge. The highest mass of data that used to be called petabytes (PB) has yielded its place to zettabytes (ZB), which is a trillion gigabytes (GB) or a billion terabytes (TB). As the volume of data increases, community is having a hard time keeping up with the universally accepted naming of the next level. Table 6.1 provides an overview of the size and naming of the modern-day data volumes.

Table 6.1 Naming for the Increasing Volumes of Data

Name	Symbol	Value
Kilobyte	kB	10^3
Megabyte	MB	10^6
Gigabyte	GB	10^9
Terabyte	TB	10^{12}
Petabyte	PB	10^{15}
ExaByte	EB	10^{18}
Zettabyte	ZB	10^{21}
Yottabyte	YB	10^{24}
Brontobyte	BB	10^{27}
Geopbyte	GeB	10^{30}

Variety

Data today comes in all types of formats—ranging from traditional databases to hierarchical data stores created by the end users and OLAP systems, to text documents, email, XML, meter-collected, sensor-captured data, to video, audio, and stock ticker data. By some estimates, 80 to 85 percent of all organizations' data is in some sort of unstructured or semi-structured format (a format that is not suitable for traditional database schemas). But there is no denying its value, so it must be included in the analyses to support decision-making.

Velocity

According to Gartner, **velocity** means both how fast data is being produced and how fast the data must be processed (captured, stored, and analyzed) to meet the need or demand. RFID tags, automated sensors, GPS devices, and smart meters are driving an increasing need to deal with torrents of data in near-real time. Velocity is perhaps the most overlooked characteristic of Big Data. Reacting quickly enough to deal with velocity is a challenge to most organizations. For the time-sensitive environments, the opportunity cost clock of the data starts ticking the moment the data is created. As time passes, the value proposition of the data degrades and eventually becomes worthless. Whether the subject matter is the health of a patient, the well-being of a traffic system, or the health of an investment portfolio, accessing the data and reacting faster to the circumstances will always create more advantageous outcomes.

In the Big Data storm that we are witnessing today, most everyone is fixated on at-rest analytics using optimized software and hardware systems to mine large quantities of variant data sources. Although this is critically important and highly valuable, there is another class of analytics driven from the velocity nature of the Big Data, called **data stream analytics** or **in-motion analytics**, which is mostly over-looked. If done correctly, data stream analytics can be as valuable, and in some business environments more valuable, than at-rest analytics. Later in this chapter we will cover this topic in more detail.

Veracity

Veracity is a term that is being used as the fourth "V" to describe Big Data by IBM. It refers to the conformity to facts—the accuracy, quality, truthfulness, or trustworthiness of the data. Tools and techniques are often used to handle Big Data's veracity by transforming the data into quality and trustworthy insights.

Variability

In addition to the increasing velocities and varieties of data, data flows can be highly inconsistent with periodic peaks. Is something big trending in the social media? Perhaps there is a high-profile IPO looming. Maybe swimming with pigs in the Bahamas is suddenly the must-do vacation activity. Daily, seasonal, and event-triggered peak data loads can be challenging to manage, especially with social media involved.

Value Proposition

The excitement around Big Data is its value proposition. A pre-conceived notion is that it contains or has a greater potential to contain more patterns and interesting anomalies than small data. Thus, by analyzing large and feature-rich data, organizations can gain greater business value that they may not have otherwise. While users can detect the patterns in small data sets using simple statistical and machine learning methods or ad-hoc query and reporting tools, Big Data means "big" analytics. Big analytics means greater insight and better decisions—something that every organization needs.

Because the exact definition of Big Data is still a matter of ongoing discussion in academic and industrial circles, it is likely that more characteristics (perhaps more Vs) will be added to this list. Regardless of what happens, the importance and value proposition of Big Data are here to stay.

Fundamental Concepts of Big Data

Big Data by itself, regardless of the size, type, or speed, is worthless unless business users do something with it that delivers value to their organizations. That's where "big" analytics comes into the picture. Although organizations have always run reports and dashboards against data warehouses, most have not opened these repositories to in-depth on-demand exploration. This is partly because analysis tools are too complex for the average user but also because the repositories often do not contain all the data needed by the power user. This is about to change in a dramatic fashion, however, thanks to the new Big Data Analytics paradigm.

With the value proposition, Big Data also brought about big challenges for organizations. The traditional means for capturing, storing, and analyzing data are not capable of dealing with Big Data effectively and efficiently. Therefore, new breeds of technologies needed to be developed to take on the Big Data challenge. Before making such an investment, organizations should justify the means. As is the case with any other large information systems investment, the success in Big Data analytics depends on many factors. Figure 6.3 shows a graphical depiction of the most critical success factors (Watson, 2012).

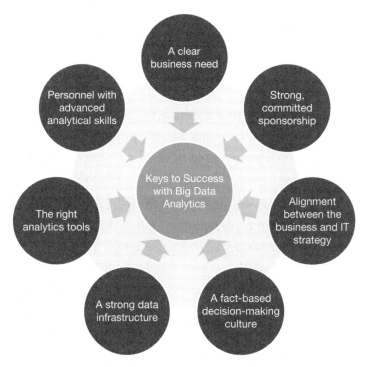

Figure 6.3 Critical success factors for Big Data analytics.

Following are among the most critical success factors for Big Data analytics:

- **A clear business need (alignment with the vision and the strategy).** Business investments ought to be made for the good of the business, not for the sake of mere technology advancements. Therefore, the main driver for Big Data analytics should be the needs of the business at any level—strategic, tactical, and operations.

- **Strong, committed sponsorship (executive champion).** It is a well-known fact that if you don't have strong, committed executive sponsorship, it is difficult to succeed. If the scope is a single or a few analytical applications, the sponsorship can be at the departmental level. However, if the target is enterprise-wide organizational transformation, which is often the case for Big Data initiatives, sponsorship needs to be at the highest levels and organization wide.

- **Alignment between the business and IT strategy.** It is essential to make sure that the analytics work is always supporting the business strategy, not the other way around. Analytics should play the enabling role in successful execution of the business strategy.

- **A fact-based decision-making culture.** In a fact-based decision-making culture, the numbers rather than intuition, gut feeling, or supposition drive decision-making. There is also a culture of experimentation to see what works and what doesn't.

- **A strong data infrastructure.** Data warehouses have provided the data infrastructure for analytics. This infrastructure is changing and being enhanced in the Big Data era with new technologies. Success requires marrying the old with the new for a holistic infrastructure that works synergistically.

As the size and the complexity increase, the need for more efficient analytical systems is also increasing. To keep up with the computational needs of Big Data, a number of new and innovative computational techniques and platforms are being developed. These techniques are collectively called high-performance computing, which includes the following:

- **In-memory analytics.** Solves complex problems in near-real time with highly accurate insights by allowing analytical computations and Big Data to be processed in-memory and distributed across a dedicated set of nodes.

- **In-database analytics.** Speeds time to insights and enables better data governance by performing data integration and analytic functions inside the database so you won't have to move or convert data repeatedly.
- **Grid computing.** Promotes efficiency, lower cost, and better performance by processing jobs in a shared, centrally managed pool of IT resources.
- **Appliances.** Brings together hardware and software in a physical unit that is not only fast but scalable and as needed.

Computational requirement is just a small part of the list of challenges that Big Data imposes on today's enterprises. Following is a list of challenges that are found by business executives to have a significant impact on successful implementation of Big Data analytics. When considering Big Data projects and architecture, being mindful of these challenges makes the journey to analytics competency a less stressful one.

- **Data volume.** The ability to capture, store, and process the huge volume of data at an acceptable speed so that the latest information is available to decision-makers when they need it.
- **Data integration.** The ability to combine data that is not similar in structure or source and to do so quickly and at reasonable cost.
- **Processing capabilities.** The ability to process the data quickly, as it is captured. The traditional way of collecting and then processing the data may not work. In many situations, data need to be analyzed as soon as it is captured to leverage the most value. (This is called Steam Analytics.)
- **Data governance.** The ability to keep up with the security, privacy, ownership, and quality issues of Big Data. As the volume, variety (format and source), and velocity of data change, so should the capabilities of governance practices.

- **Skills availability.** Big Data is being harnessed with new tools and is being looked at in different ways. There is a shortage of people (often called data scientists, which is covered later in this chapter) having the skills to do the job.

- **Solution cost.** Because Big Data has opened up a world of possible business improvements, there is a great deal of experimentation and discovery taking place to determine the patterns that matter and the insights that turn to value. To ensure a positive ROI on a Big Data project, therefore, it is crucial to reduce the cost of the solutions used to find that value.

Although challenges are real, so is the value proposition of Big Data analytics. Anything that you can do as business analytics leaders to help prove the value of new data sources to the business will move your organization beyond experimenting and exploring Big Data into adapting and embracing it as a differentiator. There is nothing wrong with exploration, but ultimately the value comes from putting those insights into action.

Big Data Technologies

Numerous technologies process and analyze Big Data. Most of these technologies are designed to take advantage of commodity hardware to enable scale-out, parallel processing techniques; employ nonrelational data storage capabilities to process unstructured and semi-structured data; and apply advanced analytics and data visualization technology to Big Data to convey insights to end users. There are three Big Data technologies that most believe will transform the business analytics and data management markets: MapReduce, Hadoop, and NoSQL.

MapReduce

MapReduce is a technique popularized by Google that distributes the processing of large multi-structured data files across a cluster of machines. High performance is achieved by breaking the processing into small units of work that can be run in parallel across the hundreds—potentially thousands—of nodes in the cluster. To quote the seminal paper on MapReduce:

"MapReduce is a programming model and an associated implementation for processing and generating large data sets. Programs written in this functional style are automatically parallelized and executed on a large cluster of commodity machines. This allows programmers without any experience with parallel and distributed systems to easily utilize the resources of a large distributed system" (Dean and Ghemawat, 2004). The key point to note from this quote is that MapReduce is a programming model, not a programming language. It is designed to be used by programmers rather than business users.

Hadoop

Hadoop is an open source framework for processing, storing, and analyzing massive amounts of distributed, unstructured data. Originally created by Doug Cutting at Yahoo, Hadoop was inspired by MapReduce, a user-defined function developed by Google in the early 2000s for indexing the Web. It was designed to handle petabytes and exabytes of data distributed over multiple nodes in parallel. Hadoop clusters run on inexpensive commodity hardware so projects can scale out without breaking the bank. Hadoop is now a project of the Apache Software Foundation, where hundreds of contributors continuously improve the core technology. Fundamental concept: Rather than banging away at one, huge block of data with a single machine, Hadoop breaks up Big Data into multiple parts so each part can be processed and analyzed at the same time.

NoSQL

A related new style of database called NoSQL (Not Only SQL) has emerged to, like Hadoop, process large volumes of multi-structured data. However, whereas Hadoop is adept at supporting large-scale, batch-style historical analysis, NoSQL databases are aimed for the most part at serving up discrete data stored among large volumes of multi-structured data to end user and automated Big Data applications. This capability is sorely lacking from relational database technology, which simply can't maintain needed application performance levels at the Big Data scale.

Data Scientist

The role of data scientist is one frequently associated with Big Data or Data Science. In a very short time, it has become one of the most sought-out roles in the marketplace. In an article published in the October 2012 issue of *Harvard Business Review*, authors Thomas H. Davenport and D. J. Patil called the data scientist "The Sexiest Job of the 21st Century." In that article, they specified data scientists' most basic, universal skill as the ability to write code in the latest Big Data languages and platforms. Although this may be less true in the near future, when many more people will have the title "data scientist" on their business cards, at this time it seems to be the most fundamental skill required from data scientists. A more enduring skill will be the need for data scientists to communicate in a language that all their stakeholders understand—and to demonstrate the special skills involved in storytelling with data, whether verbally, visually, or both (Davenport and Patil, 2012).

Data scientists use a combination of their business and technical skills to *investigate* Big Data looking for ways to improve current business analytics practices and improve decisions for new business opportunities. One of the biggest differences between a data scientist and a business intelligence (BI) user—such as a business analyst—is that a data scientist investigates and looks for new possibilities, whereas a BI user analyzes existing business situations and operations.

One of the dominant traits expected from data scientists is an intense curiosity—a desire to go beneath the surface of a problem, find the questions at its heart, and distill them into a clear set of hypotheses that can be tested. This often entails the associative thinking that characterizes the most creative scientists in any field. For example, we know of a data scientist studying a fraud problem who realized that it was analogous to a type of DNA sequencing problem (Davenport and Patil, 2012). By bringing together those disparate worlds, he and his team were able to craft a solution that dramatically reduced fraud losses.

Because data scientist is a role for a field that is still being defined and many of its practices are still experimental and far from being standardized, companies are overly sensitive about the experience dimension of data scientist. As the profession matures and practices are standardized, experience will be less of an issue while defining a data scientist. Companies today are looking for people who have extensive experience in working with complex data. They have had good luck recruiting among those with educational and work backgrounds in the physical or social sciences. Some of the best and brightest data scientists have been PhDs in esoteric fields like ecology and systems biology (Davenport and Patil, 2012). Even though there is no consensus on where data scientists come from, there is a common understanding of what skills and qualities they are expected to possess. Figure 6.4 shows a high-level graphical illustration of these skills that define who a data scientist is.

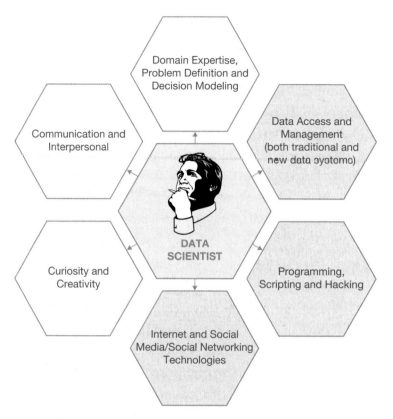

Figure 6.4 Skills that define a data scientist.

Data scientists are expected to have both soft skills—creativity, curiosity, communication, domain expertise, problem definition, and managerial (shown with light backgrounds hexagons on the left side of the figure)—as well as sound technical skills such as data manipulation, programming/hacking/scripting, Internet, and social media/networking technologies (shown with darker backgrounds, hexagons are on the right side of the figure).

Big Data and Stream Analytics

Along with volume and variety, as we saw earlier in this chapter, one of the key characteristics that defines Big Data is velocity. Velocity is the speed at which the data is created and streamed into the analytics environment. Organizations are looking for new means to process this streaming data as it comes in to react quickly and accurately to problems and opportunities to please their customers and to gain competitive advantage. When data streams in rapidly and continuously, traditional analytics approaches that work with previously accumulated data—data at rest—often either arrive at the wrong decisions because of using too much out-of-context data or arrive at the correct decisions but too late to be of any use to organizations. Therefore, it is critical for a number of business situations to analyze the data soon after it is created or as soon as it is streamed into the analytics system.

The presumption a majority of modern-day businesses are living by today is that it is important to record every piece of data because it might contain valuable information now or sometime in the near future. However, as long as the number of data sources increases, the "store-everything" approach becomes harder and harder and, in some cases, even infeasible. In fact, despite the technological advances, current total storage capacity lags far behind the digital information being generated in the world. Moreover, in the constantly changing business environment, real-time detection of meaningful changes in data as well as of complex pattern variations within a given short time window are essential to come up with the actions that better fit with the new environment. These facts become the main triggers for a paradigm that we call **stream analytics**. The stream analytics paradigm was born as an answer to these challenges—namely, the unbounded flows of data that cannot be permanently stored in order to be subsequently analyzed, in a timely and efficient manner, and complex pattern variations that need to be detected and acted upon as soon as they happen.

Stream analytics (also called data in-motion analytics, real-time data analytical, among others) is a term commonly used for the analytic process of extracting actionable information from continuously streaming data. A **stream** can be defined as a continuous sequence of data elements, which are also called **tuples**. In a relational database sense, a tuple is similar to a row of data (a record, an object, an instance). However, in the context of semi-structured or unstructured data, a tuple is an abstraction representing a package of data that can be characterized as a set of attributes for a given object. If a tuple by itself is not sufficiently informative for analysis and a correlation or another collective relationship among tuples is needed, a window of data that includes a set of tuples is used. A window of data is a finite number or sequence of tuples, where the windows are continuously updated as new data become available. The size of the window is determined based on the system being analyzed. Stream analytics is becoming increasingly more popular because of two things: time-to-action has become an ever-so-decreasing value, and we have the technological means to capture and process the data while it is being created.

Some of the most impactful applications of stream analytics were developed in the energy industry, specifically for Smart Grid (electric power supply chain) systems. The new Smart Grids are capable not only of real-time creation and processing of multiple streams of data to determine optimal power distribution to fulfill real customer needs, but of generating accurate short-term predictions aimed at covering unexpected demand and renewable energy generation peaks. Figure 6.5 shows a depiction of a generic use case for streaming analytics in the energy industry (a typical Smart Grid application). The goal is to accurately predict electricity demand and production in real time by using streaming data that is coming from smart meters, production system sensors, and meteorological models. The ability to predict near future consumption/production trends and detect anomalies in real time can be used to optimize supply decisions as well as to adjust smart meters to regulate consumption and favorable energy pricing.

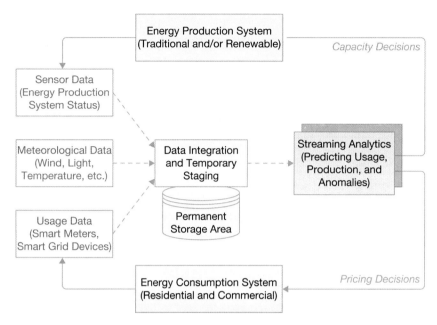

Figure 6.5 A use case of streaming analytics in the energy industry.

Application Case—Big Data for Political Campaigns

One of the application areas where Big Data and analytics promise to make a big difference is the field of politics. Experiences from the recent presidential elections illustrated the power of Big Data and analytics to acquire and energize millions of volunteers (in the form of a modern-era grassroots movement) to not only raise hundreds of millions of dollars for the election campaign but optimally organize and mobilize potential voters to get out and vote in large numbers. Clearly, the 2008 and 2012 presidential elections made a mark on the political arena with the creative use of Big Data and analytics to improve chances of winning. Figure 6.6 illustrates the analytical process of converting a variety of data to the ingredients for winning an election.

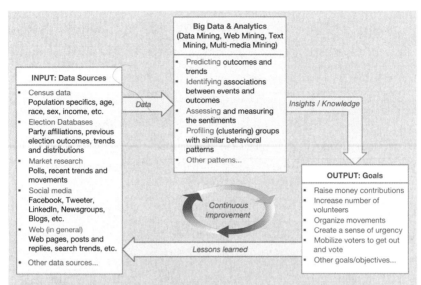

Figure 6.6 Leveraging Big Data and analytics for political campaigns.

As Figure 6.6 shows, data is the source of information; the richer and deeper it is, the better and more relevant the insights are. The main characteristics of Big Data—namely, volume, variety, and velocity (the three Vs)—readily apply to the kind of data that is used for political campaigns. Beyond the structured data (detailed records of previous campaigns, census data, market research, and poll data), vast volumes and verity of social media and Web data are used to learn more about voters and obtain deeper insights to enforce or change the outcome. Often, search and browsing history of individuals are captured and made available to customers (political analysts) who can use such data for better insight and behavioral targeting. If done correctly, Big Data and analytics can provide invaluable information to manage political campaigns better than ever before.

Source: Compiled from Shen (2013); Romano (2012); Scherer (2012); Issenberg, (2012); Samuelson (2013).

Deep Learning

AI is making a reentrance into the realm of computing, the business world, and our daily lives; this time, it's far stronger and much more promising than ever before. This unprecedented reemergence and the new level of expectations can largely be attributed to the latest trends—namely, deep learning and cognitive computing. These two latest buzzwords define the leading edge of AI and machine learning today. Evolving out of the traditional artificial neural networks, deep learning is changing the foundation of how machine learning works. Thanks to large collections of data and improved computational resources, deep learning is making a profound impact on how computers can discover complex patterns using the self-extracted features from the data (as opposed to a data scientist providing the feature vector to the learning algorithm). Cognitive computing, first popularized by IBM Watson and its success against the best human players in the game show *Jeopardy!*, makes it possible to deal with a new class of problems—the type of problems that are thought to be solvable only by human ingenuity and creativity, ones that are characterized by ambiguity and uncertainty. This chapter covers the concepts, methods, and application of these two cutting-edge AI technology trends.

Application Case—Fighting Fraud with Deep Learning

Mitigating fraud is a top priority for banks. According to the Association of Certified Fraud Examiners, businesses lose more than $3.5 trillion each year to fraud. The problem is pervasive across the financial industry and becoming more prevalent and sophisticated each month. As customers conduct more banking online across a greater variety of channels and devices, there are more opportunities for fraud to occur. Adding to the problem, fraudsters are becoming more creative and technologically savvy—they're also using advanced technologies like machine learning—and new schemes to defraud banks are evolving rapidly.

Old methods for identifying fraud, such as using human-written rules engines, catch only a small percentage of fraud cases and produce a significantly high number of false positives. While false negatives end up costing money to the bank, chasing after a large number of false positives not only costs time and money but also blemishes customer trust and satisfaction. To improve probability predictions and identify a much higher percentage of actual cases of fraud while simultaneously reducing false alarms, banks need new forms of analytics. This includes using AI.

Dankse Bank integrated deep learning with graphics processing unit (GPU) appliances that were also optimized for deep learning. The new software system helps the analytics team identify potential cases of fraud while intelligently avoiding false positives. Operational decisions are shifted from users to AI systems. However, human intervention is still necessary in some cases. For example, the model can identify anomalies, such as debit card purchases taking place around the world, but analysts are needed to determine if it's fraud or if a bank customer simply made an online purchase that sent a payment to China, then bought an item the next day from a retailer based in London.

The results of deep learning-based fraud detection systems were impressive. The bank realized a 60 percent reduction in false positives, with an expectation to reach as high as 80 percent while increasing true positives by as much as 50 percent. This allowed the bank to focus its resources on actual cases of fraud. For more details and a visual summary of this application case, the reader is referred to the following video (https://www.teradata.com/Resources/Videos/Danske-Bank-Innovating-in-Artificial-Intelligence) and the following blog post (http://blogs.teradata.com/customers/danske-bank-innovating-artificial-intelligence-deep-learning-detect-sophisticated-fraud/).

An Introduction to Deep Learning

About a decade ago, conversing with an electronic device (in human language, intelligently) would have been inconceivable—something that could be seen only in sci-fi movies. Today, however, thanks to the advances in AI methods and technologies, almost everyone has experienced this unthinkable phenomenon. You probably have already asked Siri or Google Assistant several times to dial a number from your phone address book or to find an address and give you the specific directions while you were driving. Sometimes when you were bored in the afternoon, you may have asked Google Home or Amazon's Alexa to play some music in your favorite genre on the device or on your TV. You might have been surprised at times when you uploaded a group photo of your friends on Facebook and observed its tagging suggestions, with the name tags often exactly matching with your friends' faces in the picture. Translating a manuscript from a foreign language does not require hours of struggling with a dictionary; it is as easy as taking a picture of that manuscript in the Google Translate mobile app and giving it a fraction of a second. These are only a few of the many, ever increasing applications of deep learning that have promised to make life easier for people.

Deep learning, as the newest and perhaps at this moment the most popular member of the AI and machine learning family, has a goal similar to those of the other machine learning methods that came before it: mimic the thought process of humans using mathematical algorithms to learn from data pretty much the same way that humans learn. So what is really different and advanced in deep learning? Here is the most commonly pronounced differentiating characteristic of deep learning over the traditional machine learning. The performance of traditional machine learning algorithms such as decision trees, support vector machines, logistic regression, and neural networks relies heavily on representation of the data. That is, only if we analytics professionals or data scientists provide them with relevant and sufficient pieces of information—features—in proper format, can they "learn" the patterns and thereby perform their prediction (classification or estimation), clustering, or association tasks with an acceptable level of accuracy. In other words, they need humans to manually identify and derive features that are theoretically or logically relevant to the objectives of the problem at hand and feed them into the algorithm in a proper format. For example, to use a decision tree to predict whether a given customer will return (or churn), the marketing manager needs to provide the algorithm with information such as the customer's socio-economic characteristics (income, occupation, educational level, and so on) along with demographic and historical interactions/transactions with the company. But the algorithm itself is not able to define such socioeconomic characteristics and extract such features from the survey forms filled out by the customer or from the social media.

Although such a structured, human-mediated machine learning approach may work fine for rather abstract and formal tasks, it is extremely challenging to have it work for some informal, yet seemingly easy tasks like face identification or speech recognition because such tasks require a great deal of knowledge about the world (Goodfellow et al., 2016). It is not straightforward, for instance, to train a machine learning algorithm that accurately recognizes the real meaning of a sentence spoken by a person just by manually providing it with a number of grammatical or semantic features. Accomplishing such a task requires a "deep" knowledge about the world that is not easy to formalize and explicitly present. What deep learning has added to the classic machine learning methods is in fact the ability to automatically acquire the knowledge required to accomplish such informal tasks and consequently extract some advanced features that contribute to superior system performance.

To develop an intimate understanding of deep learning, one should learn where it fits in the big picture of all other AI methods. A simple hierarchical relationship diagram, or a taxonomy-like representation, may in fact provide such a holistic understanding. In an attempt to do this, Goodfellow and his colleagues (2016) categorize deep learning as part of a representation learning family of methods. Representation learning techniques are a type of machine learning (which is also a part of AI) in which the emphasis is on learning and discovering features by the system in addition to discovering mapping from those features to the output/target. Figure 6.7 uses a Venn diagram to illustrate the placement of deep learning within the overarching family of AI-based learning methods.

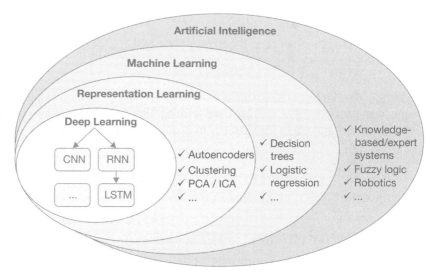

Figure 6.7 A Venn diagram showing the placement of deep learning within the overarching AI-based learning methods.

Figure 6.8 highlights the differences in the steps that need to be performed when building a typical deep learning model versus the steps performed when building models with classic machine learning algorithms. As shown in the top two workflows, knowledge-based systems and classic machine learning methods require data scientists to manually create the features—the representation—to achieve the desired output. The bottom-most workflow shows that deep learning enables the computer to derive some complex features from simple concepts that would be effort intensive (or perhaps impossible in some problem situations) if discovered by humans manually, and then map those advanced features to the desired output.

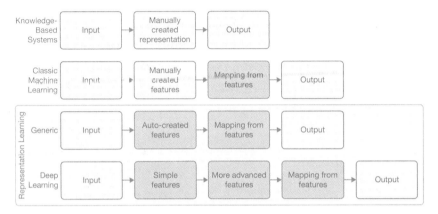

Figure 6.8 Illustration of the key differences between classic machine learning methods and representation learning/deep learning. (Shaded boxes indicate components that are able to learn directly from data.)

From a methodological viewpoint, although deep learning is generally believed to be a new area in machine learning, its initial idea goes back to the late 1980s, just a few decades after the emergence of Artificial Neural Networks, when backpropagation networks were used for recognizing handwritten zip codes. In fact, as it is being practiced today, deep learning seems to be nothing but an extension of neural networks with the idea that it is able to deal with more complicated tasks with a higher level of sophistication by employing many layers of connected neurons along with much larger data sets to automatically characterize variables and solve the problems, but at the expense of a great deal of computational effort. This high computational requirement and the need for large data sets were the two main reasons the initial idea had to wait more than two decades, until some advanced computational and technological infrastructure emerged for its practical realization. Although the scale of neural networks has dramatically increased in the past decade by the advancement of the related technologies, it is still estimated that it will take a couple more decades to have artificial deep neural networks with the comparable number of neurons and complexity that exist in the human brain.

In addition to the computer infrastructures, as mentioned earlier, the availability of large and feature-rich digitized data sets was another key reason for the development of successful deep learning applications during recent years. Obtaining good performance out of a deep learning algorithm used to be a difficult task requiring extensive skills and experience to design task-specific networks; therefore, not many were able to develop deep learning for practical or research purposes. Large training data sets, however, have greatly compensated for the lack of intimate knowledge and reduced the level of skill needed for implementing deep neural networks. Nevertheless, although the size of available data sets has exponentially increased in recent years, a great challenge, especially for supervised learning of deep networks, is now the labeling of the cases in these huge data sets. As a result, a great deal of research is focusing on how we can take advantage of large quantities of unlabeled data for semi-supervised or unsupervised learning and how we can develop methods to label examples in bulk in a reasonable time.

Deep Neural Networks

Before the advent of the deep learning phenomenon, most neural network applications involved network architectures with few hidden layers and a limited number of neurons in each layer. Even in relatively complex business applications of neural networks, the number of neurons in networks hardly exceeded a few thousand. In fact, the processing capability of computers at the time was such a limiting factor that CPUs were hardly able to run networks involving more than a couple of layers in a reasonable time. In recent years, development of GPUs, along with the associated programming languages that enable people to use them for data analysis purposes, has led to more advanced applications of neural networks. The GPU technology has enabled us to successfully run neural networks with more than a million neurons. These larger networks are able to go deeper into the data features and extract more sophisticated patterns that could not be detected otherwise.

Although deep networks can handle a considerably larger number of input variables, they also need relatively larger data sets to be trained satisfactorily. Using small data sets for training deep networks typically leads to overfitting of the model to the training data and poor and unreliable results in case of applying to external data. Thanks to the Internet and Internet of Things (IoT)-based data capturing tools and technologies, larger data sets are now available in many application domains for deeper neural network training.

The input to a regular ANN model is typically an array of size R×1, where R is the number of input variables. In the deep networks, however, we are able to use *tensors* (N-dimensional arrays) as input. For example, in image recognition networks, each input can be represented by a matrix indicating the color codes used in the image pixels. For video processing purposes, each video can be represented by several matrices, each representing an image involved in the video. In other words, tensors enable us to include additional dimensions, such as time and location, in analyzing the data sets.

Apart from these general differences, various types of deep networks involve modifications to the architecture of standard neural networks that equip them with unique capabilities to deal with particular data types for advanced purposes.

Convolutional Neural Networks

Convolutional neural networks (CNNs) are one of the most popular deep learning methods. CNNs are basically a variation of the deep MLP architecture, initially designed for computer vision applications (image processing, video processing, text recognition) but also applicable to nonimage data sets.

The main characteristic of the convolutional networks is having at least one layer involving a convolution weight function instead of general matrix multiplication. **Convolution** is a linear operation that essentially aims at extracting simple patterns from sophisticated data patterns. For instance, in processing an image containing several objects and colors, convolution functions can extract simple patterns like the existence of horizontal or vertical lines or edges in different parts of the picture. We discuss convolution functions in more detail in the next section.

A layer containing a convolution function in a CNN is called a convolution layer. These layers are often followed by a pooling, or subsampling, layer. Pooling layers are in charge of consolidating the large tensors to one with a smaller size and reducing the number of model parameters while keeping their important features. Different types of pooling layers are discussed in the following sections.

Image Processing Using Convolutional Networks

Real applications of deep learning in general, and CNNs in particular, highly depend on the availability of large, annotated data sets. Theoretically, CNNs can be applied to many practical problems today, and there are many large and feature-rich databases for such application. Nevertheless, the biggest challenge is that in supervised learning applications, we need an already annotated data set to train the model before we can use it for prediction or identification of other unknown cases. Whereas extracting features of data sets using CNN layers is an unsupervised task, the extracted features will not be much use without having labeled cases to develop a classification network in a supervised learning fashion. That is why, traditionally, image classification networks involve two pipelines: visual feature extraction and image classification.

ImageNet (http://www.image-net.org) is an ongoing research project that provides researchers with a large database of images. Each image is linked to a set of synonym words, or synset, from WordNet, which is a word hierarchy database. Each synset represents a particular concept in the WordNet. Currently, WordNet includes more than 100,000 synsets, each of which is aimed to be illustrated by an average of 1,000 images in the ImageNet. Currently, ImageNet is a uniquely huge database for developing image processing deep networks, with more than 15 million labeled images in 22,000 categories. Because of that, it is the most widely used data set as a benchmark to assess the efficiency and accuracy of deep networks designed by researchers.

One of the first convolutional networks designed for image classification using the ImageNet data set is AlexNet (Krizhevsky, Sutskever, & Hinton, 2012). It was composed of five convolution layers followed by three fully connected layers. (See Figure 6.9 for a schematic representation of AlexNet.) One of the contributions of this relatively simple architecture that made its training remarkably faster and computationally efficient was the use of rectified linear unit (ReLu) transfer functions in the convolution layers instead of the traditional sigmoid functions. With this contribution, the designers addressed the issue called **vanishing gradient problem** caused by small derivatives of sigmoid functions in some regions of the images. The other important contribution of this network to improve the efficiency of deep networks was the introduction of dropout layers to the CNNs to reduce overfitting. A dropout layer typically comes after the fully connected layers and applies a random probability to the neurons to switch off some of them and make the network sparser.

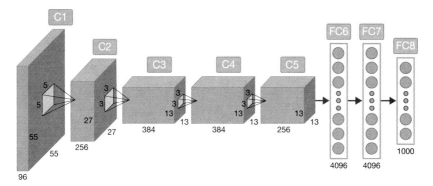

Figure 6.9 Architecture of AlexNet, a convolutional network for image classification.

From Image Recognition to Face Recognition

Face recognition, although seemingly similar to image recognition, is a much more complicated undertaking. In face recognition, the goal is to identify the individual as opposed to the class it belongs to (human). This recognition needs to be performed in a nonstatic (moving person) three-dimensional environment. Face recognition has been an active research field in AI for many decades, with limited success until recently. Thanks to the new generation of algorithms coupled with large data sets and computational power, face recognition technology is starting to make a significant impact on real-world applications. From security to marketing, applications of face recognition are increasing at an astounding pace.

Some of the premier examples of face recognition (both in advancements in technology and in the creative use of the technology perspectives) come from China. Today in China, face recognition is a hot topic, both from business and from application development. Face recognition has become a fruitful ecosystem with hundreds of start-ups in China. In personal and business settings, people in China are widely using and relying on devices whose security is based on automatic recognition of their faces.

As perhaps the largest scale practical application case of deep learning and face recognition in the world today, the Chinese government recently started a vast effort that aims at establishing a nationwide surveillance system based on face recognition, known as Sharp Eyes. The project plans to integrate security cameras already installed in public places with the private cameras on buildings and utilize AI and deep learning to analyze their videos. With millions of cameras and billions of lines of code, China is building a high-tech authoritarian future. With this system, in some cities, cameras can scan train and bus stations as well as airports to identify and catch China's most wanted. Billboard-size displays can show the faces of jaywalkers and list the names and pictures of people who don't pay their debts. Facial recognition scanners guard the entrances to housing complexes.

An interesting example of this surveillance system is the "shame game" (Mozur, 2018). The intersection, south of Changhong Bridge in the city of Xiangyang, used to be a nightmare. Cars drove fast, and jaywalkers darted into the street. Then, last summer, the police put up cameras linked to facial recognition technology and a big, outdoor screen. Photos of lawbreakers were displayed, alongside their names and government ID numbers. People were initially excited to see their faces on the board until propaganda outlets told them it was punishment. This way, citizens not only became a subject of this shame game but also were assigned negative citizenship points. Conversely on the positive side, if citizens are caught on the camera showing good behavior, like picking up a piece of trash from the road and putting it into the trash can or helping an elderly person cross the intersection, they get positive citizenship points that can be used for a variety of small awards.

Already, China has an estimated 200 million surveillance cameras—four times as many as the United States. The system is mainly intended to be used for tracking suspects, spotting suspicious behavior, and predicting crimes. But it is merged with a huge database of medical records, travel bookings, online purchases, and even social media activities and can monitor practically everyone in the country (with 1.4 billion people) and track where they are and what they do at each moment (Denyer, 2018). For instance, to find a criminal, an image can be uploaded to the system to be matched against millions of faces recognized from videos of active security cameras across the country. Going beyond narrowly defined security purposes, the government expects Sharp Eyes to ultimately be used to assign every individual in the country a "social credit score" that specifies to what extent that person is trustworthy.

Although such an unrestricted application of deep learning is against the privacy and ethical norms of many Western countries including the United States, it is becoming a common practice in countries with less restrictive privacy laws and concerns. Even the Western countries have begun to employ similar technologies in limited scale only for security and crime prevention purposes. The FBI's Next Generation Identification System, for instance, is a lawful application of facial recognition and deep learning that compares images from crime scenes with a national database of mug shots to identify potential suspects.

Sources: Mozur (2018) and Denyer (2018).

Recurrent Networks and Long Short-Term Memory Networks

Humans' thinking and understanding largely rely on the context. It is crucial for us, for example, to know if a particular speaker is sarcastic so we can fully catch all the jokes he makes. Or to understand the real meaning of the word *fall*—either the season or collapse—in the sentence "It is a nice day of Fall." Without knowledge about the other words in the sentence, there's no understanding. Knowledge of the context is typically formed based on observing events that happened in the past. In fact, human thoughts are persistent; we use every piece of information we previously acquired about an event in the process of analyzing it.

Although deep MLP and convolutional networks are specialized for processing a static grid of values like an image or a matrix of word embeddings, sometimes the sequence of input values is important to the operation of the network to accomplish a given task and therefore should be considered. There is another popular type of neural networks, called **recurrent neural networks**, or RNNs (Rumelhart et al., 1986), that are specifically designed to process sequential inputs. An RNN basically models a dynamic system where the state of the system at each time point t depends on both the inputs to the system at that time as well as its state at the previous time point $t-1$. In other words, RNNs are the neural networks that have memory and that apply that memory to determine their future outputs. For instance, in designing a neural network to play chess, it is important to consider several previous moves while training the network. A wrong move by a player can lead to the eventual loss of the game in the subsequent 10–15 plays. Also, to understand the real meaning of a sentence in an essay, sometimes we need to rely on the information portrayed in the previous several sentences or paragraphs; we need the context built sequentially and collectively over time. Therefore, it is crucial to consider a memory element for the neural network that considers the effect of prior moves (in the chess example) and prior sentences and paragraphs (in the essay example) to determine the best output. This memory portrays and creates the context required for learning and understanding.

In static networks like MLP-type CNNs, we are trying to find functions that map the inputs to outputs that are as close as possible to the actual target. In dynamic networks like RNNs, on the other hand, both inputs and outputs are sequences, or patterns. Therefore, a dynamic network is a dynamic system rather than a function; its output depends not only on the input, but on the previous output.

Technically speaking, any network with feedback can actually be called a deep network. Even with a single layer, the loop created by the feedback can be thought of as static MLP-type network with many layers. However, in practice, each recurrent neural network involves dozens of layers, each with feedback to themselves, or even to the other previous layers, which makes them even deeper and more complicated. Because of the feedback, the computation of gradients in the recurrent neural networks would be somewhat different from the general backpropagation algorithm used for the static MLP networks. There are two alternative approaches for computing the gradients in the RNNs: real time recurrent learning (RTRL) and backpropagation through time (BTT). Their explanation is beyond the scope of this chapter, but their general purpose remains the same: once the gradients are computed, the same procedures are applied to optimize the learning of the network parameters.

The long short-term memory (LSTM) networks (Hochreiter & Schmidhuber, 1997) are a variation of recurrent neural networks that today are known as the most effective sequence modeling technique and are the base of many practical applications. In a dynamic network, the weights are called long-term memory, and the feedback is short-term memory.

In essence, it is only the short-term memory (feedback and previous events) that provides a network with the context. In a typical RNN, the information on short-term memory is continuously replaced as new information is fed back into the network. That is why RNNs perform well when the gap between the relevant information and the place that is needed is small. For instance, for predicting the last word in the sentence "The referee blew his whistle," we just need to know a few words back (*the referee*) to correctly predict what's coming. Because in this case the gap between the relevant information (the referee) and where it is needed (to predict whistle) is small, an RNN network can easily perform this learning and prediction task.

However, sometimes the relevant information required to perform a task is far away from where it is needed. Therefore, it is quite likely that it would have already been replaced by other information in the short-term memory by the time it is needed for the creation of the proper context. For instance, to predict the last word in "I went to the carwash yesterday. It cost $5 to wash my car," there is a relatively larger gap between the relevant information (carwash) and where it is needed. Sometimes we may even need to refer to the previous paragraphs to reach the relevant information for predicting the true meaning of a word. In such cases, RNNs usually do not perform well because they cannot keep the information in their short-term memory for a long enough time. Fortunately, LSTM networks do not have such a shortcoming. The term **long short-term memory** network, then, refers to a network in which we are trying to remember what happened in the past for a long enough time so that we can leverage it in accomplishing the task when needed.

Computer Frameworks for Implementation of Deep Learning

Advances in deep learning owe, to a great extent, to advances in the software and hardware infrastructure required for its implementation. In the past few decades, GPUs have been revolutionized to support playing of high-resolution videos as well as advanced video games and virtual reality applications. However, their huge processing potential had not been effectively utilized for purposes other than graphics processing up until a few years back when software libraries such as Theano, Caffe, PyLearn2, Tensorflow, and MXNet had the purpose of programming GPUs for general-purpose processing and for analysis of Big Data. The operation of these libraries mostly relies on a parallel computing platform and application programming interface (API) developed by NVIDIA called Compute Unified Device Architecture (CUDA). CUDA enables software developers to use GPUs made by this company for general-purpose processing. In fact, each deep learning framework consists of a high-level scripting language and a library of deep learning routines usually written in C for using CPUs or in CUDA for using GPUs.

In the following section, we introduce four of the most popular software libraries among deep learning researchers and practitioners: Torch, Caffe, TensorFlow, and Theano.

Torch

Torch is an open source scientific computing framework (available at www.torch.ch) for implementing machine learning algorithms using GPUs. The Torch framework is a library based on LuaJIT, a compiled version of the popular Lua programming language (www.lua.org). In fact, Torch adds a number of valuable features to Lua that make deep learning analyses possible. First, it enables support of N-dimensional arrays (tensors) whereas, normally, tables are the only data structuring method used by Lua. Second, Torch includes routine libraries for manipulating tensors, linear algebra, neural network functions, and optimization. Finally, while Lua by default uses CPU to run the programs, Torch enables use of GPUs for running the programs written in the Lua language.

The easy and fast scripting properties of LuaJIT, along with its flexibility, have made Torch a popular framework for practical deep learning applications such that today its latest version, Torch7, is widely used by a number of great companies like Facebook, Google, and IBM in their research labs as well as for their commercial applications.

Caffe

Caffe is another open source deep learning framework (available at http://caffe.berkeleyvision.org). It was created by Yangqing Jia (2013), a PhD student at UC Berkeley, and then further developed by the Berkeley AI Research (BAIR). Caffe has multiple options to be used as the high-level scripting language, including the command line, python, and MATLAB interfaces. The deep learning libraries in Caffe are written in the C++ programming language.

In Caffe, everything is done using text files instead of code. To implement a network, generally we need to prepare two text files (with the .prototxt extension) that are communicated by the Caffe engine via JavaScript Object Notation (JSON) format. The first text file, known as the **architecture** file, defines the architecture of the network layer by layer, where each layer is defined by a name, a type, the names of its previous and next layers in the architecture, and some required parameters. The second text file, known as the **solver** file, specifies the properties of the training algorithm, including the learning rate, the maximum number of iterations, and the processing unit to be used for the training of network.

Although Caffe supports multiple types of deep network architectures, it is particularly known to be an efficient framework for image processing due to its incredible speed in processing image files. According to the developers, Caffe is able to process more than 60 million images per day (1 ms/image) using a single NVIDIA K40 GPU. In 2017, Facebook released an improved version of Caffe, called Caffe2 (www.caffe2.ai), with the aim of improving the original framework to be effectively used for deep learning architectures other than CNN and with a special emphasis on portability for performing cloud and mobile computations while maintaining scalability and performance.

TensorFlow

Another popular open-source deep learning framework is TensorFlow. It was originally developed and written in Python and C++ by the Google Brain Group in 2011 as *DistBelief*, but it was further developed into TensorFlow in 2015. TensorFlow, at the time, was the only deep learning framework that, in addition to CPUs and GPUs, supported tensor processing units (TPUs), a type of processor developed by Google in 2016 for the specific purpose of neural network machine learning. In fact, TPUs were specifically designed by Google for the TensorFlow framework.

Although Google has not made TPUs available to the market yet, it is reported that Google has used them in many of its commercial services, such as Google Search, Street View, Google Photos, and Google Translate, with significant improvements reported. A detailed study performed by Google shows that TPUs deliver 30 to 80 times higher performance per watt than contemporary CPUs and GPUs.

Such a unique feature would probably put TensorFlow way ahead of the other alternative frameworks in the near future if Google makes TPUs commercially available.

Another interesting feature of TensorFlow is its visualization module, called TensorBoard. Implementing a deep neural network is a complex and confusing task. TensorBoard refers to a web application involving a handful of visualization tools to visualize network graphs and plot quantitative network metrics with the aim of helping users better understand what is going on during the training procedure and debug possible issues.

Theano

In 2007, the Deep Learning Group at the University of Montreal developed the initial version of a Python library called Theano (http://deeplearning.net/software/theano) to define, optimize, and evaluate mathematical expressions involving multi-dimensional arrays, or tensors, on CPU or GPU platforms. It was one of the first deep learning frameworks, but it later became a source of inspiration for the developers of TensorFlow. Both Theano and TensorFlow pursue a similar procedure in the sense that a typical network implementation involves two sections. In the first section, a computational graph is built by defining the network variables and operations to be done on them. The second section runs that graph (in Theano by compiling the graph into a function, and in TensorFlow by creating a session). What happens in these libraries is that the user defines the structure of the network using some simple and symbolic syntax understandable even for beginners in programming. The library automatically generates appropriate codes in either C (for processing on CPU) or CUDA (for processing on GPU) to implement the defined network. Therefore, the users, without any knowledge of programming in C or CUDA and with just minimal knowledge of Python, are able to efficiently design and implement deep learning networks on the GPU platforms.

Theano also includes some built-in functions to visualize the computational graph as well as to plot the network performance metrics, even though its visualization features are not comparable to TensorBoard.

Cognitive Computing

We are witnessing a significant increase in the way technology is evolving. Things that used to take decades are now taking months, and the things that we only see in sci-fi movies are becoming reality, one after another. Therefore, it is safe to say that in the next decade or two, technological advancements will transform how people live, learn, and work in a rather dramatic fashion. The interactions between humans and technology will become intuitive, seamless, and perhaps transparent. Cognitive computing will have a significant role to play in this transformation. Cognitive computing basically refers to the computing systems that use mathematical models to emulate or partially simulate the human cognition process to find solutions to complex problems and situations where the potential answers can be imprecise. Although the term *cognitive computing* is often used interchangeably with artificial intelligence and smart search engines, the phrase itself is closely associated with IBM's cognitive computer system, called Watson, and its success in the television show *Jeopardy!* Details on Watson's success on *Jeopardy!* can be found in Application Case in Chapter 1.

According to the Cognitive Computing Consortium (https://cognitivecomputingconsortium.com/), cognitive computing makes a new class of problems computable. It addresses highly complex situations that are characterized by ambiguity and uncertainty; in other words, it handles the kinds of problems that are thought to be solvable by human ingenuity and creativity. In today's dynamic, information-rich, and unstable situations, data tends to change frequently, and it is often conflicting. The goals of users evolve as they learn more and redefine their objectives. To respond to the fluid nature of users' understanding of their problems, the cognitive computing system offers a synthesis not just of information sources but of influences, contexts, and insights. To do this, systems often need to weigh conflicting evidence and suggest an answer that is best rather than right. Figure 6.10 illustrates a general framework for cognitive computing, where data and AI technologies are used to solve a complex real-world problem.

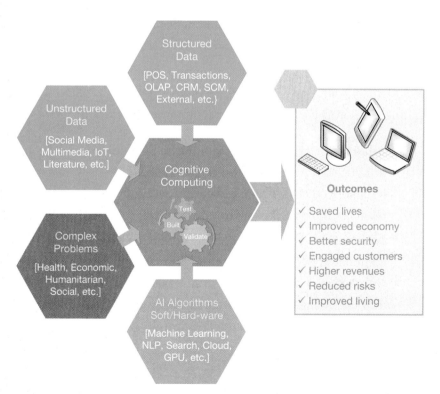

Figure 6.10 A conceptual framework for cognitive computing and its promises.

How Does Cognitive Computing Work?

As one would guess from the name, cognitive computing works much like a human thought process, reasoning mechanism, and cognitive system. These cutting-edge computation systems can find and synthesize data from various information sources and weigh context and conflicting evidence inherent in the data to provide the best possible answers to a given question or problem. To achieve this, cognitive systems include self-learning technologies that use data mining, pattern recognition, deep learning, and natural language processing to mimic the way the human brain works.

Using computer systems to solve the types of problems that humans are typically tasked with requires vast amounts of structured and unstructured data, fed to machine learning algorithms. Over time, cognitive systems are able to refine the way in which they learn and recognize patterns and the way they process data to become capable of anticipating new problems and modeling and proposing possible solutions.

To achieve those capabilities, cognitive computing systems must have the following key attributes, as defined by the Cognitive Computing Consortium (https://cognitivecomputingconsortium.com/).

- **Adaptive.** Cognitive systems must be flexible enough to learn as information changes and as goals evolve. The systems must be able to digest dynamic data in real time and make adjustments as the data and environment change.

- **Interactive.** Human-computer interaction (HCI) is a critical component in cognitive systems. Users must be able to interact with cognitive machines and define their needs as they change. The technologies must also be able to interact with other processors, devices, and cloud platforms.

- **Iterative and stateful.** Cognitive computing technologies can identify problems by asking questions or pulling in additional data if a stated problem is vague or incomplete. The systems do this by maintaining information about similar situations that have previously occurred.

- **Contextual.** Understanding context is critical in thought processes, so cognitive systems must understand, identify, and mine contextual data, such as syntax, time, location, domain, requirements, a specific user's profile, tasks, or goals. They may draw on multiple sources of information, including structured and unstructured data and visual, auditory, or sensor data.

How Does Cognitive Computing Differ from AI?

Cognitive computing is often used interchangeably with AI—the umbrella term used for technologies that rely on data and scientific methods/computations to make decisions. But there are differences between the two terms, which can largely be found within their purposes and applications. AI technologies include—but are not limited to—machine learning, neural computing, natural language processing (NLP), and most recently, deep learning. With AI systems, especially in machine learning systems, data is fed into the algorithm for processing (an iterative and time-demanding process that is often called **training**) so that the systems "learn" variables and interrelationships among those variables to produce prediction or characterizations about a given complex problem or situation. Applications based on AI and cognitive computing include intelligent assistants, such as Alexa, Google Home, and Siri. A simple comparison between cognitive computing and AI is given in Table 6.2 (Reynolds & Feldman, 2014; https://cognitivecomputingconsortium.com/).

Table 6.2 Cognitive Computing Versus Artificial Intelligence (AI)

Characteristic	Cognitive Computing	Artificial Intelligence (AI)
Technologies used	• Machine learning • Natural language processing • Neural networks • Deep learning • Text mining • Sentiment analysis	• Machine learning • Natural language processing • Neural networks • Deep learning
Capabilities offered	Simulate human thought processes to assist humans in finding solutions to complex problems	Find hidden patterns in a variety of data sources to identify problems and provide potential solutions
Purpose	Augment human capability	Automate complex processes by acting like humans in certain situations
Industries	Customer service, marketing, healthcare, entertainment, service sector	Manufacturing, finance, healthcare, banking, securities, retail, government

As can be seen in Table 6.2, the differences between AI and cognitive computing is rather marginal. This is expected because cognitive computing is often characterized as a subcomponent of AI, or an application of AI technologies, tailored for a specific purpose. Both utilize similar technologies and are applied to similar industry segments and verticals. The main difference between the two is the purpose: whereas cognitive computing is aimed at helping humans solve complex problems, AI is aimed at automating processes that are performed by humans. To the extreme extent, AI is striving to replace humans with machines at "intelligence"-requiring tasks, one at a time.

Conclusion

There is no doubt that business analytics is on a significant upward trend. The indications show that its popularity and its innovative use cases in businesses are rapidly evolving and have not come close to reaching a saturation point. Although it is not possible to know for sure what the future holds for analytics, one can conjecture that the future is bright. Even though the buzzwords that describe it may change, the fundamental reason of its existence will remain the same. This chapter touched on some of the most popular up-and-coming trends in business analytics.

In recent years, Big Data has become a synonym for data analytics. Although there is no universally accepted definition for it, the attribute that synergistically characterizes the term Big Data is mostly agreed upon and is defined with several words that start with the letter "v"—volume, variety, velocity, veracity, variability, and value. The chapter provided a concise summary of what Big Data is and how it is changing the way business decisions are being made.

As part of the futuristic view of analytics, the chapter provided a conceptual definition and brief characterization of deep learning and cognitive computing. As the new face of applied AI and machine learning, deep learning (or deep neural networks) is already making an impact on addressing seemingly unsolvable problems in many fields, especially in social media–driven marketing and healthcare. Exemplified by IBM Watson on *Jeopardy!* and then AlphaGO success in game of GO, cognitive computing and deep learning seem to be painting the picture for the leading edge of managerial decision support in the form of smart machines that make humans smarter.

References

Davenport, T. H. (2018). "From Analytics to Artificial Intelligence." *Journal of Business Analytics*, 1(2), 73–80.

Dean, J., and Ghemawat, S. (2004). "MapReduce: Simplified Data Processing on Large Clusters" at research.google.com/archive/mapreduce.html (accessed May 2014).

Denyer, S. (2018, January). "Beijing Bets on Facial Recognition in a Big Drive for Total Surveillance." *The Washington Post*. Retrieved from https://www.washingtonpost.com/news/world/wp/2018/01/07/feature/in-china-facial-recognition-is-sharp-end-of-a-drive-for-total-surveillance/?noredirect=on&utm_term=.e73091681b31

Goodfellow, I., Bengio, Y., & Courville, A. (2016). *Deep Learning*. Cambridge, MA: MIT Press.

Hochreiter, S., & Schmidhuber, J. (1997). "Long Short-term Memory." *Neural Computation*, 9(8), 1735–1780.

Issenberg, S. (2012). "Obama Does It Better" (from "Victory Lab: The New Science of Winning Campaigns"), *Slate*, October 29, 2012.

Jia, Y., Shelhamer, E., Donahue, J., Karayev, S., Long, J., Girshick, R., & Darrell, T. (2014, November). "Caffe: Convolutional Architecture for Fast Feature Embedding." In *Proceedings of the 22nd ACM International Conference on Multimedia* (pp. 675–678). ACM.

Krizhevsky, A., Sutskever, I., & Hinton, G. E. (2012). "Imagenet Classification with Deep Convolutional Neural Networks." In *Advances in Neural Information Processing Systems* (pp. 1097–1105).

Mozur, P. (2018). "Inside China's Dystopian Dreams: A.I., Shame and Lots of Cameras." *The New York Times*, June 8, 2018. https://www.nytimes.com/2018/07/08/business/china-surveillance-technology.html

Reynolds, H. & Feldman, S. (2014). "Cognitive computing: Beyond the hype" KMWorld. Jun 27, 2014, http://www.kmworld.com/Articles/News/News-Analysis/Cognitive-computing-Beyond-the-hype-97685.aspx.

Romano, L. (2012). "Obama's Data Advantage." *Politico*, June 9, 2012.

Rumelhart, David E., and James L. McClelland. (1986). "On Learning the Past Tenses of English Verbs." ERIC: 216–271.

Samuelson, D. A. (2013). "Analytics: Key to Obama's Victory." *ORMS Today*, an INFORMS publication, February 2013, 20–24.

Scherer, M. (2012). "Inside the Secret World of the Data Crunchers Who Helped Obama Win." *Time*, November 7, 2012.

Shen, G. (2013). "Big Data, Analytics and Elections." *INFORMS Analytics Magazine*, January–February 2013.

Watson, H., (2012). "The Requirements for Being an Analytics-Based Organization." *Business Intelligence Journal*, 17(2), 42–44.

Index